the
network
inside
out

the network inside out

annelise riles

Ann Arbor
THE UNIVERSITY OF MICHIGAN PRESS

First paperback edition 2001
Copyright © by the University of Michigan 2000
All rights reserved
Published in the United States of America by
The University of Michigan Press
Manufactured in the United States of America
⊚ Printed on acid-free paper

2010 2009 2008 2007   7 6 5 4

No part of this publication may be reproduced, stored in a retrieval system, or transmitted in any form or by any means, electronic, mechanical, or otherwise, without the written permission of the publisher.

A CIP catalog record for this book is available from the British Library.

Library of Congress Cataloging-in-Publication Data

Riles, Annelise.
   The network inside out / Annelise Riles.
     p. cm.
   Includes bibliographical references and index.
   ISBN 0-472-11071-3 (cloth : alk. paper)
     1. World Conference on Women (4th : 1995: Beijing, China)
2. Women—Congresses—Attendance. 3. Women's rights—International cooperation. 4. Women in development—International cooperation.
5. International organization. 6. Women—Fiji. I. Title.
HQ1106 .R54 2000
305.42—dc21
                                                            99-087959

ISBN 0-472-08832-7 (pbk. : alk. paper)

ISBN 978-0-472-11071-1 (cloth : alk. paper)
ISBN 978-0-472-08832-4 (pbk. : alk. paper)

For Eleanor Jane Riles

Contents

List of Illustrations ix
List of Tables xi
Preface xiii
A Note on Orthography xix
List of Abbreviations xxi
Chapter 1. Inside Out 1
Chapter 2. Sociality Seen Twice 23
Chapter 3. Infinity within the Brackets 70
Chapter 4. Division within the Boundaries 92
Chapter 5. Designing the Facts 114
Chapter 6. Filling in the Action 143
Chapter 7. Network! 171
Notes 185
References 215
Index 235

Illustrations

1. "Chart of the UN conferences on women and parallel NGO forums" 7
2. "United Nations Conferences: What have they accomplished?" 9
3. "Mission Statement of the *Platform for Action*" 11
4. "Flashback: UN Fourth World Conference on Women and regional and national preparatory meetings" 12
5. "What does the network look like?" 24
6. "Schematic depiction of the Asia and Pacific NGO Working Group" 49
7. "Second-order zone, with density 32 per cent" 56
8. "Information systems for the advancement of women for national machinery" 57
9. Front cover of the *Pacific Platform for Action* 71
10. Layering mats in a ceremonial space 76
11. Women layering mats for the installation of Roko Tui Bau 77
12. Paragraph 223 of the *Draft Platform for Action*, 15 May 1995 version 84
13. Early survey map of Lovonisikeci estate, Cakaudrove Province, Vanua Levu 98
14. Early (ca. 1900) survey map of Yadali estate, CG 735 100
15. Survey map of a portion of Lovonisikeci estate, CT 4321, lots 1–4 102
16. Pages from *Women's Information Network* 118
17. "Communication Line," a schematic depiction of the Fiji WIP network 122
18. "Network!" 125
19. "What you need . . . ," leaflet distributed at the Beijing NGO Forum '95 128
20. "Anatomy of the *Platform for Action*" 135

x   Illustrations

21. Sample page from *Turn the words into action! Highlights from the Beijing Declaration and Platform for Action* 157
22. "Empowerment" matrix distributed at the Seminar on Beijing and the ICPD 160
23. "Common Grounds" 163
24. Participants in the Seminar on Beijing and the ICPD 167
25. "Communication Line," a schematic depiction of the Fiji WIP network; and "Expected outputs and outcomes of activities" 168

Tables

1. Global Conferences 8
2. Women's Conferences from a Pacific Perspective, 1975–95 14
3. Some Institutions and Networks Mentioned in the Text 34
4. Networks Mentioned in the Text That Participated in the Fourth World Conference on Women (FWCW), Beijing 37
5. Fiji Participants' Affiliations at the Preparatory Conferences for the Fourth World Conference on Women and Their Funding Sources 41

Preface

This project originated in my desire to put different kinds of knowledge into practice vis-à-vis one another. At its inception, I framed this problem principally in disciplinary terms: I was interested in how I might make the ending points of legal knowledge—the puzzles, frustrations, facts, and commitments the theory and practice of law entailed—beginning points for anthropological reflection and vice versa. The idea was to make use of the tensions between disciplines while recognizing the intellectual commonalities between the concerns and impasses of each.

To harness the potential of engagement between disciplines would require a different stance than the one advocated by contemporary legal and anthropological approaches to "interdisciplinarity." In one way or another, these approaches imagined a wide gulf between law and anthropology; they presented the results of anthropological work as the outsider's knowledge about the law and stressed the moral imperative of empirical studies of law's "context." This led to an entire generation of work dedicated to exploiting a space between disciplines by imagining that the disciplines, their subject matter, or their component parts somehow needed to be "related" to one another (Riles 1994). Although in recent years the strategies for creating relationships and the definitions of relationships themselves had become ever more sophisticated and detailed, one had the sinking feeling that the project could no longer hold. The gulf between disciplines, and the relating strategy anthropologists and their legal sympathizers claimed as their own, somehow failed to captivate the imagination.

My approach has been to background the interdisciplinary question so that the issues might reemerge in a different guise. In other words, although this book is very much the artifact of an interdisciplinary venture, I consider its methodological contribution to the anthropology of law to be its movement beyond the explicit topics of "law" and "culture" to other subjects, which will have resonance for lawyers and anthropologists of law alike, albeit in somewhat different ways. Fieldwork has brought into view a series of artifacts that are ubiquitous but untheorized elements of international legal practice. These include, for example, the "networks" of nongovernmental organizations (NGOs) that now proliferate in the Pacific or the documents of United Nations

(UN) conferences. Although I "knew" much about these artifacts prior to living and working in Fiji, they were not accessible to me as subjects of study. They became thinkable only through the practice of working with Fijian government workers or activists and rediscovering these subjects as what mattered to them.

A second interest of the project, in actuality a facet of the first, was to investigate more fully the causes and character of the collective anxiety that seemed to hang over many academic enterprises, whatever their disciplinary genre. In both law and anthropology, people seemed to feel that their strategies were spent, that a different kind of world now was upon them that dwarfed attempts to understand or make use of it. In some cases (particularly in legal scholarship) this was expressed as a problem about the fallout from lessons about the death of the subject, the impossibility of originality, the collapse of meaningful differences into the homogeneity of pastiche, or the lack of defensible grounding from which to make an authoritative moral critique. In other cases (particularly in anthropological scholarship) this was expressed as the intellectual effects of the encapsulation of all locality (both as a phenomenon and as an analytical tool) in global forms of culture or of the deconstruction of key conceptual tools such as the notion of society, culture, or context that left doubt as to what conceptual tools might remain. It also found expression in the uneasy tone in which ethnographic writing about new conditions and effects of knowledge proceeded. It always has been the subject's job to produce the symbols and the anthropologist's job to do the analysis, so to speak. Yet what is one to make of a subject, such as the international institutional practices considered in this book, that one encounters already analyzed? How might one transform this kind of ending point into a beginning point of one's own?

It seemed worthwhile, therefore, to explore in greater ethnographic detail some of the aspects of contemporary knowledge that so captivated and concerned scholars in both fields, as elaborated in one set of institutional contexts. Was there indeed something new and disorienting about the forms of knowledge that people in the world of international bureaucratic practice worked and lived through? If so, what were its elements, how was it conceived, and what responses did it elicit? Who or what were the subjects and objects of such knowledge and what were its effects?

I arrived in Suva, Fiji, in late September 1994 and began to work with international aid agencies, government offices, and nongovernmental organizations. The first step—a matter of survival as much as of interest—was to try to understand what mattered and what received emphasis there. I proceeded by attempting to identify some of the important "artifacts" of institutional activity. These were not hidden themes in the subtext of life; they were what actually captivated attention—what people devoted time to making, what defined ties, what was worth taking risks for, what problems blocked their activity. This task was not a purely transparent observational endeavor, of course. In retrospect, it is clear that the themes I identified resonated with knowledge practices already familiar to me. Yet if there were connections to my own analytical problems they were backgrounded for awhile to resurface as I went about the work of "gathering information" and using it to think with, as did those described in the pages below.

At the outset, I encountered problems familiar to most ethnographers of contemporary institutions (cf. Rabinow 1996). All of the people who eventually became friends, coworkers, and resources for this study were busy public figures for whom the prospect of becoming the subject of sustained study held no inherent novelty or intrigue and who had little time to spare to discuss the kinds of details of their daily lives that form the basis of anthropological inquiry. There was also a practical problem concerning how to locate myself, since there was no singular place to "find" people and important interactions often occurred in private encounters that were not immediately accessible to observation. Finally, as discussed further in the chapters that follow, the circle of both expatriate and Fijian institutional actors was a small and tight one characterized by a certain degree of distrust of outside involvement or interference, whether it be from the "home office" in the case of some international institutions, from "white women" in the case of some activist organizations, or simply from publicity and the unpredictable dispersion of information in the case of many more.

Slowly, these difficulties were overcome through diverse and unpredictable paths. In key instances, the Part-European clerical staff of these institutions, intrigued by my interest in and knowledge of their family histories, owing to prior research concerning an international arbitration case involving the descendents of American citizens in Fiji (Riles 1995), opened their offices to me. In several other important cases, I gained access to institutions through rewarding personal friendships with other young professional women. As my attention turned to the "women in development" activities of international institutions, I also benefited from Fiji's rich tradition of feminist academic thought now carried on at the University of the South Pacific. Needless to say, I am grateful to all those who first took this chance and hope that the text that follows does not betray the trust they showed in the project.

Over the fifteen months that followed, I participated in the daily work of five or six networks and institutions preparing for the Fourth World Conference on Women (Beijing Conference) and became tangentially involved in many more, providing what participants called "technical assistance" such as helping to plan meetings, drafting documents, writing and preparing the layout for newsletters, transcribing conference proceedings, collecting survey materials, assisting with research, or helping to reorganize an institution's library. I also represented organizations at meetings and conferences when the group's coordinator or other members could not attend. From this vantage point, I was able to participate in the major preparatory meetings for the Beijing Conference, which were held in Suva and at the UN headquarters in New York during this period. In March and April 1995 I attended the final preparatory conference (PrepCom) for the Beijing Conference, held at the UN headquarters, where I observed and participated in the activities of Pacific governments and NGOs. Then, in September 1995, I attended the Beijing Conference as a representative of one Fiji-based NGO and participated in the activities of Pacific delegates at the parallel "NGO Forum."

This work was interspersed with fieldwork among so-called Part-Europeans in Suva and the Savusavu area of Vanua Levu. Initially, this fieldwork represented something of a leap of faith since there was no obvious analytical connection between my interest in the Part-European community and my interest in international institutions beyond my gratitude to certain Part-European employees of those institutions for their assistance with my research. In retrospect, however, it is clear that the very incongruity at the level of "analysis" helped bring other themes and possibilities into view. I eventually chose to focus primarily on one singular clan.[1] This research is also informed by archival work at the Public Records Office in London, the National Archives of Fiji, the Salem Museum in Salem, Massachusetts, the National Archives in Washington, D.C., and the Church of Latter Day Saints Family History Library in Salt Lake City, Utah.

The subject matter of this book requires some patience on the part of any reader, therefore. It is not a society, nor is it even a community. Its contribution to the ethnography of the Pacific region lies in fragmentary resonances rather than overarching models or positions in debates. The subject cannot be defined satisfactorily by a sense of geographic place, as much of the activity takes place in New York, Bangkok, Beijing, or over electronic mail networks or satellite connections as well as in Suva. Indeed, often it seemed that I alone stayed rooted in Suva, while all others came and went. More than a place or society, what the persons and institutions described here share is a set of informational practices. These include the constant meetings and conferences, the ubiquitous coordination tasks, the endless cataloging and discussion of documents, and the numerous exercises of drafting and redrafting. They include the funding such entities receive from international aid agencies and the procedures they must go through in order to secure this funding. They include travel to meetings and the contacts they develop with similar organizations in the Pacific and other parts of the world. These practices partake in a certain aesthetic.

I have used pseudonyms or initials or omitted names throughout the text with two exceptions. First, where I comment at length upon the design work of particular individuals, it has seemed appropriate to credit the designers for these achievements. Second, I have referred to Susanna Ounei, a Kanak activist, by name, as she would not want to be referred to by a pseudonym. Because the institutions and persons at issue in the text are public figures in Fiji, it also regretfully has been necessary to disguise institutions in the descriptions of some incidents.

As the above account makes plain, my debts are tremendous. First, I am grateful to the Fiji government for allowing me to conduct this research. I wish to thank Margaret Patel and her staff at the National Archives of Fiji for their tireless efforts on my behalf. I am especially indebted to the Fiji government's Department of Women and Culture, and its director, Ms. Sereima Lomaloma, for granting me access to their records and for including me so readily in many of the department's activities.

I wish to express my warmest thanks to the many persons in Fiji who generously shared of their knowledge and time to teach me about their work, who allowed me to participate in so many of their activities, and whose friendship was one of the great joys of this research. I regret that the sensitivity of the material makes it inappropriate to thank them individually. However, I can mention my special thanks to Susanna Ounei, who taught me much more than a social scientific account can convey; to Lili King and Jim Whippy, whose remarkable designs literally brought the subject matter into view for me; and to Arthur Whippy, Frank Whippy, Florrie Whippy, Alex Whippy, Charlotte Whippy, Barbara Whippy, and Ephraim Whippy, and the many members of the Whippy clan in Suva and Kasavu, who shared so much with me with patience, warmth, and humor. My thinking was refined by the academic guidance of Vanessa Griffen, Redge Sanday, and Claire Slatter, whose knowledge of all the issues at stake in the pages below is humbling.

I wish to express my appreciation to Andy Adede and Phillippe Sands for arranging official access to the PrepCom, to Ming-ya Teng for arranging access to the Fourth World Conference on Women, to Gina Houng-Lee of AusAID Fiji, to Susan Whitlock of the University of Michigan Press, to Irene Berkey of Northwestern University's International Law Library, and to Elizabeth Olds. Jane Campion, the most wonderful research assistant and friend that one could hope for, has held this project together over the last two years with intelligence, grace, and wit. Conversations with colleagues at Northwestern University's School of Law and Department of Anthropology have proven invaluable. Finally, I wish to thank Bryant Garth and the research fellows of the American Bar Foundation for their faith in this project and for a most engaging dialogue.

The project has been enriched by comments and criticism from Tony Anghie, Debbora Battaglia, Leigh Bienen, Abram Chayes, John Comaroff, Tim Earle, Debbora Elliston, James Ferguson, Martha Fineman, Peter Fitzpatrick, Günter Frankenberg, Simon Harrison, Michael Herzfeld, Bonnie Honig, Steven Hooper, Margaret Jolly, Paul Kahn, David Kennedy, Martii Koskenniemi, Sally

Merry, Beth Mertz, Nancy Munn, Kunal Parker, Paul Rabinow, Lawrence Rosen, Marshall Sahlins, Sarita Sandham, Helen Schwartzman, Art Stinchcombe, Verena Stolcke, Chris Tennant, Nicholas Thomas, Christina Toren, David Van Zandt, and Pål Wrange. Numerous conversations with Don Brenneis and Adam Reed have substantially shaped the direction of this work. I thank them for laboring through so many drafts but most of all for their friendship.

This book is the artifact of my many debts to Marilyn Strathern. It was the inspiration of her elegant and imaginative ethnography of modern knowledge practices that initially framed my anthropological interests and ultimately led me back to anthropology from law. Only in retrospect did I come to understand the extraordinary intellectual freedom she allowed me as a doctoral student and the patience with which she shared of her time and tolerated my fumbling about awkwardly amid her work. I thank her for the example she continues to provide.

Finally, this work is only one outcome of a most rewarding intellectual and personal collaboration with Hiro Miyazaki, whose unwavering commitment to this project, as well as his subtlety and generosity of spirit, sustained me and refined my work at every juncture. I thank him for all the joy his friendship has brought me and for the challenges he never ceases to pose.

Research and writing were funded by grants from the American Bar Foundation; Cambridge Commonwealth, Livingstone and Overseas Trusts; the Ford Foundation; the Northwestern University School of Law; the Richards Fund; the Smuts Fund; Trinity College; and the William Wyse Fund.

Chapter 3 appeared in print in slightly different form as "Infinity within the brackets," *American Ethnologist* 25 (3) (August 1998): 378–98, copyright American Anthropological Association, 1998. Substantial portions of chapter 4 appeared as "Division within the boundaries," *Journal of the Royal Anthropological Institute* 4 (September 1998): 409–24, copyright Royal Anthropological Institute of Great Britain and Ireland. Sections of chapter 4 also appeared in "Part-Europeans and Fijians: Some Problems in the Conceptualisation of a Relationship," in *Fiji in Transition*, ed. Brij V. Lal and Tomasi R. Vakatora, Research Papers of the Fiji Constitution Review Commission, vol. 1 (Suva: School of Social and Economic Development, University of the South Pacific, 1997).

A Note on Orthography

In conformity with standard Fijian orthography, the letters below are pronounced as follows when they appear in Fijian-language words or names:

b is pronounced *mb* as in number

c is pronounced *th* as in thus

d is pronounced *nd* as in sand

g is pronounced *ng* as in sing

q is pronounced *ng* as in linger

Abbreviations

ADB	Asian Development Bank
AIDAB	Australian International Development Assistance Bureau
APC	Association for Progressive Communications
APDC	Asian and Pacific Development Centre
APWG	Asia and Pacific NGO Working Group
APWIP	Asia-Pacific Women in Politics
AusAID	Australian Agency for International Development (formerly AIDAB)
British ODA	Great Britain Overseas Development Administration
CAA	Community Aid Abroad
CAC	critical areas of concern (thematic sections of the *Global Platform for Action*)
CEDAW	Convention on the Elimination of All Forms of Discrimination against Women
CETC	Community Education Training Center
CIDA	Canadian International Development Agency
CONGO	Conference of Non-Governmental Organizations in Consultative Status with ECOSOC
Corso	New Zealand Association for International Relief, Rehabilitation and Development
CSW	Commission on the Status of Women (a subdivision of ECOSOC)
DAC	Development Assistance Corporation
DAWN	Development Alternatives with Women for a New Era
DWC	Department of Women and Culture (Fiji)
ECOSOC	United Nations Economic and Social Council
ECOWOMAN	a collective of NGOs involved with women and environment in the Pacific
ENGENDER	Center for Environment, Gender and Development

Abbreviations

ESCAP	United Nations Economic and Social Council for Asia and the Pacific
EU	European Union
FIJI WIP	Fiji Women in Politics
FNCW	Fiji National Council of Women
FWCC	Fiji Women's Crisis Centre
FWCW	United Nations Fourth World Conference on Women (Beijing 1995)
FWRM	Fiji Women's Rights Movement
G77	Group of 77 (traditional voting bloc of states from the developing world)
GAD	gender and development
GPFA	Global Platform for Action
GROOTS	Grassroots Organizations Operating Together in Sisterhood
ICPD	United Nations International Conference on Population and Development (Cairo, 1994)
ILO	International Labour Organization
INSTRAW	United Nations International Research and Training Institute for the Advancement of Women
IWDA	International Women's Development Agency
IWTC	International Women's Tribune Centre
NCW	National Council of Women
NFIP	Nuclear Free and Independent Pacific Movement
NFLS	Nairobi Forward Looking Strategies (document produced at the United Nations End of the Decade Conference on Women, Nairobi, 1985)
NGO	nongovernmental organization
NZODA	New Zealand Official Development Assistance Programme
Pac-Y	Pacific YWCA
PAWORNET	Pacific Women's Information/Communication Network
PCRC	Pacific Concerns Resource Centre (secretariat of the NFIP)
PEACESAT	Consortium for International Pacific Education and Communication Experiments by Satellite
PNGOCG	Pacific NGO Coordinating Group
POPIN	Pacific Population Information Network
PPFA	Pacific Platform for Action
PPSEAWA	Pan-Pacific and Southeast Asian Women's Association

PrepCom	Preparatory Committee of the UN CSW
PSDNP	Pacific Sustainable Development Network Programme
PWRB	Pacific Women's Resource Bureau (a division of the SPC)
PWRC	Pacific Women's Resource Centre
SIDA	Swedish International Development Authority
SO	strategic objectives
SPACHEE	South Pacific Action Committee for Human Ecology and Environment
SPC	South Pacific Commission (an organization of Pacific governments that became the Secretariat of the Pacific Community in February 1998)
SPF	South Pacific Forum
SVT	Sogosogo Ni Vakavulewa Ni Taukei
TAF	The Asia Foundation
TST	Technical Support Team
UN	United Nations
UNCED	United Nations Conference on the Environment and Development
UNDP	United Nations Development Programme
UNFPA	United Nations Population Fund
UNICEF	United Nations Children's Fund
UNIFEM	United Nations Fund for Women
USP	University of the South Pacific
WAC	Women's Action for Change
WACC	World Association for Christian Communication
WAINIMATE	Women's Association for Natural Medicinal Therapy
WCC	World Council of Churches
WEDO	Women's Environment and Development Organization
WHO	World Health Organization
WID	Women in Development
WIN	Women's Information Network (newsletter of the FNCW)
WINAP	Women's Information Network for Asia and the Pacific
YWCA	Young Women's Christian Association

CHAPTER 1
Inside Out

In *Walbiri Iconography,* Nancy Munn brings her reader to terms with an artifact that eclipses anthropological tools of understanding. Her subject is the networklike designs of Walbiri artists, and the difficulty for anthropological understanding, she notes, lies in the way the artifacts are at once "maps" and "designs" (1973: 136), entities that describe a specific path a person might take across a territory but also work as representations of particular ancestors or animals *and* as nonrepresentational patterns or designs (126). While an observer might imagine these as disparate concepts or levels of interpretation to be brought into a relationship through analysis, Munn notes that "the use of one graphic element to represent different meaning items simply reflects the premise that these items are 'the same thing'" (171). She insists, contrary to a diversity of midcentury analytical tools, that Walbiri designs neither map out a social structure nor reflect a set of inherent patterns in the mind. Instead, she directs attention to the way patterns refer precisely to the animals or paths they represent and thus ultimately to the drawings themselves.

The problem this book addresses might be termed the "inside out" version of Munn's. Like *Walbiri Iconography,* it is an experiment in the ethnographic observation, description, and critical reflection on analytical phenomena for which we lack tools of description. Like Walbiri designs, the phenomena addressed in this book are what anthropologists conceptualize as of different "orders"; they are both "designs" and "paths across territory." In other words, they resist traditional anthropological methods of making sense by relating disparate elements (Strathern 1992b), as, for example, we habitually separate and then relate the artifacts of the mind and social or historical context.[1] The book follows on from Munn's puzzling insistence, then, that Walbiri designs are not a smaller scaled, after the fact version of the paths Walbiri have taken, or contexts for the paths people might take, but rather one and the "same thing."[2]

Yet unlike Walbiri designs, the phenomena at issue in this book resist interpretation precisely because they are all too familiar; they share with our interpretive tools a singular aesthetic and a set of practices of representation. In this sense, they direct our attention to a problem of anthropological analysis that does not inhere in our encounter with knowledge practices "outside" our own, but rather is endemic to the "inside"[3] of modern institutional and academic analysis—the production of funding proposals, the collection of data, the drafting of documents or the organization of meetings, for example. In other words, my "subject"—the character and aesthetics of information, the manner in which information is elucidated and appreciated, its uses, and its effects[4]—deserves ethnographic attention because it is equally indigenous to the subjects of this study and to the tradition of social science of which this study is a part.[5]

From 1994 to 1996, most of the persons and activities described in this book were associated with the national, regional, and international governmental and nongovernmental organizations based in Suva, the capital city of Fiji, and involved in the United Nations Fourth World Conference on Women (the Beijing Conference). In describing the "networks" and "networking" as well as the many other activities that captivated these persons' passions and commitments, I hope to understand the flurry of international activity, of which the UN women's conference is a part, as an *effect* of a certain aesthetic of information of which the world of NGOs, nation-states, international institutions, and networks is only one instantation.

International networking activities of the kind at issue in this book have now become subjects of great interest. In anthropology, the study of the transnational[6] is taken to bring with it the risks and possibilities of a "methodological shift . . . testing the limits of ethnography, attenuating the power of fieldwork, and losing the perspective of the subaltern" (Marcus 1995: 95). International relations scholars avidly promote transnational issue networks as the new, more creative, more principled register of international political action (Brysk 1993; Finger 1994b; Fisher 1993; Keck and Sikkink 1998; Lipschutz 1992; Luard 1990: 113–15; Mathews 1997; Princen 1994; Spiro 1994; Tarrow 1998: 188–93; Wapner 1995; cf. Moisy 1997). Anthony Giddens places his hope in transnational "social movements" (Giddens 1990: 158–63), as do the political philosophers Ernesto Laclau and Chantal Mouffe (1985), Jürgen Habermas (1984), and many others.

The anthropological orientation of the policy studies and political theory literature on transactional networks might give anthropologists reason to pause. Consider, for example, the following evocation of a sociality outside and beyond the here and now:

> [Networks reach] back . . . before simple human relationships became obscured by hierarchy and bureaucracy. In other respects, networks . . . leap forward . . . with globe-encompassing capability that subsumes the enduring aspects of authority and bureaucracy. (Lipnack and Stamps 1984: 294–96)

Central to this modernist sociological vision is a notion of relations characterized by systemic complexity. Arturo Escobar describes the interest the political philosophers Laclau and Mouffe take in new social movements, for example, as an outcome of the breakup of political alliances into more complex groups (1985). Writing from within the world of international institutions, likewise, Paul Ghils argues that

> The emergence in the human sciences of the notion of complexity and interaction between phenomena is reflected today, in international policy studies, in a growing interest in entities other than states and international organizations as subjects of analysis. (1992: 417)

This new application of familiar paradigms has in turn reflected possibilities back onto modernist sociology.[7] The sociologist Leslie Sklair writes that "[t]he argument that, even when they are not apparently interested in seizing state power, [new social movements] can still be as sociologically interesting as, say, revolutionary movements, has in some ways liberated the study of them" (1998: 292).

Although my subject is the concrete activities of those involved in such transnational issue networks, throughout the book I take the Network as a broader class of phenomena. By the "Network," I mean to refer to a set of institutions, knowledge practices, and artifacts thereof that internally generate the effects of their own reality by reflecting on themselves. In a recent article, Scott Lash has called for a new kind of critical theory suited to the information age that grasps the aesthetic dimension of "reflexive modernity" in order to bring into view modernity's "doubles" (1994: 11). Likewise, George Marcus has written that "[t]here appears to be no real or powerfully imagined 'outside' to capitalism now, and where oppositional space is to be found, or how it is to be constructed within a global economy, is perhaps the most important fin-de-siècle question of left-liberal thought" (1996: 6). Indeed, for those concerned with the intersection of modernist epistemologies and liberal political philosophies, the Network offers a poignant case study of institutionalized utopianism, an ambition for political change through communication and information exchange, of universalism *after* cultural relativism and the "incredulity toward the metanarrative" (Lyotard 1984). In the Beijing Conference and the networks it spawned, we have an opportunity to explore one highly reflexive elaboration of a modernist epistemology and radical neoliberal political vision, albeit one defined by its refusal of particularity, that is, by its own universalizing claims.

To date, there has been little sustained observation of such activity (cf. Fisher 1997: 441).[8] For the most part, globalization has been understood as a matter of theory, and late modernity's theorists proceed rather at the level of reflections and thought experiments. Frederic Jameson, for example, suggests, "[l]et's start from the principle that we already somehow know what globalization is," and the assumption, it turns out, is that "[w]e have a sense that there are both denser and more extensive communicational networks all over the world today" (1998: 55). Giddens, for his part, imagines that each one of us enters into a "bargain with modernity" (1990: 90) and describes the modern, globalized world as if it were a giant machine (151). An anthropologist might bristle at such fictions, and indeed, although certain features of popular and academic fantasies about the nature and effects of information will be borne out in the practices of the networkers described here, many others are not.

More importantly, in the activities and discourse of these networks, we will find the purchase of many of these fantasies already spent. The assumption that information technologies "stretch" time and space (Poster 1990: 2), for example, and cause the intensification of social relations (Giddens 1990: 64), or that bureaucratization has brought about a delegation of authority to "experts" in the face of new degrees of phenomenological complexity (84), are all accounts the networkers described in this book already deploy at particular moments, images they photocopy and distribute in their newsletters, to great effect. The same could be said of the notion of the network as a tool of sociological analysis: where the people described in this book already understand themselves to create networks in order to generate realities by studying, analyzing, or communicating about them, discovering a "network" no longer can evoke the surprise of uncovering hidden analytical truth as it once did (see chap. 2). This replication of the work of sociologists—an example of what Lash (1994) terms "modernization's doubles"—offers an opportunity, I think, for developing ways of thinking that do not resort to surprise discoveries, do not uncover hidden generalities, and yet do not treat cultural phenomena as uninteresting or undeserving of analysis because they are already understood, elaborated on, and even critiqued by those who used to provide the raw "data" for our analyses.

The armchair approach to global institutional knowledge that characterizes the literature is ethnographically significant in its own right and derives precisely, I think, from the methodological problem at the heart of this book, namely, the comfort or fear that all is already *known* to the theorist, that the knowledge practices at stake in networking activities are those he or she encounters and acts through every day—that we are already "inside" the Network, in other words.[9] If there is a covert cynicism about the possibility of generating new insight in the late modern world latent in this assumption that is somewhat at odds with the utopian appeal of the transnational activity the theorists endorse in the first place, it points, I believe, to the critical importance of the ethnographic apprehension of these phenomena precisely as a means of developing tools for accessing what we already "know," that is, for critical engagement with the place of informational practices in our lives and with the fantasies, academic and popular, that they inspire.

Consider for example, the methodological problems that anthropologists now understand as endemic to the ethnography of globalization. Despite the excitement surrounding this literature, in practice, studies of transnationalism have tended to yield familiar analytical paradigms writ large—notions such as "community" or "tradition" long outmoded in other anthropological domains. In my view, this traditionalism springs from a methodological source. What renders the field of transnationalism "new" is not so much the discovery of a new field site or set of material conditions but rather the ethnographic encounter with knowledge practices already familiar to, and indeed in use by, the anthropologist at precisely the moment at which he or she seeks insight through fresh ethnographic observation. We might understand the impulse to exoticize through notions of community, identity, or tradition that characterizes this literature, then, as a methodological device, an effort to render the familiar strange so that it might be apprehended as ethnography. If exoticism is ultimately unsatisfactory as a solution, the problem is inescapably central to the practice of contemporary anthropology.

This lack of an "outside" on and against which to work our analytical devices yields another related problem. The insights of anthropological studies of globalization often seem oddly anticipated by the subjects of transnational ethnographic inquiry themselves (cf. Dezalay and Garth 1996). As with all analysis, in order for these moves to succeed, that is, to elicit the proper effect, the reader must feel that there has been an innovation on what was known before, as, for example, when David Edwards invokes the image of Afghan rebels turning to the Net (1994). Yet there is an irony in these techniques of evocation: an expansion of something that already lays claim to the aesthetic of infinite expansion such as "the global" creates no feeling of innovation at all. James Clifford's insight concerning diaspora that "old localizing strategies . . . may obscure as much as they reveal" (1994: 303) finds its work already done and redone in the activities of international institutions whose work depends on the continual redeployment and then critique of both "global" and "local" positions. Likewise, the critical observation that "the 'naturalness' of the nation can be radically called into question" (Gupta 1992: 64; cf. Malkki 1992) belies institutional actors' pragmatic appreciation of this point and may even obscure these actors' creative deployments of notions of the nation or the state at particular moments only to take these concepts apart again.[10]

In such a condition, the anthropologist's analytical moves are not so much insights as the very elements of the analysis that one seeks to describe: Anthropological analysis is reduced to restatement, to repetition, to generating reflexive modernity's "doubles." All one can do, it seems, is to identify instances of globalization, as when Clifford identifies the diaspora and Edwards points to the Net. This does not transform the subject, however, as we imagine academic analysis transforms "data," so much as it replicates the work this "data" already has done.[11] One of the ethnographic subjects, and methodological problems of this book, therefore, concerns the way in which this analysis does not feel like analysis anymore. I will attempt to show how "failure" is endemic, indeed, is the effect of the Network form.

The discovery of "the global," "the transnational," and "the network," then, does indeed represent a significant moment and one that calls for fundamental reconfigurations of sociological inquiry. Yet the methodological argument of this book is that the focus of the engagement must lie in the problem of how to render the familiar accessible ethnographically, not in the identification of new multisited "places," diasporic "groups," or technological phenomena for anthropological study. This will require finding a point of access from *within* the ethnographic material—it will require turning the Network Inside Out.

Yet, before tackling the question of the contribution of such an experiment, I must render such mundane practices as information gathering and sorting ethnographically visible in the first place. An overview of some of the artifacts at issue in this book may provide an initial sense for the achingly familiar and overanalyzed feel of the material and hence of the ethnographic problem at hand.

Modern Knowledge

In September 1995, the United Nations convened a three-week "global conference" of governments to assess the condition of women and to formulate proposals for its improvement. CONGO (Conference of NGOs), an organization of UN-affiliated NGOs, convened a parallel NGO Forum.[12] Known officially as the United Nations Fourth World Conference on Women (FWCW or Beijing Conference) in reflection of its kinship with three previous UN women's conferences since 1975 (Nadel 1975; Fraser 1987; Stienstra 1994; Jacquette and Tinker 1987; Winslow 1995)[13] (fig. 1), the Beijing Conference and NGO Forum drew approximately fifty thousand participants from 189 member states, plus UN observers, in the largest UN meeting ever convened. Forty-two governmental and NGO representatives attended the conferences from Fiji.

The Beijing Conference was the culmination of a post–cold war explosion of UN global conferences (table 1) aimed at building a new regime of international law and global civil society (e.g., Chayes and Chayes 1995; Groom 1989; cf. Scelle 1953). From 1990 to 1998, the UN convened fourteen such conferences.[14] For those who might initially find the purpose of this global outpouring of effort confusing, a United Nations Public Information Department web page entitled "United Nations Conferences: What Have They Accomplished?" makes the case in archetypal terms (see fig. 2). As you scroll down, the text continues with a discussion of the relatively small cost of these conferences, and thus the value for money that they represent, and concludes

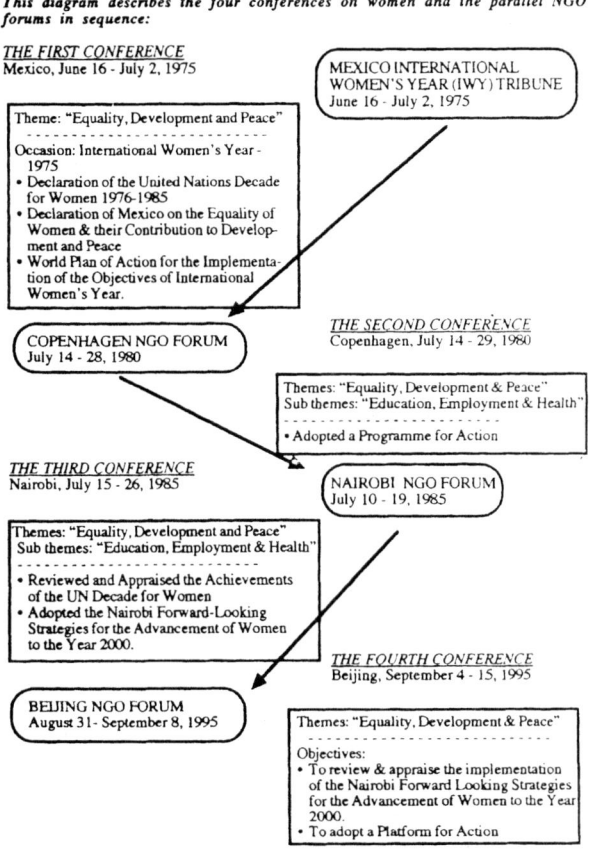

Fig. 1. "Chart of the UN conferences on women and parallel NGO forums" created by WACC for its *Pacific Handbook* (1995: 6. Reproduced courtesy of World Association for Christian Communication—Pacific Region.)

with a summary of the outcomes of the most important conferences in chronological order.

As this public relations release implies, UN global conferences have taken place in an atmosphere in which international institutions struggle to defend their legitimacy on many fronts (e.g., Morgenstern 1986: 135). Global conferences have proven an effective tool for securing legitimacy for both the United Nations and international law more generally in the context of the proliferation of new members of the "family of nations" and of concurrent challenges to the universalist claims of international legal norms. These conferences exemplify a movement in international law toward the recognition of "soft law," that is, of international agreements that do not carry threats of sanctions for their violation (Szasz 1997: 32). In general, these conferences remain low-status events from international lawyers' point of view owing to the "nonbinding" nature of conference agreements and resolutions.[15] The hope of their proponents, however, is that, as "language" is quoted and repeated from one conference document to the next and as states begin to conform their practices, or at least their discourse, to the norms expressed therein, some of what is agreed upon at global conferences gradually will become rules of "customary international law"

TABLE 1. Global Conferences

A. Global Conferences, 1990–98

1990	World Summit for Children	New York, USA
1992	United Nations Conference on Environment and Development	Rio de Janeiro, Brazil
1993	World Conference on Human Rights	Vienna, Austria
1994	Global Conference on the Sustainable Development of Small Island Developing States	Bridgetown, Barbados
1994	International Conference on Natural Disaster Reduction	Yokohama, Japan
1994	International Conference on Population and Development	Cairo, Egypt
1994	World Summit on Trade Efficiency	Columbus, Ohio, USA
1995	World Summit for Social Development	Copenhagen, Denmark
1995	Fourth World Conference on Women	Beijing, China
1996	Ninth United Nations Conference on Trade and Development	Midrand, South Africa
1996	Second United Nations Conference on Human Settlements	Istanbul, Turkey
1996	World Food Summit	Rome, Italy
1997	Earth Summit +5	New York, USA
1998	World Conference on International Cooperation of Cities and Citizens for Cultivating an Eco-Society	Tokyo, Japan

B. Global Women's Conferences, 1975–95

1975	First World Conference on Women	Mexico City, Mexico
1980	Second World Conference on Women	Copenhagen, Denmark
1985	Third World Conference on Women	Nairobi, Kenya
1995	Fourth World Conference on Women	Beijing, China

United Nations Conferences: What Have They Accomplished?

Some 30,000 people journeyed to Istanbul to seek solutions to urban problems at the Habitat II Conference. Nearly 50,000 went to Beijing to set new standards for the advancement of women. And some 47,000 converged on Rio de Janeiro to find a better balance between environmental protection and economic development at the Earth Summit.

To some, the recent series of large-scale United Nations conferences may seem like an extravagant talk-fest. But most of the world's leaders and policy-makers view these events as a worthwhile investment -- and even a watershed -- in shaping our global future.

Making an impact

Global conferences have made a long-term impact by:

- mobilizing national and local governments and non-governmental organizations (NGOs) to take action on a major global problem;
- establishing international standards and guidelines for national policy;
- serving as a forum where new proposals can be debated and consensus sought;
- setting in motion a process, whereby governments make commitments and report back regularly to the United Nations.

Breaking new ground

Conferences have played a key role in guiding the work of the UN since its inception. In fact, the world body was born when delegates from 50 nations met in San Francisco in April 1945 for the United Nations Conference on International Organization. The recent high-profile conferences on development issues, which have continued a series that began in the 1970s, have broken new ground in many areas:

By involving Presidents, Prime Ministers and other heads of State -- as pioneered at the 1990 World Summit for Children -- these events have put long-term, difficult problems like poverty and environmental degradation at the top of the global agenda. These problems otherwise would not have the political urgency to grab front-page headlines and command the attention of world leaders.

The participation of thousands of NGOs, citizens, academics and businesspeople, in both the official and unofficial meetings, has turned these conferences into true "global forums". The UN has encouraged this, knowing that the support of a wide spectrum of society is needed to implement the policies being discussed.

Fig. 2. "United Nations Conferences: What have they accomplished?" (http://www.un.org/News/facts/confrncs.htm, reproduced courtesy of the United Nations.)

(Chinkin 1989; Gunning 1991). Indeed, the press release's closing reference to a chronology of conferences stretching back to the founding of the United Nations highlights this hope that the "chain" of conferences and documents will produce a set of practices and norms that over time will take on the status of "norms."

There is much in this that is familiar to anthropologists. It is a sociological vision of an "international community" governed by its own elaborate rituals (Kennedy 1993) and informal methods of social control (Chayes and Chayes 1995), an emphasis on what sociologists of law call "law in action" rather than "law on the books" (Abel 1973). The UN secretary-general Mr. Boutros-Ghali, for example, admonished the Advisory Group on the Beijing Conference to understand the full significance of the conference in the paradigmatic modernist sociological terms of coherence, holism, and context:

> I am more than ever convinced that the global conferences are a continuum. They can be shaped into a coherent whole. You should regard the Beijing Conference as a crucial link in the great chain of global conferences that are being organized in this decade.... All of the great global concerns—the environment, human rights, population, social development—directly affect the situation of women. Equally, improvements in the situation of women will bring positive change in each of the great global issues. Our task is to bring all these concerns and possibilities together in coherent plans of action. Our task is to integrate, one with another, the gains, and the conceptual and political advances, made at each of the global conferences. (1995: 1)

The idea, repeated in countless newsletters, speeches, and private conversations among Beijing Conference delegates, was that one could only grasp the new emerging global society from the vantage point of an appreciation of this great network of conferences as "a continuum, a cohesive series of events devoted to interrelated issues," in the words of UN secretary-general Kofi Annan (Annan 1997). This network of conferences in turn proved to be something worthy of defending in itself: at the Beijing Conference, NGO representatives wore buttons that read "don't go back on the Cairo Consensus" to indicate that agreements on women's health made in Cairo should be honored at this meeting.

UN global conferences have also expanded the scope of international institutions' legitimacy by incorporating a much larger number and broader range of participants into their activities (Willetts 1996: 31–58).[16] Indeed, much of the activity described in this book is the product of a concerted effort to include organizations other than governments in international institutional practices and to foster the development of institutions that can participate in international meetings in parts of the world where they have not existed before. It is widely understood that both UN institutions and NGOs gain legitimacy from this broadening of participation: NGOs contribute to the "success" of the conferences, but the conferences, whatever their "subject matter," are claimed in retrospect by the NGO community as a validation of the significance of NGOs and their causes domestically and internationally (Ginger, Wagley, and Markfield 1996).

Finally, a reader of the UN web page may notice the kind of "impact" conferences are advertised as having. Conferences serve as forums, they "mobi-

Chapter I

MISSION STATEMENT

1. The Platform for Action is an agenda for women's empowerment. It aims at accelerating the implementation of the Nairobi Forward-looking Strategies for the Advancement of Women and at removing all the obstacles to women's active participation in all spheres of public and private life through a full and equal share in economic, social, cultural and political decision-making. This means that the principle of shared power and responsibility should be established between women and men at home, in the workplace and in the wider national and international communities. Equality between women and men is a matter of human rights and a condition for social justice and is also a necessary and fundamental prerequisite for equality, development and peace. A transformed partnership based on equality between women and men is a condition for people-centred sustainable development. A sustained and long-term commitment is essential, so that women and men can work together for themselves, for their children and for society to meet the challenges of the twenty-first century.

2. The Platform for Action reaffirms the fundamental principle set forth in the Vienna Declaration and Programme of Action, adopted by the World Conference on Human Rights, that the human rights of women and of the girl child are an inalienable, integral and indivisible part of universal human rights. As an agenda for action, the Platform seeks to promote and protect the full enjoyment of all human rights and the fundamental freedoms of all women throughout their life cycle.

3. The Platform for Action emphasizes that women share common concerns that can be addressed only by working together and in partnership with men towards the common goal of gender equality around the world. It respects and values the full diversity of women's situations and conditions and recognizes that some women face particular barriers to their empowerment.

4. The Platform for Action requires immediate and concerted action by all to create a peaceful, just and humane world based on human rights and fundamental freedoms, including the principle of equality for all people of all ages and from all walks of life, and to this end, recognizes that broad-based and sustained economic growth in the context of sustainable development is necessary to sustain social development and social justice.

5. The success of the Platform for Action will require a strong commitment on the part of Governments, international organizations and institutions at all levels. It will also require adequate mobilization of resources at the national and international levels as well as new and additional resources to the developing countries from all available funding mechanisms, including multilateral, bilateral and private sources for the advancement of women; financial resources to strengthen the capacity of national, subregional, regional and international institutions; a commitment to equal rights, equal responsibilities and equal opportunities and to the equal participation of women and men in all national, regional and international bodies and policy-making processes; and the establishment or strengthening of mechanisms at all levels for accountability to the world's women.

Fig. 3. "Mission Statement of the *Platform for Action*." (UNFWCW 1995a: 10. Reproduced courtesy of the United Nations.)

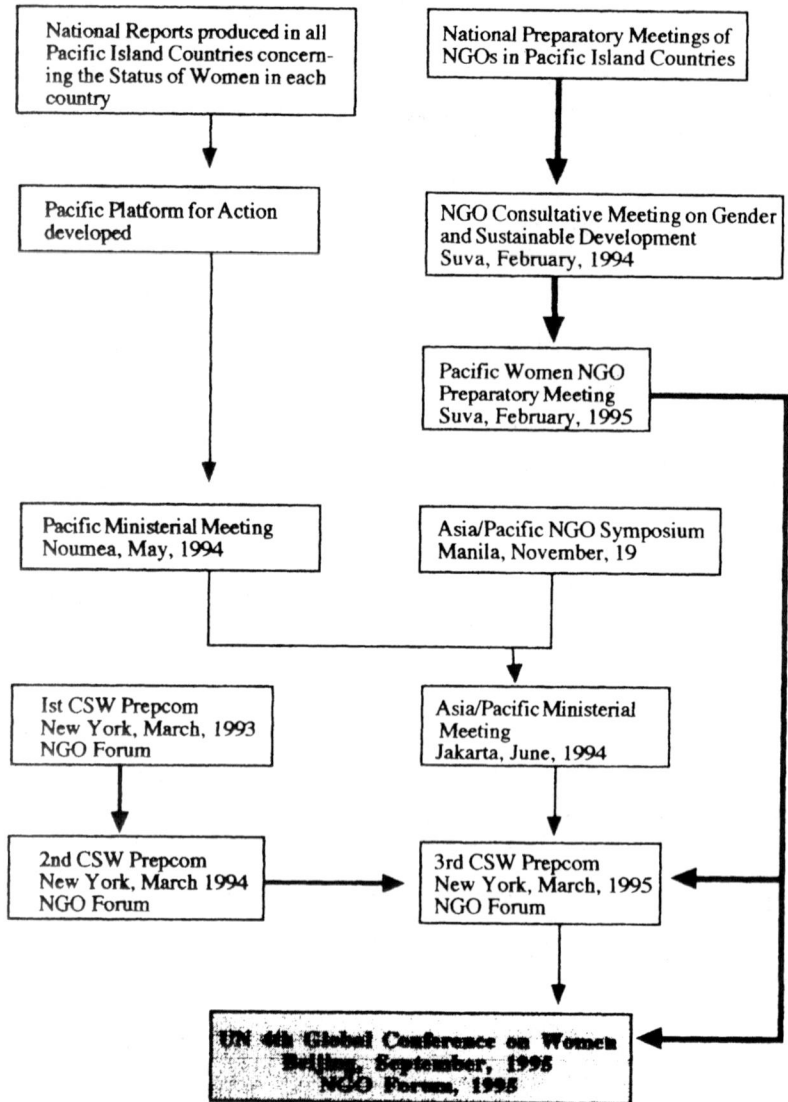

Fig. 4. "Flashback: UN Fourth World Conference on Women and regional and national preparatory meetings" created by WACC for its *Pacific Handbook* (1995: 18. Reproduced courtesy of World Association for Christian Communication—Pacific Region.)

lize," they "[set] in motion a process," they generate publicity, and most of all they draw in a wide variety of participants. Yet the purpose of this flurry of rather processually oriented activity is always described in wider instrumental terms. There is an urgent "problem" *other* than the building of an international community—women's rights, the environment, population control—that gives the conference its reason for being. It is a classic modernist vision of the power of knowledge to solve problems outside itself (Rabinow 1989).[17]

Officially, the task of the Beijing Conference was to produce and ratify a document, the "Platform for Action" (UNFWCW 1995).[18] A text of 150 pages, the platform lists twelve "critical areas of concern" (CACs)[19] and proposes an extensive set of "Strategic Objectives" (SOs) in response. The introductory paragraphs capture something of the aesthetic of the artifact as well as of the spirit in which it was drafted (see fig. 3).

The work of producing this document began over two years prior to the Beijing Conference with national, regional, and international negotiations over draft versions (see fig. 4).[20] The most important of these preparatory meetings from the point of view of Fiji's participants were the Asian and Pacific Regional Meeting held in Jakarta in June 1994; the Pacific Ministerial Meeting and the Regional Pacific Women's Conference held in Nouméa in May 1994; and the Asian and Pacific NGO Symposium held in Manila in November 1993. The final preparatory meeting, known as the PrepCom, was held at UN headquarters from 15 March to 7 April 1995.[21] Over one hundred government delegations and fourteen hundred nongovernmental organizations attended that meeting (United Nations Division for the Advancement of Women 1995).

Many organizations in the Pacific,[22] and especially in Fiji and Papua New Guinea, devoted the majority of their time from 1993 to 1995 to preparations for the Beijing Conference and the NGO Forum (see table 2). Pacific women who had attended each of the preceding UN conferences on women were those most bewildered by the UN practices of document production because they are relatively new. At the Nairobi Conference of 1985, for example, the government delegate apparently simply wrote the Fiji statement on her own, and Pacific attendees from outside government directed their energies toward the NGO Forum and the workshops and other issue-centered activities organized there rather than toward the intergovernmental negotiations.

After Rio, Pacific NGOs therefore began to participate in the "conversation" at the UN. They learned that, as one person put it, "the only way to counter a text is with a better text."[23] Only a small number of people—mostly academics—privately expressed concern about the impact of this new orientation. This concern usually was phrased in terms of a conflict between text and issues, meaning that Pacific participants "knew their issues" but were not skilled at drafting text or that once the conversation about "text" got started they would find it impossible to move the discussion to the level of the underlying issues.

TABLE 2. Women's Conferences from a Pacific Perspective, 1975–95

Date	Conference	Location
19 June–2 July 1975	International Women's Year United Nations World Conference and NGO Forum	Mexico City, Mexico
20–27 November 1978	Second Pacific Women's Conference	Suva, Fiji
14–24 July 1980	United Nations Mid-Decade Conference on Women and NGO Forum	Copenhagen, Denmark
1980	Subregional Follow-Up Meeting for Pacific Women on the World Conference of the United Nations Decade for Women	Suva, Fiji
20 July 1981	Seminar of South Pacific Women	Papeete, Tahiti
19–23 March 1985	Regional Meeting of Pacific Islands Women's Non-Governmental Organizations	Rarotonga, Cook Islands
25–27 March 1985	Second Regional Conference of Pacific Women	Rarotonga, Cook Islands
10–19 July 1985	NGO Forum	Nairobi, Kenya
15–26 July 1985	Third World Conference on Women	Nairobi, Kenya
1–6 December 1986	Regional Seminar on the Development of Women's Information Network System	Saitama, Japan
23–26 March 1987	Third Regional Conference of Pacific Women	Naboutini, Fiji
17–23 September 1988	Fourth Regional Conference of Pacific Women	Suva, Fiji
2–5 December 1991	Fifth Regional Conference of Pacific Women	Agana, Guam
4–15 May 1992	Pacific Subregional Workshop on the Technical Processing of Information concerning Women in Development	Suva, Fiji
29–30 June 1993	South Pacific Commission Women in Development Aid Coordination Meeting	Suva, Fiji
16–20 November 1993	Asia and Pacific Symposium of Non-Governmental Organizations on Women in Development	Manila, Philippines
February 1994	NGO Consultative Meeting on Preparation for Beijing	Suva, Fiji
February 1994	Pacific NGO Follow-Up Workshop to the Asia-Pacific NGO Symposium	Suva, Fiji
2–4 February 1994	Melanesian Women's Caucus	Suva, Fiji
14–23 February 1994	Regional Workshop on Training of Trainers in Gender-Responsive Planning	Suva, Fiji
25 April–6 May 1994	Global Conference on the Sustainable Development of Small Island Developing States	Bridgetown, Barbados
2–6 May 1994	Sixth Triennial Regional Conference on Pacific Women	Nouméa, New Caledonia
7–14 June 1994	ESCAP Second Asian and Pacific Ministerial Conference on Women in Development	Jakarta, Indonesia
July 1994	Consultative Meeting of NGOs	Suva, Fiji

17 August 1994	PEACESAT Meeting of Pacific Women	Suva, Fiji
October 1994	Women in Development Donors' Conference	
18–21 October 1994	South Pacific Commission Twenty-First Meeting of the Committee of Representatives of Governments and Administrations	Port Vila, Vanuatu
23 November 1994	PEACESAT Meeting of the Melanesian Caucus	
29 November–22 December 1994	Meeting of Asia/Pacific NGO Working Group (in preparation for Beijing)	Bangkok, Thailand
14–16 December 1994	Meeting of Women from Non-independent Territories	Nadi, Fiji
15–18 December 1994	ESCAP Regional Meeting of National Machineries for the Advancement of Women	Manila, Philippines
18–19 January 1995	Fiji Conference on the Implementation of the Cairo Declaration and Preparation for Beijing	Suva, Fiji
23–28 January 1995	Pacific Regional Conference on the Ratification of the Convention on the Elimination of All Forms of Discrimination against Women	Suva, Fiji
February 1995	NGO Editing Committee Meeting	Upstate New York
1 February 1995	PEACESAT Meeting of Pacific Women	
20–24 February 1995	Pacific NGO Coordinating Committee Regional Training Workshop in Negotiation and Strategizing Skills for Beijing	Suva, Fiji
March 1995	Sub-Regional Caucus, Polynesia	Western Samoa
13–14 March 1995	NGO Consultation Meeting	New York, USA
14 March–5 April 1995	Commission on the Status of Women 39th Session: Final PrepCom for the World Conference on Women	New York, USA
April 1995	Sub-Regional Caucus, Micronesia	Chuuk, Federated States of Micronesia
12 April 1995	Regional PEACESAT Meeting of Pacific Women	
26 April–5 May 1995	Fourth Sub-Regional Caucus for Melanesian Women	Port Vila, Vanuatu
15–18 May 1995	Meeting of the Committee of Representatives of Governments and Administrations	Nouméa, New Caledonia
30 August–8 September 1995	NGO Forum '95	Beijing, China
4–15 September 1995	United Nations Fourth World Conference on Women	Beijing, China

Inside Out

The text of the previous section is largely mine. The point of the enactment is to demonstrate how seamlessly the knowledge practices I describe in this book fade into our own. For example, as we will see in later chapters, the reprinting of excerpts from UN documents is exemplary UN practice. Participants in UN drafting projects in Fiji as elsewhere were continually quoting, excerpting, and reprinting sections of this and every document.

And yet, perhaps the previous section seems somewhat out of place in an ethnographic introduction. Perhaps it is too familiar to engage our ethnographic sensibilities and yet too strange to engage our disciplinary ones. Herein lies the problem: where the subject of study is configured according to analytical categories, devices, and practices that approximate anthropological analysis, to begin with anthropology's own categories is to doom the project to a mere replication of indigenous representations. In the systemic nature of the artifact, sociological analysis already is complete, part of the indigenous exegesis.[24] How is one to "get outside" an artifact like the international legal document described in chapter 3, which presents itself as a given totality, in order to analyze it in the totalizing terms of social science? Neither defending what is outside the Network as a "truer" form of reality nor taking its "sociological" realities at face value will do.[25]

My response to these conditions is, first, to recognize that these are only partially familiar institutional practices—to attempt what Sarah Franklin describes as a "differently comparative" enterprise (1997). At a second level, however, I hope to work the parallels between late modern institutional knowledge and social science, to make use of or enact the very devices of replication that render the study of the transactional problematic in the first place. My hope is that, following other new ethnographies of institutions (Born 1995; Brenneis 1994; Galtung 1986; Ginsburg 1994; Harper 1998; Herzfeld 1992; Nader 1969; Rabinow 1989; Radway 1997; Schwartzman 1989), this focus on the aesthetics of bureaucratic practices will contribute in equal parts to an ethnographic understanding of the character of contemporary institutional knowledge, on the one hand, and an understanding of how "information" becomes an anthropological subject on the other. Like Walbiri designs, therefore, informational practices might come into view as "designs" in their own right and also as maps across a territory, a path we might have taken or might take.

My first awareness of this came in my own process of reacclimatization from the field. One might not imagine that my daily life of producing funding proposals and drafting documents in Fiji would be very distant from life back in my departmental office, and indeed, I initially experienced no sense of discontinuity between my work in the field and the academy. Slowly, however, I began to notice my colleagues' puzzled reactions to my prose; to the way I took too much care in matters of procedure and too little in matters of substance; to my excessive interest in punctuation and formatting when I read their drafts. Without ever realizing it, I had been assimilated into the patterned quality of Network communication, what Gregory Bateson terms its aesthetics (Bateson 1987b, 1987c).

Two examples that contrast with what I am describing may highlight the subtle differences to be found in seemingly universal practices. In a recent study of the currency of the image of flexibility in American culture, Emily Martin has drawn attention to the notion of the person, institution, or group as a flexible system elaborated, for example, in employee training programs similar to those organized and attended by the networks described here (1994: 207–24). Martin alludes to connections between this concept of systemic flexibility and the anthropological tradition of which she is a part in her observation that Bateson "aptly captured the notion of the flexible, constantly adjusting, constantly changing person, long before its appearance in ads for athletic shoes and temporary employment services" (1994: 159). The parallel she draws between anthropologists' and institutional actors' interest in system is illuminating for the present case as well. It is comparatively interesting, however, that while Fijian networkers participated enthusiastically in discourses of flexible systems they never entertained the notion that this flexibility might apply to their person or body, as in the American case described by Martin.

A second example is particularly close to the materials that follow. Donna Haraway has proposed the chain of UN conferences on women as an example of the feminist politics she advocates ([1989] 1992: 286–87). Noting in particular a well-known document prepared for the 1985 UN women's conference entitled *Women, a World Report* that stitches together the contributions of feminist writers from different parts of the world, each reporting on the condition of women in regions other than their own, she interprets these conferences and their documents as deconstructions of universalism into a new field of global possibilities:

> The UN Decade for Women perhaps should be read as a "post-modern" phenomenon, offering a vision of possible connection and hope for global futures only on condition of accepting the permanent refusal of closure of identities, adequacy of descriptions, and master narratives about what it means to be female, woman and human. ([1989] 1992: 286–87)

The report Haraway describes here—a network of information pieced together from various parts of the globe and produced in document form—would be quite familiar and accessible to the subjects of this book. As we will see, it is the sort of document they "input into" every day. Yet the aspiration she finds in it is ours, not theirs. The concern with questions such as "what it means to be female," and the possibilities for a utopian feminist project would seem utterly foreign to the document producers I know. Rather, their interest would be in the document's production process, in its language and graphics, in its anticipated outcomes including future documents, and of course in its funding sources.

These subtle variations in the assumptions and aesthetics of institutional knowledge, then, afford opportunity for elucidating the differences that coexist with modernity's universal claims through traditional ethnographic techniques. As I have argued in this introductory chapter, however, finding and describing "difference" is no longer enough, for the subjects of a study like this one resist anthropology's relativizing moves. How is one to study the points not of difference but of commonality, of universality even?

Recent rethinking of anthropological theory has noted the ways in which analytical models often draw on the terms and practices of the cultures of the anthropologists who do the modeling. The same might be said of the absences of terms from academic consciousness, for as we will see what is most effective about "information" is precisely its relative paucity of "content" or "meaning," its ability to create a "gap." Yet in *Partial Connections* (1991), Marilyn Strathern has done the work of bringing information into anthropological view. Her comparison of the problems of ethnographic representation that gripped anthropologists in the 1980s with knowledge practices the same generation of anthropologists had encountered in other societies brings to the forefront issues of quantity and scale in informational form. For example, Strathern demonstrates that the late modern conception that all phenomena are infinitely complex and that all perspectives are only partial because the same information can be seen differently from another point of view is an effect of an aesthetic that places a central emphasis on the quality of information and in particular on the possibility of always moving the analysis to another level of scale.[26] The insight is important for a study such as this one, which straddles "global" and "local" concerns, because it emphasizes the way in which anthropologists' and other moderns' concerns with the intensification of "global/local relations" is in itself an effect of the way we order information, an effect of our aesthetic devices (cf. Riles 1995).

Summarized as an argument, as I have done here, this observation may seem unsurprising precisely because, as Strathern notes, the necessity of the exercise stems from the way in which it is *already known* from the start. The achievement, then, lies not in the discovery of new knowledge but in the effort to make what we already know analytically accessible. But what inspires the present study is the way in which Strathern inverts the relationship between models and data as they traditionally are put into practice by anthropologists. Recognizing that while she can render anthropology's knowledge practices explicit, she cannot step outside of them, Strathern instead "exploits orthodox anthropological analysis as itself a literary form" (Strathern 1988: ix). We might say that Strathern turns those knowledge practices inside out—treating anthropological devices as the subject as well as the organizing stylistic device of her account. In *Partial Connections,* for example, she borrows a fractal as an organizing structure for her ethnography of the aesthetics of complexity;[27] the form of *The Gender of the Gift*, likewise is borrowed from two particularly ubiquitous anthropological models—essentialist we/they oppositions and the practice of playing one viewpoint off another.

One way of thinking about this is to view *Partial Connections* as the inside out version of the autobiographical approaches to ethnographic writing of the 1980s it describes. Starting from the same premise as those ethnographies—that it is impossible to speak of ethnographic "data" independent of their collector and analyst—the account does the opposite of putting the ethnographer in the picture, that is, it makes of the ethnographic state of mind a frame or form. The ultimate result does more than render the ethnographer as a character in the story. In recognizing that there is nothing outside the ethnographic mind, one might say, it turns that mind inside out.[28] The effect is to recreate aesthetically the possibility of anthropology after poststructuralist critiques: in turning our model inside out, the very modern knowledge practices that are the subject of Strathern's analysis are confirmed by their enactment even as a critical distance on those practices is achieved.

Informational Gaps

In other words, where the differences between, for example, relating to a person as academic colleague or "network focal point" are both too explicit to warrant analysis and too subtle to analyze explicitly, ethnographic description must become demonstration.[29] The approach I have taken, then, is not so much an argument as an enacting or exemplifying of a genre. For this reason, I have borrowed institutional actors' own forms and designs—designs such as the drawings they make of their "networks," the matrices donor agencies use for calculating objectives, or the divisions that rural Part-Europeans chart onto their land—as tools for bringing what is already known into view.

A reader will notice that certain "information" one typically expects of an ethnographic account is lacking from the pages that follow. It may not even feel like ethnography at points. One of the problems with studying global phenomena ethnographically, it is said, is that it is impossible to produce "thick description" (Geertz 1973: 3–10), that is, to elucidate the requisite description of social relations, because the phenomena are dispersed and the cultures are many. The assumption is that the ethnographer is generalizing from a social complexity of a new order and in so doing is losing the very complexity that renders social phenomena real and therefore interesting. One might refer to this absence as another example of aesthetic *failure* that I take as endemic to the Network form. As we will see, bureaucratic practices also point again and again to their own incompleteness (chap. 6). In the course of working with UN bureaucrats, government employees, and NGOs, I have come to appreciate that failure is a powerful aesthetic of its own.

Borrowing this device from the materials at hand, I have purposely resisted writing about this subject as if all that was required was to apply familiar methods to a new body of data. To do so would render the account more familiar. Yet I believe this tack would be doomed to fail in a more fundamental sense. For, where there is no place "outside" the subject matter from which to describe it, the old contextualizing tools of thick description, which work precisely by appealing to all that is "outside" the artifact (the problem or ritual, for example), will not produce the requisite effect.

Conversely, where the social scientists and institutional actors' knowledge practices are perfectly compatible but also mutually eclipsing (they share a singular model, the Network), each comes into view only through a careful blindness to the other form—a *failure* to see the other side, an agnostic lack of attention to the figure's well-delineated gaps.

This is not simply a matter of presentation style. A central argument of this book is that the ethnographic problem posed by globalization is not one of how to generalize from, to categorize, or to simplify phenomenological complexity but rather that the global does not exist in the first place, at least as it is imagined as a sphere or place of social action open to study rather than as an aspect of late modern informational aesthetics (chap. 3). In other words, I hope to demonstrate that anthropologists err where they take simulations of the artifacts of academic analysis, such as networks or slogans, as indigenous signposts that phenomenological complexity, or social reality, stands behind them (as we understand to be the case of our own analysis). One could also state the ethnographic problem in reverse: when phenomena are too well known to be described, what is needed is not greater detail but a selective erasure thereof, as, for example, the abstractions of modern art have brought modernity itself into view.

Ultimately, then, what is significant about this account is what is taken away. I became aware of the possibility of evocation by rendering the composition "thin" from my participation in institutional actors' many projects of design. Design, a networked craft[30] of visual manipulations of the aesthetics of communication, does not purport to describe fully but rather to channel attention. Drawing upon the designs that animate intellectual activity in the institutions described below, therefore, I wish to propose a different means of generating the effect of "being there" (Geertz 1988: 23). Like the stark lines of the graphic designs or the tables and data sets, I have made aesthetic choices, and it is these choices that demonstrate the subject and render it accessible.[31]

Finally, some readers may feel that I have failed sufficiently to reflect on my own place in the story. Rather than a repudiation of the reflexive turn in anthropology, however, I understand this project as its inside out version. What is problematized, in other words, is not so much my position in the field as the way the field is both within and without myself. To do so is to collapse the distinction between argument and ethnography—to abandon one of the most powerful aesthetics of our trade. Yet to frame the project in these terms also places the field, rather than the ethnographer, in the foreground.

Overview of the Book

The book is organized around a series of "analytical forms." In chapter 2, the form at issue is the "network," as it is deployed by social scientists on the one hand and institutional actors on the other. In chapter 3, it is the "bracket" used by negotiators of international agreements to resolve conflicts over proposed texts. Chapter 4 contrasts the bounded rectangular form of one Part-European clan's land with the form of the family tree produced by urban and overseas members of the same clan. Chapter 5 examines the form of "system" as it is represented and deployed in networkers' tasks of graphic design. Chapter 6 focuses on the matrices used within institutions as analytical tools.

I view each chapter as an experiment in working with these forms to find ways to apprehend what is already too familiar. In this sense, each chapter takes on a different aspect of the ethnographic problem I have laid out in the preceding pages. Chapter 2 sets up the "ethnographic context," including the problems of ethnographic method at issue in a subject that *defies* context as an analytical device. The ethnographic focus of the chapter is on the networks that institutional actors say define their collectivity and to which they devote so much time and energy. The puzzle here is the fact that despite this talk and activity networkers in Fiji take little interest in doing what they say networks do, that is, in expanding their personal connections or their knowledge. Moreover, the personal relationships outside the Network are hardly the anonymous and distant relationships envisioned in the Network's self-description. A preliminary problem concerns the absence of society, culture, or any form of "community" beyond what those involved term "personal" relations. What might be the subject of anthropological inquiry in such a condition, and what analytical tools are at the ethnographer's disposal?

In chapter 3, the problem is the relationship of global to local, as it is encountered in the ethnography of transnationalism and in the negotiation of UN documents. The experiment involves the use of an analogy—the analogy of UN documents to Fijian mats—which comes out of ethnographic observation but is not entirely "theirs"—and thus is neither "data" nor "analysis" in the typical anthropological understanding. The argument of the chapter is that globalization is an effect of the pattern, not a condition outside of knowledge.

The chapter also introduces the book's central motif of pattern and design through an examination of the patterns of the drafted text. The international legal document will be shown to be a form that generates its own context in the patterned levels it contains within itself. In UN documents, pattern emerges precisely when the counting (of paragraphs, brackets, or text in the course of negotiations) fails. This in turn provides a first instance of another central theme, that is, the way "failure" is internal to the aesthetics of the forms of transnational institutional practices and indeed engenders its own important effects.

The subject matter of chapter 4 is the geometry and arithmetic entailed in the division of finite parcels of land among a pair of Part-European clans in the rural Savusavu area of Fiji. In contrast to understandings of analysis as an activity that transforms its raw material (information), this division of land does not leave its subject matter altered. Division is a grounded, literal operation that exists a priori to the analyst, since the rules of division are given at the start, and therefore it does not take individuals or groups as its point of reference. The material provides a point from which to query the notion of information that underlies much of the anthropology and social theory of globalization.

Chapter 5 focuses on the character of network design. A twin aesthetic of heterogeneity and system characterizes this work. The argument of this chapter is that, in contrast to the high modernist tradition of activist "design," networks do not refer to a reality outside themselves. Distances and differences of culture that the designs are taken to transcend are internal features of the composition, therefore, not "real" entities outside the figures. This insight then is extended to a consideration of the systemic aesthetics of fact.

Chapter 6, "Filling in the Action," addresses the problem networkers experience in turning forms into "action" through a consideration of funding practices on the one hand and activism on the other. The chapter describes its logic of slots or internal gaps and the way the entities that fill these slots—words, people, symbols, or funds, for example—are material, thinglike entities, kernels of the Real. The argument here is that the Real is internally constituted by the gaps in the design. The chapter considers how the apprehension of the figure's empty spaces spurs matrix users to Action by demanding its completion. Action, then, is also internally generated by the form.

Chapter 7 concludes with a consideration of some of the implications of the Network form the previous chapters elucidate for international law and politics and, in particular, for the place of the academic critique of global processes.

One might summarize this project as an exercise in finding a vantage point from which to approach what is too familiar to apprehend with ease. While conducting fieldwork and later writing this book, I often thought of a deceptively simple exercise in graphic design I once was asked to perform in an art class at primary school. The teacher piled a jumble of ordinary stools on the table and asked us to draw not the shape of this mundane form but the shape generated by the spaces between the stools—to see the other figure that was in front of us. My frustration at my inability to see what was in front of me that day was replicated numerous times in the field. What took me a while to understand, however, is that, in attempting to see the gaps in the figure through fieldwork, I already was enacting what I hoped to describe, what in this book I have called the network inside out. It remains to elucidate the figure in the pages to follow.

CHAPTER 2

Sociality Seen Twice

In early 1990, the Pacific Regional YWCA initiated an ambitious project of "women's development." Known as PAWORNET (the Pacific Women's Information/Communication Network), it was the innovation of a Tongan woman trained as a lawyer in New Zealand and the United States who had been active in international circles since she represented Tonga at the UN End of the Decade for Women Conference in Nairobi in 1985. As presented in its funding proposal and newsletters, and as described to board members, donors, and women's groups, the project proposed to create one of the most elaborate, far-reaching, and structurally complex information networks in the Pacific. The network would extend from radio stations in Fiji to villages in Tuvalu and from the UN headquarters in New York to women's clubs in the outer islands of each Pacific nation.

The project involved the appointment and training of "national information officers"—communications experts—in six Pacific Island states. These officers would serve simultaneously as the outer "focal points" of PAWORNET and the central focal points of their own national information networks, and they would collect and disseminate information within their countries. They in turn would pass information on to the "regional focal point" at the Pacific YWCA, thus networking in several directions (see fig. 5). A regional assistance team would supervise activities and train women in each country in networking skills deemed necessary for participation in the national networks coordinated by the national information officers. The program included a clipping service, which would accumulate and redistribute news articles on women's issues, and a series of questionnaires distributed by the thousands, which, once collated by the regional focal point, would reveal what "issues" mattered most to Pacific women.

As those involved in the project later remembered, its appeal to participants and donors alike lay in a particularly satisfying confluence of communications idioms. On the one hand, it emphasized technical expertise, efficiency, well-defined lines of communication, and "support teams." On the other hand, it identified a new category of clients—"women"—united in a new need—"information"—and addressed these clients' isolation and powerlessness in the friendly and accessible ethos of the network. Project materials (often copied di-

What does the Network Look Like?

at the regional level

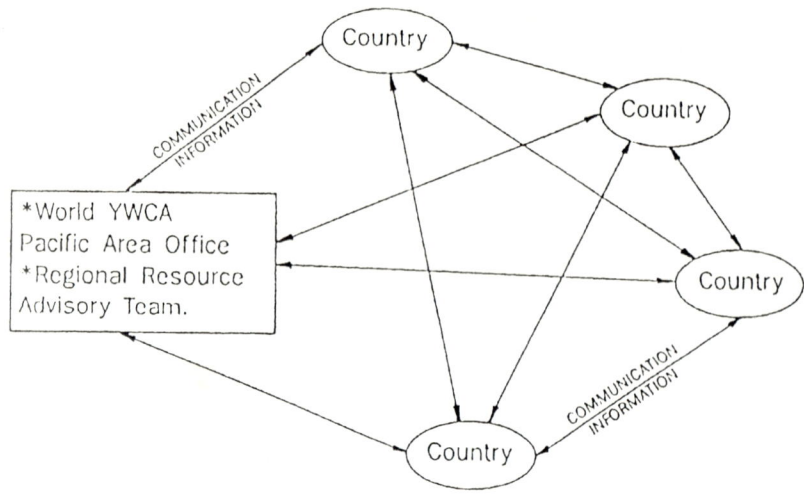

at the national level

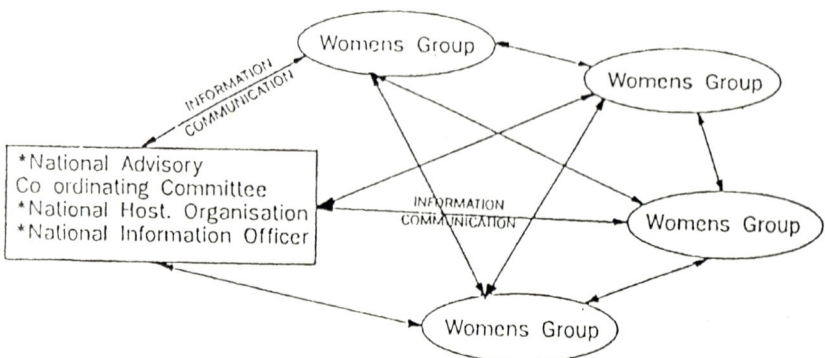

Fig. 5. "What does the network look like?" (schematic depiction of PAWORNET). (From the report of the Pacific Subregional Workshop on the Technical Processing of Information Concerning Women in Development 1992: 6. Reproduced courtesy of PAWORNET.)

rectly from the pages of the newsletters of the New York–based International Women's Tribune Centre, or IWTC) listed easy steps to establishing one's own network on a small scale and encouraged women to recognize that they already were networking and therefore needed only to concentrate on it more explicitly and formalize their existing networks. One PAWORNET newsletter explained the concept as follows:

> A "Network" is a group of people who have a common interest and link together to share information, skills, ideas, and resources. A "Network" can be large or small. It can link individuals to each other, individuals to small groups, small groups to large groups and so on. No matter what the size all networks have one common theme—SHARING! (1990: 4)

Throughout the Pacific NGO community PAWORNET was received as a new and exciting project, and the Australian for International Development Agency (now known as AusAID) bought into that excitement by funding it at a rate far exceeding any other locally administered women in development project in the Pacific.

The Pacific regional YWCA was largely synonymous with the person of its Tongan director. She had come to Fiji to found the office, an offshoot of the World YWCA housed in a small bungalow in an affluent neighborhood of Suva, which was to "coordinate" national YWCAs in the Pacific. She had been chosen for the position by the expatriate founder of the Fiji YWCA, who had observed her activities at the 1985 United Nations Women's Conference in Nairobi and had been impressed with her intelligence and eloquence. In Suva, she cut an intimidating figure, drawing allies and friends into positions as national information officers and board members, while maneuvering to block her enemies' projects and shunning them during the coffee breaks at the meetings that filled everyone's schedule.

The PAWORNET project got off to a successful start with the appointment and training of the first class of national information officers. Articles and radio programs began to appear under the PAWORNET banner throughout the Pacific, surveys were distributed and collected, and what those involved described as an elegant and cheerful PAWORNET newsletter made its way to a vast number of people and organizations across the region and the globe. Yet in 1992, just as PAWORNET seemed poised to become a showcase of women's development, the project suddenly collapsed. Expenditures ceased to be "documented," funds ceased to flow from the center to the regional focal points that awaited them, and some whispered that the network had begun to produce such illegitimate outputs as elaborate parties for friends and dignitaries. AusAID withdrew further funding, and the network ceased to exist in formal terms. An anthropologist might ask why a network endowed with all of the tools necessary for its operation, perpetuation, and expansion on a global scale (Callon 1991)—funding, trained staff, equipment, a prestigious reputation, and a purpose or task at hand—would collapse after producing not information flow but a series of personal gatherings.[1] As a caveat to the actor-network theorists' term *interessement* (Callon 1986), one argument of this chapter will be that technology "for reaching out" cannot extend networks where the notion of extension fails to capture the imagination.

Traditionally, the second chapter of an ethnography offers something of a context for the argument that follows. This work has two "contexts," in this anthropological sense. The first is the history and social relations that I encountered in Suva—or rather, as we shall see, the *problem* of the lack thereof. The second is the history and status of a set of standard modernist analytical tools commonly deployed by anthropologists. The second kind of context concerns precisely the way in which the former context—"social relations"—fails as an explanatory device. As we will see, the subjects of this book do not form a "society," or a "culture," nor do they offer the observer any other model of relationality with which one might seek to explain the proliferation of networks such as PAWORNET. More precisely, the model of relationality they offer is the Network itself—the very thing an anthropologist might wish to explain. Another way to put this is that everything that can be explained already has been explained indigenously; there seems to be no way to analyze the phenomenon beyond the explicit language it offers for itself.

By now, the problems with contextualizing moves have become the subject of considerable anthropological and other social theory. One of the paralyzing insights of late-twentieth-century critical theory has been the understanding that there is no "outside" to our analyses, no position beyond our own knowledge from which we can reflect critically on them (e.g., Baudrillard 1994). In anthropology, this insight has taken the form of an increasing dissatisfaction with processes of entextualization and contextualization that have characterized the disciplinary mode of analysis throughout the century (e.g., Clifford 1988: 38; Goodwin and Duranti 1992; Thomas 1991; Crapanzano 1992: 207–11; Silverstein and Urban 1996; Appadurai 1996). Yet if there is a problem with the notion of "context," anthropologists by now also widely understand that deconstruction in itself, too, is not enough (e.g., Ortner 1998). Nor is it sufficient to simply accept others' representations of their actions at face value, for to do so would be to take the ideology of the Network as reality and to participate in its expansion. One also might wonder in such a scenario what anthropology's contribution might be.

As it turns out, this problem is also familiar to the people who are the subject of this book. In this chapter, therefore, I introduce and put to work a device I have borrowed from them that I call a phenomenon "seen twice." As we will see, for networkers in Suva, the Network and "personal relations" are versions of one another seen twice. It will be important to understand how different this is from traditional anthropological understanding in which either of the two (Network or relations) could be understood as context and thus as an explanatory device for the other (cf. Wagner 1975). Networkers in Suva do not make sense of their personal relations in terms of their networks or vice versa; rather, like in the double view of the hologram as described by Baudrillard (1994: 105–9), it is in seeing the form of each in turn that both become real.

My objective, then, is to work with some problems of modernist knowledge concretized by the diverse uses of the Network, as an analytical form in the social sciences on the one hand, and the networks I encountered in Suva, on the other. Borrowing from the practices of the networkers I know there, I do not aim to make sense of or explain one kind of network in terms of the other; whether, for example, the ideas of modernist sociology somehow spawned the institutional networks that proliferate the globe or what kinds of networks a sociologist might see in these persons' relations and activities are questions I simply do not address. What else analysis might be about is the puzzle I take from Nancy Munn's assertion, quoted at the outset of this book, that Walbiri designs and the paths the Walbiri have taken are to be understood as "the same thing." A postexplanatory anthropology might turn instead to the enactment of the knowledge practices we once described.

Versions of an Issue

Fiji gained independence from Britain in 1970, at the height of the exportation of second-wave feminism to the developing world, and the history of "women's issues" in Fiji is inseparable from that of the transition from colonial to postcolonial registers of transnational influence.[2] In the early twentieth century, "women" became an *issue* for the government of Fiji, as for other colonial powers in the Pacific. The government established the Soqosoqo Vakamarama (Fijian Women's Society), an organization under the leadership of chiefly women in 1924, and, as one friend long active in the organization put it, the government "poured money into it" until independence when the organization turned to village-based "fundraising" for its income. The Soqosoqo Vakamarama was active at the time of the Beijing Conference, although it was considerably less influential than during the colonial period. It sent a delegate to Beijing.

During the same period, American interests in the Pacific also frequently took the form of an interest in women and their "issues." The Pan-Pacific and Southeast Asian Women's Association (PPSEAWA), the first international women's organization to include Fijians, was founded in 1930. This organization was to be the "women's arm" of a high-level American-led political and economic alliance aimed at ensuring Pacific "security" in the post–World War

I reconstruction era through "mutual understanding" (Hooper n.d.). From its inception, PPSEAWA was intended to be an association of elite women from the Pacific Rim countries who would discuss questions of child nutrition, education, and other nonpolitical issues, although the founding conference organized by the American feminist activist Jane Addams set a somewhat different tone.

Fijian delegates attended this founding meeting of PPSEAWA and every subsequent one, and from 1978 to 1981 a Fijian woman held the position of international president (PPSEAWA 1978). During the 1950s, PPSEAWA served as an umbrella organization of women's clubs and groups in Fiji, what contemporary institutional actors described to me as "a precursor to the National Council of Women." Like the Soqosoqo Vakamarama, PPSEAWA still had a chapter in Fiji during the period of my fieldwork, and with partial funding from PPSEAWA International it sponsored a delegate to the Beijing Conference,[3] although it rarely held meetings.[4] Yet, despite the waning of these two organizations, the influence of PPSEAWA and the Soqosoqo Vakamarama on the present state of "women's organizations" was palpable: women of fifty years of age or older who participated in so-called women in development programs had come into these activities almost exclusively through leadership roles in these two organizations, and many alliances and conflicts had their roots in the friendships and misunderstandings that accompanied the transitions from these associations to those that followed.

One of the most significant events in the history of the emergence of "women's issues" as an arena of international activity in Fiji was the founding of the YWCA. In 1962, two Australian women arrived in Fiji at the request of a group of elite Europeans in one of many efforts to bring the social institutions of the colonial center to Fiji (YWCA 1962; "X looks back" 1973). Imagined by their European patrons as middle-class women skilled in running kindergartens and art programs, they saw themselves as covert activists who would broker their white middle-class credentials into programs to promote racial and gender equality in Fiji. They did indeed found a kindergarten—Fiji's first multiracial educational institution—and they did teach art classes, although the emphasis lay more on the needs of unemployed urban youth and the uses of design for poster and newsletter making. As an Australian journalist now working as the director of information for the University of the South Pacific, who had emigrated to Fiji as a young woman, recalled of her involvement in the YWCA in the early years:

> It's not an organization I would belong to somewhere else, but in Fiji it was different—a catalyst for many of the things that happened for women and also a key venue for the development of some of the important individuals in the movement. . . . The "Y" took off because [the directors] seemed to have a knack for getting young Fijian women involved. . . . It

was far more outspoken than other organizations. Others tended to be social welfare oriented. The "Y" had its social welfare angle, too, but it was able to respond to what young people really wanted. It taught skills.

She credited the YWCA with "politicizing a generation of young women about themselves as citizens and as young women." As she put it, "What was happening among that small group was not happening in the larger community."

Central to the success of the endeavor was the use the founders made of all of the resources available to members of the colonial establishment during that era. Every year, the Adi Cakobau School, the school for elite Fijian girls whose headmistress was a New Zealander and a patron of the Y's founders, held an "open day." The pupils performed Fijian dances, served tea to the visitors, and sold potted plants, and the proceeds went to the YWCA. One Fijian woman recalled how, as a young student at Adi Cakobau, she would take the bus once each week into the city to prepare coffee for the "ladies at the Y." The school's old girls felt they had "built the Y," she said, and she added that owing to this history they should be entitled to an office in the YWCA building today. Another recalled how the women ingeniously cajoled the mayor of Suva, and virtually every member of the colonial establishment, into making contributions in administrative favors, cash, kind, and labor to build a four-story "community center" in the center of Suva, which in 1996 still housed a hostel for women, counseling programs, training programs, and the offices of the YWCA.

By all accounts, the YWCA did indeed create a forum and meeting place for an emerging cadre of young Fijian, Indian, and Part-European women who saw themselves as feminists, critics of colonial and chiefly power, and opponents of segregation and racism in Fiji. Thirty years later, this group of local women spoke about the YWCA with fondness. They remembered their experience of the 1960s with a certain amount of nostalgia as the first time that women of different races met on an equal footing in Fiji. They associated the YWCA with the watershed moments in Fiji's contemporary history—for example, they told of taking physical refuge together at the YWCA building during the anti-Indian "Taukei" marches in the days of the political coup in 1987. As in the case of the leaders of the Soqosoqo Vakamarama and PPSEAWA, those who "grew up together" in the YWCA, as they said, remained personally close and committed to the activist values of that institution. A significant number of the women involved in WID programs at the time of my research had ties to the YWCA. Within the Department of Women and Culture alone, the director was a former general secretary of the YWCA; the minister for education, women and culture, science and technology, whose portfolio included the department, was a former president of the YWCA; and the department's statistician had worked for the YWCA for ten years, and served as secretary to the YWCA from 1994 to 1996, before joining government.

The UN International Women's Year in 1975 provided these young initiates with new international exposure. Several attended the NGO Women's Tribune, organized in conjunction with the UN International Women's Year Conference in Mexico City (Planning Committee 1975), and returned to organize a regional meeting of Pacific women (Griffen 1975, 1976). This regional conference founded a Pacific Women's Association and Pacific Women's Resource Centre (PWRC) based in Suva with a Third World activist agenda and the particular aim of bringing together women in the independent and still colonized territories of the Pacific. Several of these women attended university and training programs overseas. Others became lecturers at the University of the South Pacific and in 1996 constituted core members of the academic feminist community in Fiji and the Pacific.

After independence, one of the two YWCA founders left Fiji to do postgraduate studies in education in the United States, focusing, interestingly enough, on alternative communications conduits among women in Fiji.[5] She ultimately founded the International Women's Tribune Centre based at the UN headquarters in New York (chap. 5). The other YWCA founder soon handed authority over to a Fijian activist chosen early on for the task. The latter steered the Fiji YWCA in more explicitly activist directions and ultimately into a conflict with its elite European patrons, whose slogan, some of these patrons recalled, was "put the C back into the YWCA."[6]

In some respects, the new leaders of the YWCA simply rendered more explicit the activist agenda of their expatriate predecessors. Yet in other respects, their agenda was different. The new leaders saw little reason to limit their activities to traditional "women's issues" or to frame their commitment to political causes such as postcolonial capitalism, decolonization, nuclear testing, and peace in terms of the relevance of these causes to women. During this period, the YWCA leadership forged strong ties with academics, male and female, and with other activists in Fiji and abroad (Subramani 1998: 148). The new leaders of the YWCA also began to rethink the colonial system of privilege that had enabled two European women to found a Fijian organization in the first place and confronted them explicitly about the legitimacy of their leadership at several junctures.

In extending their political critique to the power structures of the colonial elite in Fiji, the young Fiji-born activists of the YWCA also alienated their financial and power base. The Pacific Women's Resource Centre soon closed its doors due to funding problems, conflicts among board members, and a concern among its administrators that it lacked the "grassroots support" of the women it aimed to help (PWRC n.d.). In 1996, early Fijian members and later leaders of the YWCA were sidelined from current WID (women in development) projects, and some had left Fiji.[7] Like PPSEAWA and the Soqosoqo Vakamarama, the YWCA still existed but only as a shadow of what members said it used to be. Its building had fallen into disrepair, and its programs were limited. One of the two founders remained in Fiji, although she rarely participated in the activities of either this group of activists or the WID specialists who ultimately replaced them.

The 1987 coup[8] also fundamentally changed the atmosphere. Multiracial and activist organizations such as the YWCA became more suspect. At the same time, the postcoup instatement of Sitiveni Rabuka, the soldier who had led the coup, as prime minister ironically served as a source of inspiration to some urban educated Fijian women. As one such person commented, "if Rabuka can be PM, why can't I be in politics?" The coup also left some people in search of their place in contemporary Fiji and thus created a new need for institutional affiliations. For example, the Rev. Lian-hong Ch'ien, one of only three female Methodist ministers and the only "nonindigenous person" ministering to the indigenous Fijian community, attended the Beijing Conference as the Pacific representative of the World Association for Christian Communication (WACC), an international ecumenical group based in London. The organization's stated objective is to train people to share information more effectively. In the Pacific, the beneficiaries of the program were not necessarily Christian groups. For example, WACC funded members of the Fiji Women's Rights Movement and the Fiji Women's Crisis Centre to attend a regional meeting for "communicators" in Bangkok.

Lian-hong's interest was in the conflict between religion and political activism. She saw herself as pushing Pacific churches to do more for women and to acknowledge the limitations they placed on the participation of women, on the one hand, and as pushing activist women to question why their religious faith and their work in government or international organizations were seen to be incompatible on the other. She planned to accomplish this through what she called a "documentation project"—a "handbook" summarizing the history of the international women's conferences and the international ecumenical groups' commitment to women's causes and explaining Pacific preparations for Beijing.

Originally a Taiwanese citizen (and employee of the Taipei YWCA), Lian-hong emigrated to Brazil with her parents, where she farmed and ran a flower stall and then moved to the United States to study to become a minister. There she met her husband, a Tongan raised in Fiji, and the two moved back to Fiji after the completion of their studies twelve years prior to the Beijing Conference to serve as Methodist ministers. After the coup (supported by the Methodist Church), an ardent nationalist took over as president and redirected church activities toward more direct involvement in politics.[9] Lian-hong lost her position in the upper echelons of the seminary and was assigned to running the Methodist bookshop. Her role in the World Association for Christian Communication global network therefore literally gave her a place.

At the same time, the 1980s saw the rise of "women in development" as a major international concern. Women's issues became issues of "development," and with this new focus on development came a new technocratic relationship between the former colonial powers and women's groups (cf. Mueller 1986). New institutions emerged: Where the earlier Pacific Women's Resource Centre had floundered because of lack of funds and angst over its relationship to the "grass roots," the Pacific Women's Resource Bureau (PWRB), founded at the SPC in 1982,[10] remained a wealthy, powerful institution in 1996, staffed by experienced administrators, communications experts, and high-level political appointees rather than activists and funded principally by the governments of Australia, New Zealand, and France. The 1985 UN Women's Conference's call for "national machineries" saw the establishment of National Councils of Women (NCW) throughout the Pacific as well as the emergence of a new form of organization, the Network. As one of the most active participants in the Beijing process explained, "after the first women's conference we got organizations. But at Nairobi, we got networks"[11] (table 3). From the early 1980s, conferences aimed at producing documents became the dominant genre.[12]

In Fiji, an entirely new cadre of women came to the forefront—educated professionals and persons with institutional experience in fields unrelated to women and activism, much more skilled in interfacing with aid agencies on these organizations' terms, accustomed to travel and life overseas, knowledgeable about the procedures of the UN and other international institutions, and less interested in the overt politicization of causes that had animated the YWCA. A University of the South Pacific scientist explained to me that she became involved in the ECOWOMAN network and attended the Beijing Conference only because "ECOWOMAN had funds. I substituted for someone else." The Department of Women and Culture's senior civil servant had been transferred to the department from the higher prestige Central Planning Office with no background or particular interest in WID issues, but during her tenure in the department she became president of Fiji's National Council of Women on a pledge to bring a new standard of efficacy and accountability to the organization. The members of the Pacific NGO Coordinating Group for the Beijing Conference, who directed Pacific NGOs' participation in the Conference, likewise, were all relative newcomers to women's issues with strong personal ties to particular international funding sources.

The evolution of feminist activism into a set of WID bureaucracies coincided with the development of the city of Suva into the administrative hub for a wide range of regional and international organizations working in the South Pacific. The major UN development institutions—the United Nations Development Programme (UNDP), the United Nations Fund for Women (UNIFEM), the United Nations Population Fund (UNFPA), the United Nations Children's Fund (UNICEF), and others—have offices in Suva from which they direct projects throughout the Pacific, as do large governmental and international aid agencies such as AusAID or the World Council of Churches (WCC) and international pressure groups such as Greenpeace. During the period 1994–96, typical projects of these international institutions included providing training courses in areas such as "rural development skills" and "data management," sponsoring regional and international meetings on banking policies and water sanitation methods, producing legal documents and pamphlets for popular audiences, lobbying Pacific Island governments for the ratification of international agreements, gathering demographic data, and mounting public awareness campaigns.

Suva also serves as the administrative base for numerous regional intergovernmental bodies. The South Pacific Commission,[13] an organization of Pacific Island states and colonial powers in the region, operates many of its programs from Suva. Likewise, the South Pacific Forum (SPF),[14] an economic and political alliance of Pacific Island states, headquarters its secretariat in Suva. The work of these organizations includes negotiating regional and international agreements, devising and implementing development programs, conducting studies, maintaining data bases, providing "technical assistance" to Pacific Island governments, and representing Pacific concerns in other international forums. At the top management level, these organizations are staffed by university-educated Pacific Islanders with diplomatic experience drawn from the region at large or in some cases by expatriates. Most of the remaining staff of the Fiji offices are Fiji citizens of diverse cultural and educational backgrounds.

Branches of the Fiji government also participate directly in numerous international legal and institutional arenas. Pacific governments rely on interaction and support from international aid agencies to fund many of the projects they wish to pursue. A large amount of time and energy is devoted to regional meetings, joint projects with other states, attendance at international conferences, and the preparation of documents for international conferences. In preparation for the UN Fourth World Conference on Women, for example, the Department of Women and Culture, a division of the Ministry for Education, Women and Culture, Science and Technology, worked on an almost daily basis to coordinate and prepare for national, regional, and international consultations. These tasks included "liaising" with other governments and regional and international organizations involved in the preparations, producing newsletters explaining the conference to a national audience, and drafting documents and position papers. Finally, whatever their capacities, those working in this area also spent a large amount of time traveling in the region and throughout the world, as participants attended conferences abroad and made frequent visits to counterpart organizations overseas for "study tours" or "networking" activities.

TABLE 3. Some Institutions and Networks Mentioned in the Text

Governmental and Intergovernmental Organizations	Origin Date	Type[a]	Principal Issues	Staff[b]	Principal Donor
UNIFEM—Pacific Mainstreaming Project	1986	Inst	WID	3	UNDP; AusAID; NZODA
ESCAP—Women's Information Network (WINAP)	1987	Net	WID (information)	n/a	ESCAP
SPC—Pacific Women's Resource Bureau (PWRB)	1982	Inst/Net	WID	(5)	NZODA; France; AusAID
Fiji Government—Department of Women and Culture (DWC)	1987	Inst	WID	12	AusAID; NZODA; Fiji government
NGOs (international)					
Development Alternatives with Women for a New Era (DAWN)	1984	Net	Political/economic analysis	(1)	MacArthur Foundation; Ford Foundation
International Women's Tribune Centre (IWTC)	1975	Inst	WID (information)	(16)	UNIFEM; UNFPA; Australia; Canada
NGOs (regional)					
Gender and Development Programme (GAD), Asian and Pacific Development Centre (APDC)	1980	Inst	WID	(7)	CIDA; SIDA
Asia and Pacific NGO Working Group (APWG)	1993	Net	Beijing coordination	n/a	UNIFEM
IWDA Beneath Paradise	1993	Proj	Beijing documentation	(4)	AusAID
Omomo Melen Pacific	1994	Net	Decolonization	1	APDC; Corso; Bread for the World

Organization	Year	Type	Focus	Staff	Funders
Pacific Concerns Resource Centre (PCRC)	1980	Inst	Decolonization, demilitarization	9	CAA; Bread for the World
Pacific NGO Coordinating Group (PNGOCG)	1994	Net	Beijing coordination	none	AusAID; NZODA; UNDP; TAF; British ODA
Pacific POPIN	1991	Net	Population information	1	USP; ESCAP
Pacific Sustainable Development Networking Project	1994	Net/Proj	Information technology	4	UNDP; TAF
Pacific YWCA	1991	Inst	WID	2	WCC
PAWORNET	1990	Net	WID (information)	7	AIDAB
SPACHEE ECOWOMAN	1994	Net	Environmental education	2	CIDA
WACC—Pacific	1979	Inst	Media information	1	WACC
WAINIMATE	1993	Net	Indigenous medicine	none	CIDA; NZODA
Women and Fisheries Network	1992	Net	Network	none	CUSO; Greenpeace

NGOs (domestic)

Organization	Year	Type	Focus	Staff	Funders
Catholic Women's League	1968	Net	Rural development	none	self-funded
Fiji National Council of Women	1986	Inst/Net	WID coordination	1	AusAID; DWC
Fiji Women's Crisis Centre (FWCC)	1984	Inst	Domestic violence	4	AusAID; IWDA; CAA
Fiji Women's Rights Movement (FWRM)	1986	Inst	Legal/economic rights	3	OXFAM; TAF; AusAID
Fiji Women in Politics (FIJIWIP)	1994	Inst	Political participation	2	TAF
Fiji YWCA	1962	Inst	WID education	6	self-funded: World YWCA
Soqosoqo Vakamarama	1924	Inst	Rural development	none	UNFPA; DWC
Women's Action for Change (WAC)	1990	Inst	Drama, political change	1	AusAID; South Pacific People's Foundation

[a] Inst = institution; Net = network; Proj = project. This typology is based purely on the institution's official self-description.

[b] "Staff" includes persons who administer the project or work for the institution on a full or part-time basis as employees or volunteers. It does not include members, focal points, representatives, consultants, or other categories of participants. Numbers in parentheses indicate staff outside of Fiji.

A multitude of national and regional nongovernmental organizations based in Suva also make use of international conferences and instruments, and participate in international "networks," as part of their work on issues ranging from "environmentalism" to "indigenous rights" to "Christian communication."[15] In Suva, these organizations are staffed by Pacific Islanders of widely varying educational, cultural, and status backgrounds out of small offices and using a minimum of equipment (usually a computer, a photocopy machine, a telephone, and a fax machine) in their work.

Approximately fifty Suva-based networks participated in preparations for the UN Fourth World Conference on Women (tables 3 and 4). Almost all of these had emerged in the previous ten years as a result of the new and vigorous prioritization of WID funding by a handful of traditional donor institutions (tables 3 and 5) that paralleled a dramatic increase in attention to WID during this period throughout the developing world.[16]

The majority of the women in development projects funded in the Pacific from 1994 to 1996 were concentrated in two often overlapping areas. The first involved activities related specifically to the Beijing Conference and its preparatory process. These included funds for attendance at the many preparatory conferences; for the completion, rewriting, or publication of reports; for the purchase of computer equipment for producing documents; and for the hosting of meetings and workshops. The second category consisted of "training" and "information dissemination" activities. These included funds for short-term training sessions in areas such as statistics, rural development, or gender awareness, and the beneficiaries ranged from high-level bureaucrats to village-based "community workers." These projects also included the publication of newsletters, the organization of satellite radio conferences by the Consortium for International Pacific Education and Communication Experiments by Satellite (PEACESAT),[17] the hosting of large open public education events and small invited "workshops," the production of videos and television and radio programs, the organization and funding of study visits overseas, the provision of an expatriate consultant to conduct a management review or lead a workshop, and the provision of basic "institutional support." There were a number of projects, such as PAWORNET, directed at teaching information management skills to "grassroots people" (PWRB 1994a). For example, a principal element in the PWRB "work programme" for 1995–97 involved training rural Pacific women in the collection and evaluation of statistics. Only a small number of projects were directed at providing infrastructure,[18] and very few were directed at recipient institutions outside the city areas. In essence, WID funding was a market for information in various forms.

The sums at issue were substantial. The cost of attending the Beijing Conference, for example, equaled the yearly salary of the average full-time worker in the capital city. A single project to produce several issues of a newsletter—

TABLE 4. Networks Mentioned in the Text That Participated in the Fourth World Conference on Women (FWCW), Beijing

Governmental and Intergovernmental Networks	Principal Focal Point/ Network Co-ordinator	Focal Points[a]	Newsletter	Technical Networks[b]	Affiliated Networks
Pacific Mainstreaming Project	UNIFEM-Pacific	Cook Islands; Marshall Islands; PNG; Tuvalu	Pacific Mainstreaming News	PEACESAT; Internet	PNGOCG; UNIFEM; IWTC
Women's Information Network (WINAP)	ESCAP	national women's ministries and national NGOs	WINAP Newsletter	n/a	n/a
SPC Network	PWRB	national women's ministries and NCWs in SPC member states	Women's News	PEACESAT	FWCW—regional focal point
WID Steering Committee (DWC-WID)	Fiji government, Department of Women and Culture (DWC)	government ministries; NGOs	News of Women	PEACESAT	n/a
NGOs (international)					
Development Alternatives with Women for a New Era (DAWN)	Women and Development Unit (WAND); University of West Indies	Pacific regional coordinator; Pacific research coordinator	DAWN Informs	Internet	WEDO; IWTC
International Women's Tribune Centre (IWTC)	IWTC	NGOs in developing world	Tribune	Internet	WEDO; World YWCA—Pacific Area Office; DAWN

(continued)

TABLE 4.—(Continued)

Governmental and Intergovernmental Networks	Principal Focal Point/ Network Co-ordinator	Focal Points[a]	Newsletter	Technical Networks[b]	Affiliated Networks
Global FaxNet	IWTC	NGOs in developing world	Global FaxNet	n/a	PNGOCG
Nuclear Free and Independent Pacific (NFIP)	Pacific Concerns Resource Centre (PCRC)	grassroots movements/activist organizations	Pacific News Bulletin	Internet	WEDO
Women's Linkage Caucus	Women's Environment and Development Organization (WEDO)	PCRC: Women and Fisheries Network: World YWCA. Pacific Area Office	Advocacy Documents	Internet	IWTC: DAWN
Women Weaving the World Together	Khemara, Cambodia	FNCW: PNGOCG: APWG	Beijing	n/a	n/a
NGOs (regional)					
n/a	Gender and Development Programme (GAD), Asian and Pacific Development Centre (APDC)	n/a	Issues in Gender and Development	n/a	APWG; IWTC: WEDO: NFIP: USP: DAWN
Asia and Pacific NGO Working Group (APWG)	PPSEAWA: Pacific YWCA	subregional contact points; regional task forces; project co-ordinators	Reaching Out	Internet	NGO Planning and Facilitating Committee: IWTC
Beneath Paradise	IWDA	n/a	Beneath Paradise	n/a	n/a
Omomo Melen Pacific	Pacific Concerns Resource Centre	Activist women's organizations from Pacific colonies and occupied	n/a	n/a	Beneath Paradise; Women of Colour Network

Pacific NGO Coordinating Group (PNGOCG)	UNIFEM: Pacific YWCA; FNCW	NCWs in each Pacific country; WACC—Pacific	S'Pacifically Speaking	PEACESAT; Internet	APWG; Women Weaving the World Together; IWTC; WEDO; WCC
PAWORNET	Pacific YWCA	national information officers	Tok Belong Ol Meri	n/a	SPC; IWTC; YWCA
ECOWOMAN Project	SPACHEE	environmentalist NGOs in the Pacific	n/a	PEACESAT; Internet	Once & Future Action Network; Women and Fisheries Network; IWTC; WEDO; YWCA
Pacific Women in Christian Communication	WACC—Pacific	n/a	n/a	PEACESAT	PNGOCG; WCC; WACC; IWTC
WAINIMATE	SPACHEE	national WAINIMATE networks	n/a	PEACESAT	n/a
NGOs (domestic)					
Pacific Women against Violence Network	Fiji Women's Crisis Centre	n/a	Pacific Women against Violence	PEACESAT; Internet	DWC—WID
Women and Fisheries Network	USP Academic	activists and researchers	Fishnet	n/a	Greenpeace; NFIP; WEDO
Women's Information Network	Fiji National Council of Women (FNCW)	affiliate organizations	Women's Information Network	n/a	DWC—WID; PWRB; PNGOCG; WEDO; IWTC; YWCA

(continued)

TABLE 4.—(*Continued*)

Governmental and Intergovernmental Networks	Principal Focal Point/ Network Co-ordinator	Focal Points[a]	Newsletter	Technical Networks[b]	Affiliated Networks
n/a	Catholic Women's League	n/a	Mai na Ruku ni Kali	PEACESAT	World Union of Catholic Women; GROOTS International
n/a	Fiji Women's Rights Movement (FWRM)	n/a	Balance	PEACESAT	DWC—WID; WCC; Women of Colour Network
Fiji WIP (see fig. 17)	FNCW	NGOs; government; political parties	Fiji WIP	n/a	APWIP
n/a	Soqosoqo Vakamarama	n/a	n/a	n/a	DWC—WID; Associated Country-women of the World
n/a	Women's Action for Change (WAC)	n/a	Changing Times	n/a	n/a

[a] "Focal Points" here include only entities explicitly mentioned in the networks' official self-descriptions.
[b] In addition to these technical networks, all of the networks listed here make use of telephone and facsimile connections, and all have at their disposal word processing and photocopying equipment.

TABLE 5. Fiji Participants' Affiliations at the Preparatory Conferences for the Fourth World Conference on Women and Their Funding Sources

Delegate[a]	Asia-Pacific NGO Symposium, Manila, November 1993	Funding Sources	Pacific Ministerial Conference and Regional Pacific Women's Conference, Nouméa, May 1994	Funding Sources	Asia-Pacific Ministerial Meeting, Jakarta, June 1994	Funding Sources	PrepCom (39th Session of the Commission on the Status of Women), New York, March–April 1995	Funding Sources	Fourth World Conference on Women and NGO Forum	Funding Sources
TVN	FNCW	AusAID	FNCW Fiji government		FNCW	UNICEF	PNGOCG FNCW UNIFEM Fiji government	AusAID British ODA	PNGOCG	NZODA
ITA	UNIFEM	UNIFEM	UNIFEM	UNIFEM	UNIFEM Fiji government	UNIFEM	PNGOCG UNIFEM	AusAID British ODA	UNIFEM PNGOCG	NZODA
LKI	FNCW	TAF	FNCW Fiji government				Fiji-WIP	TAF	Fiji Women in Politics Fiji government FNCW	TAF
CSI	DAWN	DAWN			ENGENDER	ENGENDER			DAWN	DAWN
IJA	FWRM	TAF								
BPE			SPC	SPC (NZODA)	SPC	SPC	SPC	SPC (NZODA)[b]	SPC	SPC
FCA			SPC	SPC	SPC	SPC	SPC	SPC (NZODA)	SPC	SPC
KMA			DWC	SPC (AusAID)	Fiji government (DWC)	SPC (AusAID)			Fiji government	FPTL/Fiji government
SOS			Beneath Paradise PCRC	PCRC			Omomo Melen Pacific PCRC	PCRC	Beneath Paradise Omomo Melen Pacific PCRC	IWDA/Corso
DSI			UNIFEM	UNIFEM					WAC *Fiji Times*	AusAID

(continued)

TABLE 5 (Continued)

Delegate	Asia-Pacific NGO Symposium, Manila, November 1993	Funding Sources	Pacific Ministerial Conference and Regional Pacific Women's Conference, Nouméa, May 1994	Funding Sources	Asia-Pacific Ministerial Meeting, Jakarta, June 1994	Funding Sources	PrepCom (39th Session of the Commission on the Status of Women), New York, March/April 1995	Funding Sources	Fourth World Conference on Women and NGO Forum	Funding Sources
SAR			UNDP	UNDP						
KPT			Fiji government (Ministry of Finance and Economic Planning)	SPC (NZODA)	Fiji government (Central Planning Office)	AusAID				
PFD			SPC (RPF)	ESCAP	ESCAP	ESCAP			UNDP	UNDP
DTO			UNICEF	UNICEF						
SAL			FWCC Violence against Women Network Beneath Paradise	IWDA						
KSS			British ODA Fiji government	British ODA						
JNA			Fiji government (Ministry of Education)	SPC (NZODA)						
PLO			FNCW Fiji government							
BRG					Pacific Media Desk Fiji government		PNGOCG Fiji government	AusAID British ODA	Pacific Media Desk PNGOCG Fiji government	UNFPA

	Tonga	UNFPA	PNGOCG Tonga	AusAID British ODA	Pacific YWCA PNGOCG	
SFU						
TVA	Fiji government	SPC (AusAID)			Fiji government	SPC (AusAID)
SMA	Fiji government (Central Planning Office)	Fiji government				
SRO	Fiji YWCA FNCW Media	UNFPA			Pacific Media Desk Fiji TV One Fiji YWCA Fiji government	AusAID
LMA	Fiji government (Ministry of Health)	SPC			Fiji government	WHO
TVE			Fiji government (DWC)	UNFPA	Fiji government	Fiji government
EO			Women and Fisheries Network	AusAID	Women and Fisheries Network	
EDU			SVT Fiji government	NZODA		
ALC			SVT Fiji government	Fiji government PNGOCG		
HT					Fiji government (Ministry of Health)	WHO
XY					South Pacific Forum	SPF
GHL					AusAID	AusAID

(continued)

TABLE 5—(Continued)

Delegate	Asia-Pacific NGO Symposium, Manila, November 1993	Funding Sources	Pacific Ministerial Conference and Regional Pacific Women's Conference, Nouméa, May 1994	Funding Sources	Asia-Pacific Ministerial Meeting, Jakarta, June 1994	Funding Sources	PrepCom (39th Session of the Commission on the Status of Women), New York, March–April 1995	Funding Sources	Fourth World Conference on Women and NGO Forum	Funding Sources
APA									PPSEAWA	PPSEAWA International/ partially self-funded
SEV									Catholic Women's League FNCW	Local fund-raising
MTT									WACC-Pacific PNGOCG	WACC
LSA									PCRC	WEDO
PSH									FWRM	WCC
KCO									Beneath Paradise FWCC	IWDA
SMA									FM96 Islands Business Pacific Islands News Association	APDC
VDU									Beneath Paradise FWRM	IWDA

VBI						Women and Fisheries Network SPACHEE ECOWOMAN Network	CIDA
ADA						WAINIMATE SPACHEE Fiji YWCA	CIDA
MBA						FNCW Fiji government	SPC
IJN						Individual Fiji government	Self-funded
CMO						USP Students Association	APDC
SLO						Fiji government	SPC
KRO						WACC	WACC
SSM						USP Forum '95 *Fiji Times*	NGO Forum
RLE						World YWCA, Pacific Area Office SPACHEE	CIDA
GFO						Women and Fisheries Network	
AKO						USP Students Association	APDC
KNA						Soqosoqo Vakamarama Fiji government	UNFPA

(continued)

TABLE 5—(Continued)

Delegate[a]	Asia-Pacific NGO Symposium, Manila, November 1993	Funding Sources	Pacific Ministerial Conference and Regional Pacific Women's Conference, Nouméa, May 1994	Funding Sources	Asia-Pacific Ministerial Meeting, Jakarta, June 1994	Funding Sources	PrepCom (39th Session of the Commission on the Status of Women), New York, March–April 1995	Funding Sources	Fourth World Conference on Women and NGO Forum	Funding Sources
VGR									APDC DAWN	APDC
MTO									Pacific Media Desk Radio Fiji (Fiji Broadcasting Commission) Fiji government	SPC[b]

[a] Initials denote individual delegates. Actual names withheld.
[b] Indicates funding from NZODA channeled through SPC.
[c] RP = Resource person (nondelegate).

a task requiring several weeks of work—could procure funding at a rate that exceeded the yearly starting salary for a university-educated civil servant. The salaries paid to employees of women's NGOs in Fiji, likewise, made a lucrative and respected career of activist work. Such positions tended to attract the few young women from Fiji who held foreign university degrees, and several of these women readily pointed out to me that were it not for the availability of these positions they would not have returned from abroad after completing their studies.

For example, one young Part-European woman, the niece of a prominent feminist academic, had recently returned to work as news director at a local radio station, reporting on women's issues, and she attended the Beijing Conference as a journalist funded by international women's groups. She had grown up and attended university in Australia and had returned to Fiji on her aunt's urging because of the opportunity for a young woman fresh out of university to direct radio news reporting. Several other women in their early twenties who had grown up in Fiji but attended university in Australia or New Zealand, where they had studied social sciences or women's studies, returned to serve as project officers at the Fiji Women's Rights Movement (FWRM) and the Fiji Women's Crisis Centre (FWCC).

The individuals who had emerged as the direct beneficiaries of donors' enthusiasm for WID projects usually maintained multiple affiliations with diverse networks, institutions and projects, and often received two or more "project" disbursements at once in their alternative institutional capacities. Despite the bureaucratic spirit of objective document-based evaluation of funding proposals that proceeded as if there was anonymity between donor and applicant, in virtually every case, the applicant was personally known to the donor staff, or at the very least the application was brokered by an intermediary who was personally known. Funding recipients moved from project to project as funds became available and then were spent. For example, upon the collapse of PAWORNET, Fiji's national information officer, a young Indo-Fijian woman with a gift for writing, went to work for UNIFEM as a project officer, then moved on to the South Pacific Commission as an information officer, then returned to work as a journalist for the *Fiji Times*. Upon her return to Fiji, she became involved in Women's Action for Change (WAC), a group specializing in theater performances with feminist and antiracist messages. Three years after the termination of her employment with PAWORNET, she attended the Beijing Conference in her capacity as a journalist and a member of WAC with funds from AusAID.

A Closed System

This brings us to the Network. For many delegates, groups, and institutions, in Fiji as elsewhere, the Network was one of the great innovations of the 1995

United Nations Women's Conference and indeed of the global women's movement of the 1980s and 1990s.[19] As a radio journalist and AIDS educator who attended the NGO Forum at Beijing told a Lautoka Village audience upon her return, her task was to collect materials, share experiences, and disseminate information in Fiji, and they could do the same:

> You can *network* with some of us in Suva. That's what the whole idea of Beijing was all about, was to network. That's one big lesson I learned. When you go to these meetings, take a lot of business cards with you so that you can exchange, 'cause when they are talking to you, they are giving out the business card.

In the ten years prior to the Bejing Conference, with the financial support of international donors, for whom both "regionalism" and "women in development" had become key priorities, hundreds of Pacific governmental and nongovernmental "networks" had emerged. These networks differed considerably in their degree of institutional formality, in the nature of their aims, in the extent of their reach, and in the identity of their participants (table 3). For example, networks involved in the Beijing preparatory process with focal points in Suva included Development Alternatives with Women for a New Era (DAWN), a network of academic activists from developing countries; a Women in Development Network of governmental and nongovernmental institutions established by the Fiji Government's Department of Women and Culture (DWC); the regional Women and Fisheries Network of Pacific academics, activists, and fisherwomen; the Asia-Pacific Women in Politics (APWIP) network; Omomo Melen Pacific, a network of activists from the colonies and nonindependent territories in the Pacific; and many others.

The Network also provided the official organizational form for the NGO Forum that accompanied the Beijing Conference, a system of regional, subregional, and national "focal points" through which official information and UN documents were circulated and recommendations for amendments were conveyed to NGOs (fig. 6). One focal point was designated for each of the UN regions—Asia-Pacific, Africa, the Caribbean and Latin America, Europe and North America, and Western Asia.

In the Pacific, each government also designated a "focal point" within its own bureaucracy (in most cases, its Department for Women), which participated in a "network" organized by the South Pacific Commission's Pacific Women's Resource Bureau (PWRB) as "regional focal point." PWRB received and distributed among these focal points funds, documents from UN headquarters, and information such as details of living conditions in Beijing and procedures for procuring visas. The bureau, as regional focal point, convened three

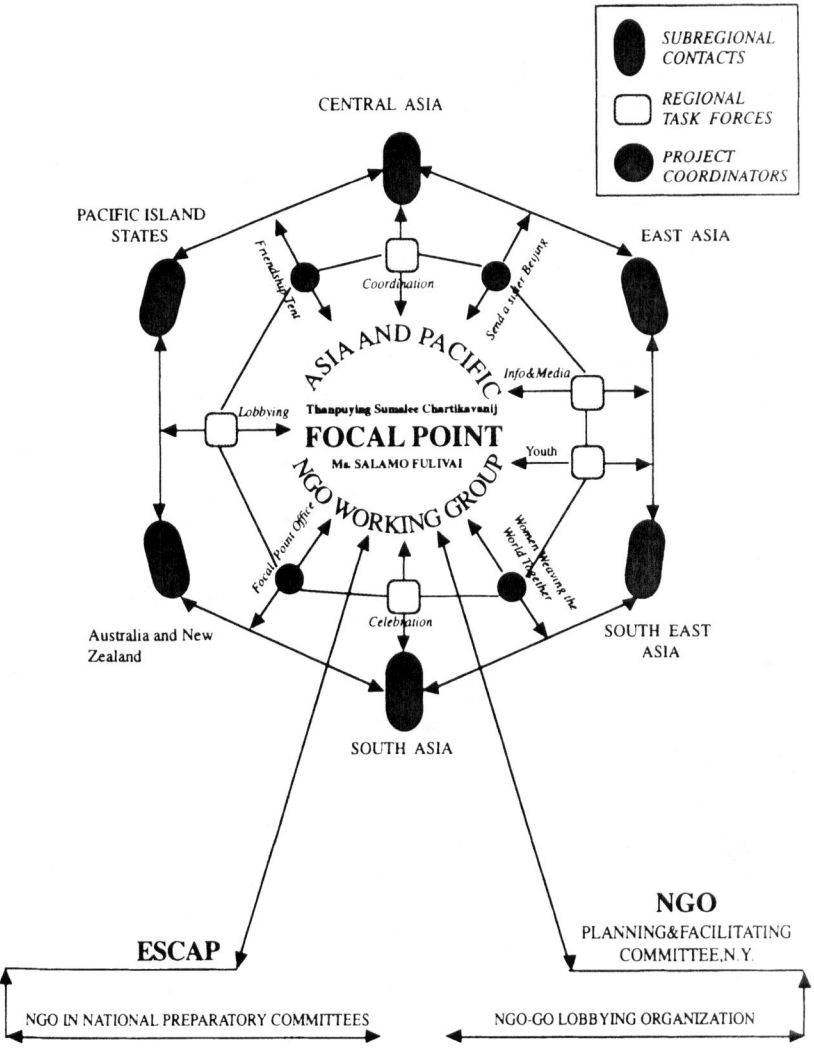

Fig. 6. "Schematic depiction of the Asia and Pacific NGO Working Group." (From Asia-Pacific souvenir booklet distributed at the NGO Forum, Beijing '95.)

preparatory meetings ("subregional caucuses") for the states of "Melanesia," "Polynesia," and "Micronesia," respectively. It held monthly satellite meetings of focal points, and it organized a daily caucus for government delegates at the Beijing Conference. PWRB planned the agenda and circulated minutes or formal reports of these meetings. It also convened a Technical Support Team (TST) of Pacific experts to prepare draft amendments to the Platform for Action on behalf of the Pacific Island states.

As the PAWORNET newsletter quoted at the outset of this chapter made plain, the ostensible purpose of all network activities was information sharing. For example, the Pacific Sustainable Development Network Programme (PSDNP), funded by the United Nations Development Programme (UNDP) and based in a small wooden house at the South Pacific Commission's Suva site, maintained an electronic mail network for governments and nongovernmental organizations, organized teleconferences between groups throughout the Pacific, and compiled and distributed what its project summary termed "metainformation"—"directories of information sources within and outside the region"—in addition to "providing support for the information dissemination requirements of other regional sustainable development programs." As its coordinator explained to me:

> Information technology is the most revolutionary. In the Pacific we have always heard that the problem is geographic isolation. All that tourism is made possible through civil aviation. For me, Internet takes that bridging technology one step further. When you have access to Internet, you can work with someone as if they were in the next room. First we had the steamship, then airplanes, and now we have this.

The precise purpose of information exchange rarely was articulated, however. Verbs like *networking* or *liaising* often carried no subject or object. If pressed, focal points listed functional benefits to the flow of information—information empowers people, they said, or information makes people feel less isolated or allows them to do things they could not do before. Yet the instrumental functions of information did not elicit much reflection, nor were they cause for making connections between problems, persons, or institutions.

Instead, networks were described and imagined by those participating in them as tools for creating further, more extensive networks. Networkers often made statements such as "the purpose of this meeting is to bring us all together so that we can exchange information about how best to plan our activities so that we can all coordinate" or, as a focal point of the Women and Fisheries Network put it, "the idea is basically to link all the women through communication so we can exchange ideas." One of the features of Network activity, in other words, was its dual quality as both a means to an end and an end in itself. This was reflected in a general fascination among focal points with process. At conferences, in newsletters, or in casual conversation, those involved in networks engage in frequent and intensive debate about how best to coordinate: Should they use e-mail? Should they create a data base? Should they produce and circulate reports? (cf. Schwartzman 1989).

In fact, according to their own standards of network activity as proclaimed in newsletters, mission statements, and panel discussions, the focal points, networks, and linkages in Suva were hardly "networking" at all. Notwithstanding the claims made in newsletters and interviews about their network's activities, networkers took considerably greater care in the interrelationship of the system's components than in their extension across distances of space, time, or scale.[20] One can put the matter more bluntly: the networks I observed in Suva showed little interest in using the Network to share information or extend their institutional connections.

People involved in the production or exchange of public documents often discouraged others from reading them. For example, the International Labour Organization (ILO) Conventions on the Rights of Indigenous Peoples often were invoked by indigenous Fijian politicians and activists as a justification for denying political and economic rights to the non-Fijian population of Fiji. As a result, the ILO office in Suva often was approached for assistance in interpreting these conventions. Although the staff members had a firm opinion about this interpretation of the conventions (they felt it was erroneous), they invariably responded that the interpretation of documents was a highly "technical" process not to be undertaken by laypeople, that they lacked a "technical expert" on staff who could read them but they could make a referral to such an expert at the ILO headquarters in Geneva—knowing full well that an expert in Geneva was out of the reach of most Fijians.

Nor was it the case that the Network, in Fijian participants' imagination, was nonhierarchical. Formal meetings, and many individual encounters, adhered to institutionalized expressions of Fijian norms of hierarchy.[21] Conferences usually began with a prayer delivered by a senior person and the presentation of *salusalu* (flower garlands) to guests of honor, including persons of chiefly rank. In the course of a meeting, older persons and persons of rank always spoke first, while younger persons usually spoke only if explicitly asked to do so. Within the Department of Women and Culture staff, members of staff sat on a mat on the floor at lunchtime while the director sat on a chair, and in departmental meetings the director always sat "above" (*i-cake*) while others sat "below" (*i-ra*) (cf. Toren 1990: 35). However, despite these formal displays of hierarchy, most of those involved in networks were Fijian commoners and non-Fijians, and when asked, they asserted that while chiefly rank should be accorded supremacy within a certain sphere ("in the village," one put it) their own status as educated professionals should dictate leadership within networks.

The concentration rather than the extension of networks in informational terms is illustrated in the much-loved panel discussion format, a network held within a singular point in space and time. People involved in networks attended at least one or two panel discussions each week. Organizers of panels explicitly aimed to "share information." The audience they had in mind for these panels was what they called "the community," that is, anonymous strangers outside their networks. In practice, however, little information moved beyond the Network's perimeter.[22] Sometimes this was intentional on the part of focal points and resented as such by attendees, who interpreted it as an act of information hoarding. Yet often the failure to extend outside the circle inhered in the form of the event. Often there *was* no anonymous audience of community members eager to absorb the Network's information, for example, and it fell upon the focal points to sit in the audience's place and fill its role. In fact, on the occasions when true anonymous outsiders attended publicly advertised meetings concerning the Beijing Conference (such as an anthropologist beginning her fieldwork), organizers treated them with measured suspicion, as if they must have some other motive or identity, thus showing a certain disbelief in the very notion of anonymous communication they espoused.[23] Although speakers often expressed a *desire* to communicate with outsiders, they peppered their presentations with acronyms and references to particular documents or conferences and therefore spoke in terms that were both too general and too specific for anyone but a seasoned participant to follow. Resigned to this simulation of anonymous communication, the organizer of one such panel discussion shrugged, "it will be good to discuss things, even if, as usual, we're just talking to ourselves."

Even within the sphere of any one network, there was little formal communication. Many regional networks met and exchanged information among focal points in each country only once or twice each year, in preparation for or as a follow-up to an annual meeting, for example. The circulation of network newsletters, likewise, usually occurred far less frequently than networks professed. Even when published, newsletters often presented only information that was widely known and "after the fact" so that focal points rarely read newsletters for their news content. The sunny, friendly, personal tone of newsletters and circulars from the PWRB, for example ("Dear Colleagues, Very warm greetings from all in the Bureau! 1994 has been an extra busy year for everyone and it is most pleasing to see the progress and efforts put in to the development of Women in the Pacific by all concerned. Well done everyone!" [1994b]), actually blocked the flow of information, some more peripheral networkers said.

Regional in scale, but hardly "representative" of their region, focal points entailed a particular form of subjectivity. In the flurry of preparatory activities that preceded the Beijing Conference, for example, the Asia-Pacific "region" could be accounted for simply by communicating with one focal point. AusAID served as "Pacific regional lead donor" for the Beijing Conference. As its representative explained, "this is basically an information collecting and disseminating role." AusAID received and collated funding proposals, identified government donor priorities and the ability to fund, and then linked the two when possible. "It also involves an obligation to report to DAC [Development Assistance Corporation] in London—to disseminate the information globally so other donors in other parts of the world can pick up on parts of the project." This collating work resulted in two major documents—an "information kit" for recipients of aid funds, which included photocopies of letters, UN documents, newsletters, AusAID policy statements, and bibliographies of works on women in development; and a "funding matrix" for donors, which listed proposed projects and the amount of funding they had received (chap. 6). The objective was to "streamline information, to avoid the duplication of projects." AusAID's role implied no commitment or competency to represent the Pacific in any way, and when an international donor such as DAC looked to AusAID or its representative it did not see the Pacific, its organizations, Pacific women, or even Pacific donor institutions. Yet at the same time, in turning to AusAID, a donor had taken the Pacific into account.

The enhancement of a focal point emanated from its status as a point at which information accumulated. One heard again and again in Network newsletters and conversations among focal points that "information is power," and the focal point was a locus of information. Officially, focal points were exhorted to "share" the information they received. "But we all know that they're not going to do anything," others repeatedly said. When the Pacific Population Information Network (POPIN) trained its focal points in "technical skills," it trained them in how to gather—how to maintain a collection of population statistics, how to catalog materials, how to use a data base—not in how to transmit their data to other focal points. It was this collection and containment, not the connections per se, that made a focal point a regional entity, that is, a subjectivity of a different scale.

The focal point therefore loomed larger than life; it dwarfed other entities (organizations, people, facts) in a field. As such, it often floated free from either the field it accounted for or the Network in which it participated. People could produce lists of government and nongovernment focal points on their own, free of any organizational device, united only by their appearance together as a list in a document. A Network ceased to "function" in formal terms when the linkages collapsed, people said. But a focal point, in contrast, could continue to gather and contain without connection. The collapse of PAWORNET, for example, by no means meant the disappearance of its regional focal point. She continued to embody PAWORNET's transactions, information, and commitments. This enhanced status was recognized by the organizers of the nongovernmental portion of the Beijing Conference in her appointment as the "substantive regional focal point" for the entire Asia-Pacific region. In this role, she provided a focus for the "region" in a sense that PAWORNET could only aspire to do.

One of the features of this structure of linked focal points is that it appeared to be self-generating. How focal points came to be focal points or how a project began or even how funds came to be acquired remained outside the formal networks of communication. No one in Suva seemed to know for certain who had "selected" the Pacific and Asia-Pacific NGO Coordinating Group focal points for the Beijing Conference or why. The focal points almost always described their appointments in the passive voice: "A call went out for better organization, and a committee was formed," one explained to me. Another stressed at a public meeting that "a group of women were asked by the nongovernmental organizations at a meeting in Jakarta last year to be the coordinating group." Never was initiatory action portrayed as the result of personal agitation.[24]

Perhaps this lack of interest in collecting or disseminating people, institutions, and facts in facilitating information flow within or without the Network explains why, despite all the fanfare surrounding the effort to establish the Pacific Sustainable Development Network Programme electronic mail network alluded to earlier, in 1995 only eight governmental or nongovernmental organizations had enrolled and several of these were foreign aid agencies.[25] Likewise, despite the excitement in preconference literature concerning the "computerization" of the Beijing Conference, and despite donors' enthusiasm about providing NGOs with computers, few bothered to take advantage of the offer.[26] The regional focal point of POPIN, a network of population statistics and statisticians, praised the uses of electronic media not for their functions in facilitating the rapid dissemination of information, but as a tool for generating interest in information in the first place:

> The average person is not going to go out and look for the information. They're sitting waiting for it to come. *But* once exposed to the technology—the technology's the catchy bit, not the information. The information comes second. The technology is fascinating and that's what gets them into it. Later, they realize that there's all this information out there, I didn't know this, I didn't know that. But initially, the attraction is the technology. You can sit down and put a CD in a machine and have it play music, multi-

media stuff, some pictures, some music, and somebody explaining it to you. This is good life! [*laughs*] Information is something that grows on you. Once you've discovered something and say, this is information, people are off, and they get into it.

In practice, then, personal and informational linkages connected points within a very limited sphere. Indeed, the problem for networkers was not so much how to expand connections as how to keep connections from expanding sui generis; how to stop the flow of information, resources, and commitments; and how to close the circle when all of their public rhetoric centered around "keeping in touch," "soliciting your views," or "reaching out" (cf. Strathern 1996). One Fijian holder of an important institutional position in Suva claimed that she was rarely invited to meetings or asked to speak on panels because she too often had violated other networkers' collective desire to keep information among those who "know each other": "[A]fter several workshops they know that I am not very diplomatic with things and probably that is what they don't like. I don't believe in diplomacy if the facts need to be shared."

The particular information she had in mind here concerned "misappropriations" of funds by network focal points. Yet she also extended the point: "There are lots of conferences that I've been to with other women and they just go there for the sake of going and visiting places. When they come back, you know, they just shelve everything." When she accused these networks of purposely keeping "grassroots" women out, she criticized them precisely for failing to network properly in terms evocative of modernist anthropological notions of how one should extend one's knowledge:

> You have to know how to network at the local level. And what I really fear is that people are very good at negotiation at national level and also at international level but when it comes to actual practicality, they look very small when they go right down to grassroots women. That is my experience. I believe when you go to any place you have to be part of the community. You eat whatever they eat. You sleep with them, you don't expect to be successful in any project you do, when you go to talk to them in the daytime and in the night you go to the hotel and have a comfortable bed and everything, no. You have to go down to them, and they will believe in you, because these days you cannot say that you can fool around with them. They are very clever. They have to see you living practical, you know the practical part of what you say.

As the Pacific focal point of the Grassroots Organizations Operating Together in Sisterhood (GROOTS) network aptly put it, "to network is just link

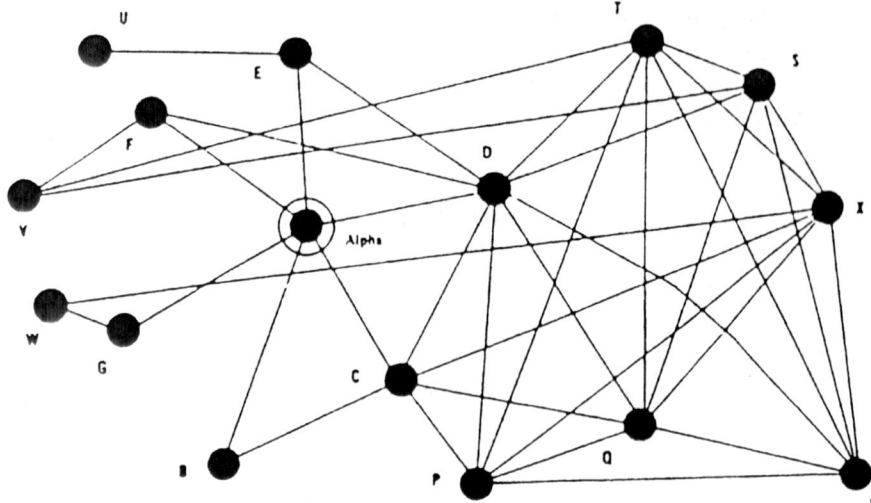

Fig. 7. "Second-order zone, with density 32 per cent." (From Barnes 1968: 116.)

with other women that are in the same category." Yet a category is defined as much by its stability, and by what it leaves out, as by its metamorphoses and what it includes. A lack of "analysis" was grounds for keeping certain persons out of the DAWN network, for example, while a lack of "political commitment" was grounds for exclusion from Omomo Melen Pacific, the network of activists from the Pacific colonies and nonindependent territories. This closure rather than extension of networks also took a visual form. Indeed, one of the insights to be gained from fieldwork among networks is the realization that unlike the star-shaped form of the networks of social network analysis (see fig. 7), the Network is a circular form (see fig. 8).

This was true in significant and trivial ways. At a meeting of Omomo Melen Pacific, Susanna, a veteran activist and the meeting's convenor, had allowed a local employee of AusAID working on Beijing preparations to attend as an observer. In the course of the meeting, suspicion began to mount about this person. She would report their conversations to the Australian government, people said; in any case, the representative of an aid agency funded with money made from indigenous people's land should not be welcomed. Susanna's insistence that "I know this girl, she is OK" and the AusAID employee's own reminder that "I am a Pacific woman, too, and I care about the same things you do" satisfied no one. In the end, the network demonstrated its own efficacy by asking her to leave.

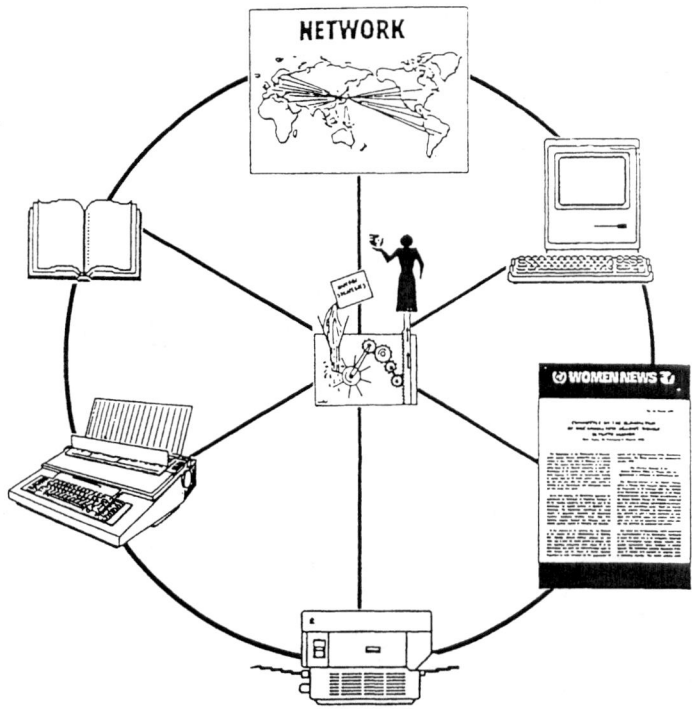

Fig. 8. "Information systems for the advancement of women for national machinery." (From UN Branch for the Advancement of Women 1988: 1.)

Nevertheless, the lives of institutional actors in Suva were devoted to attending conferences, producing newsletters, applying for funding, speaking at panel discussions, drafting documents, and participating in training sessions. They attended at least several conferences or large meetings each week. Some spent a part of almost every day in such activities. It would be too simple to understand this as merely the effect of outside demands (e.g., Hulme and Edwards 1997), for these activities truly engaged participants' collective passions. Whether they pursued this activity on a salaried basis or as "volunteers," networking was a full-time commitment, not a means to some greater end. What remains to be explained, then, is the enormous investment of time, energy, aspiration, and funds on the part of networkers, the long hours of work on behalf of the Network. Wherein lay the interest that sparked their commitment?

An Apposite Analytical Tool? Networks and Personal Relations

By virtue of their positions, those who directed these projects participated in Fiji's expanding urban middle class. For the most part, they felt cut off from their rural kin, and many found the periodic visits their jobs demanded to the "grassroots" to be uncomfortable experiences (cf. Humphrey 1995). In Suva, they lived alone or in nuclear family arrangements. Their lifestyle was emblematic of the new consumption that had accompanied the explosion of expatriate aid workers, embassy staff, and UN officials in Suva. They drank cappuccino at outdoor cafes, met for drinks and jazz at the Travelodge Hotel after work, attended aerobics classes at a private gym, bought groceries imported from Australia, and dressed in clothing purchased on their many work-related visits to Sydney, Geneva, and New York.[27]

In anthropological terms, it is difficult to identify what exactly this "group" had in common. It was a racially and culturally diverse collection of Fiji Indians,[28] indigenous Fijians, Part-Europeans, Europeans, and Chinese as well as persons who had come to Fiji from Tonga, Taiwan, New Caledonia, Indonesia, Australia, and New Zealand. There were important differences of educational background among participants. Some held advanced degrees in academic and professional subjects, others held Australian or New Zealand undergraduate degrees in the social sciences or had studied as undergraduates at the University of the South Pacific or the University of Papua New Guinea, and others had completed secondary school in Fiji. There were lawyers, nurses, government bureaucrats, teachers, politicians, journalists, secretaries, television and radio personalities, a Catholic nun, an Anglican priest, a Methodist minister, and several academics as well as career directors or coordinators of nongovernmental organizations. A small number identified themselves as "feminist"; most did not. Some were seasoned activists in self-determination, environmental, and peace movements in the Pacific; others were newcomers to "development issues." Still others had moved to their current positions or causes from organizations working in other areas of donors' priority such as disability, environmental, or population issues. Some were practicing Christians, others were nominal Muslims, and a significant number were self-consciously against the intrusion of the church into affairs of state and urban life in the postcoup political environment of Fiji.

My problem of description found a complement in these persons' own sense of the multiple gulfs that divided them. Networkers did not understand themselves to share a set of values, interests, or culture. Rather, a myriad of cultural, educational, political, and institutional differences were imagined to exist within a spatial radius of several blocks in downtown Suva. People saw themselves as separated by age, political commitments, nationality, and educational background.[29] Like the Pintupi "polity," whose meetings, as described by Fred Myers, bear a resemblance to those here,[30] this community had no "clearly defined social center in which authority resides. It [was] never quite certain who should be included in considering a problem, who believes he or she has a right to be consulted" (1996: 250). For example, a person from a particular island group was expected to support politicians and persons of chiefly rank from her region and also had a freedom in her "projects" in that region that she did not have elsewhere. Others working in Suva interpreted that person's actions with stereotypes of regionality in mind. At the same time, the mix of people from different regions rendered it more difficult to negotiate relations with one another in an idiom of kinship.[31]

Likewise, generalized conceptions of "race" and "culture" were ubiquitous divisive elements in institutional politics.[32] Informal coalitions of institutions had developed largely around the racial identity of their leadership. Institutions were praised or disparaged as "Indian" or "indigenous," and persons' activities were explained in terms of their conformity to cultural stereotypes: "Indian women never come help us because their husbands won't let them leave the house"; "Fijians are too lazy to finish anything on time"; and so on. In some cases, the racial composition of organizations was explicitly celebrated, while in others it was vehemently denied. There were also numerous "personal conflicts," and virtually everyone complained about their personal and professional victimization because of the jealousy and "bad talk" of others.

What these people understood themselves to share, therefore, was their involvement in local, regional, or global *networks*—institutionalized associations devoted to information sharing, which had certain indicia such as a bona fide source of "funding" and a "newsletter." In conversation, my friends often referred to one another by the names of the organizations that served as the official focal points in these networks—"Fiji WIP" or "Pacific YWCA" or "Department of Women," for example. They described themselves as "focal points" and understood their interactions to be acts of "regional" networking since they often served as "Pacific" focal points in international networks.

Despite talk of their "technical skills" in information sharing, what defined networkers most of all was the fact that they were personally and institutionally "connected"—knowledgeable—about the world of Pacific institutions and networks.[33] Although positions as network focal point administrators sometimes were advertised publicly, in practice I know of only two occasions on which a person utterly outside the circle of persons already involved in these institutions and known to each other was hired for one of those positions.[34]

A handful of persons, mostly from Suva, attended each of the regional and international conferences as Pacific representatives to the virtual exclusion of representatives from the states of Micronesia, Polynesia, and even Papua New Guinea (table 4). For example, several months prior to Beijing, three close friends linked their organizations—the Pacific YWCA, the Pacific office of UNIFEM, and the Fiji YWCA—into a Pacific NGO Coordinating Group (PNGOCG), which in turn was to serve as the hub of a network of NGO "national focal points" consisting of each country's National Council of Women and other organizations around the Pacific. A fourth friend established a "Pacific Media Desk" for the network and with funding from the Asia Foundation (TAF), an American donor, produced a periodic newsletter, *S'Pacifically Speaking!* That the three "focal points" of the Pacific NGO Coordinating Group—three close personal friends—were based in Fiji in offices several blocks from one another became a source of overt dissent in Beijing when delegates from Papua New Guinea confronted these focal points and demanded to know why none of their members were accorded leadership roles in the network. What is most interesting for our purposes, however, is that the committee's coordinating work broke down just prior to the PrepCom, when a conflict broke out between two of the three friends. When the friendship ceased, the network ceased as well.

As this story implies, there was an underbelly of personal relations to the formal linkages of the Network.[35] Given their differences, networkers related to one another "on a personal level," they said.[36] Everyone maintained one or two close relationships with other networkers. Some of these had their origin in a teacher-student relationship that continued as an ongoing association and form of mutual protection. Others were personal friendships given formal expression as coworker relations when one friend brought another into a project. Others were relationships between former classmates or friendships that developed out of what began as a coworker relationship. These relationships were known to all—they were given knowledge about the networks. One assumed, for example, that if one person in such a pair or that person's institution took a position on a certain institutional conflict, the other person and institution would already have agreed to the same position. The personal deliberation would have taken place prior to the institutional one.

What was outside a network, likewise, was "personal." For example, a critic of networkers' failure to share information accused focal points of "shelving" the knowledge they gained rather than sharing it. "Shelving" is precisely what focal points do as they gather documents, facts, and relationships into themselves and their institutional libraries. Yet, when one wished to emphasize the way in which the Network excludes, rather than expands, one labeled the exclusion a "personal matter." In one typical statement, one person explained others' failure to include her institution in panel discussions, workshops, or training projects, as follows: "I think it's more the personal differences than totally not knowing that I'm existing. They know that I am here, and I know that it is just personal differences."

Likewise, since the Network professed an ethic of inclusion and expansion, stopping the flow of information usually was accomplished in a "personal" rather than an institutional guise. People often simply failed to remember to notify unpopular network members of a meeting, and no one took such an omission as benign oversight. One former member of an organization told me that, once appointed to office, others began "just letting me know that they wished I wasn't there."

In this respect, personal relationships beyond the purview of the Network provided a means of resolving tensions within the formal structure. For example, IWTC advertised that its publications were available to organizations in "the South" free of charge, thus claiming a formal willingness to extend its network infinitely across the developing world. This ambition confronted practical and material constraints. A problem developed when Lian-hong requested large numbers of publications, thus stretching the resources of the IWTC network beyond their limits. The executive director of IWTC, who was personally acquainted with Lian-hong, resolved this problem by speaking to her by telephone and, without explicitly refusing to send materials, communicating that she had overstepped her bounds.

One of the classic strategies in the personal conflicts among networkers was to accuse one's enemies of having brought personal matters into the Network. A typical case involved the recipient of coveted funding to attend the Beijing Conference from one particular foreign donor. Several contenders began to speak ill of the means by which the recipient had acquired the funds, whispering that she had been awarded them only because of her personal friendship with a member of the staff of the funding agency. When relayed by another person, the complaint merged with stories of how the same person on several occasions had networked in an overtly careerist fashion, for professional gain rather than "friendship" or "commitment to the issues." When I heard the complaint a third time, another piece had been added—it was recalled that at a conference some years back she had "got involved with someone else's husband and then found herself in for one of those Pacific vendettas." The person was largely ignored and subtly disparaged at meetings and conferences in the tone of public introductions or in the seating accorded to her in panel discussions.

Seen Twice

We might find a precursor to my problem of description and networkers' problem of organization in midcentury social anthropologists' interest in "social network analysis."[37] When J. A. Barnes first proposed social network analysis in 1954, it was as a response to the understanding that with increasing social complexity came new problems of description that the familiar tools such as kinship, institutional organization, or economic-based collectivities seemed incapable of accounting for. Barnes emphasized that while it would be possible to apply network analysis to "traditional tribal society," such a project would be fundamentally uninteresting, and "all too easy," for anthropologists encountered the "multiplex" relations in such societies already well defined. In the urban or semiurban context, in contrast, the possibility of strangerhood generated a problem for analysis (1968: 127). Network analysis therefore held out the hope of explaining actions and relations "which could not be understood in terms of the more formal industrial and territorial systems of social relationships" (Mitchell 1973: 15). For example, coalitions among Sicilian peasants could be shown to have been formed partly along kinship lines, partly along commercial lines, partly along lines of affinity, and partly around the consequences of acts of violence (Blok 1973). Network analysis, then, provided a tool for understanding how linkages of friendship, for example, might become conduits for information flow.[38]

In recent years, interest in transnational informational flows, on the one hand, and the epistemological foundations of modern knowledge, on the other, has led to the resuscitation of this tool of anthropological knowledge. Ulf Hannerz, among others, has called for the application of social network analysis to the "global ecumene." The appeal of the Network for Hannerz lies in its "openness" (1992b: 39), particularly with respect to its ability to grasp asymmetry of scale in relationships: "Networks, that is, can be seen to cut across more conventional units of analysis" (40). The impetus for the project, then, is a fascination with a form that keeps both the analytical system and the heterogeneity of the system's elements in view: "There is a need here for one coherent yet flexible language of form for social relationships and the relationships between relationships" (41).[39]

In its emphasis on the complexity of system in the global ecumene, the call for a new network analysis evokes another era. In the years following World War II, another tradition of network thinking known as cybernetics drew from and exerted a powerful influence over a variety of fields from military technology to medical science to anthropology. Cybernetics consisted of the study of self-correcting feedback loops, systems of "thinking" that incorporated a heterogeneous collection of entities, human and nonhuman (Foerster 1951; Makarov 1987). Its principal interest, however, was no longer "social" linkages but *informational connections*. Gregory Bateson, one of the strongest anthropological proponents of cybernetics, explained in 1967 that "the subject matter of cybernetics is not events and objects but the *information* 'carried' by events and objects" (1987a: 407).[40] The form of communication, what Bateson referred to as "pattern," had become the very subject of analysis (1987a: 412).

Cybernetics in turn has been ironically resuscitated of late by writers seeking an alternative image through which to theorize the politics of the postmodern technological world (e.g., Haraway 1995: xiii; 1990; Crary and Kwinter 1992; Latour 1993; Harvey 1996). In contrast to social network analysis and cybernetics, the emphasis of "cyborgology" (Gray, Mentor, and Figueroa-Sarriera 1995) is on the heterogeneous rather than the systemic quality of the cybernetic world. Yet the network form reappears in allusions to the systemic aspects of a new world order (Haraway 1995: xii)[41] or in the cyborg's citizenship in the heterogeneity of the information age:

> Information, impatterned and wild, is the very context of life, whether it is called consciousness, personality, individuality or a unique cognitive system. We now live in the Information Age, and what metaphor could be more fitting than that of the organism as an information system linked to prosthetic machines—the cybernetic organism. (Gray and Mentor 1995: 454)

As an example of the radical political possibilities latent in their approach, Chris Gray and Steven Mentor quote UN secretary-general Boutros Boutros-Ghali's assertion that "nothing can match the UN's global network of information-gathering and constructive activity, which reaches from modern world centres of power down to villages and families" (1995: 462) and offer as a cautionary comment only the existence of other counternetworks of governments or international monetary funds (462).

The aesthetic power of the Network form has yet another incarnation of late. In the 1980s and 1990s, actor-network theorists have publicized the Network, and the material relationality it encapsulates, as a way of simultaneously drawing attention to the limitations and expansive qualities of modern knowledge: the Network, as a chain of relationships between entities of any kind—people, facts, documents, computers, villages, or institutions, for example—allows very concrete and localized truths to hold elsewhere. It is

> a new topology that makes it possible to go almost everywhere, yet without occupying anything except narrow lines of force and a continuous hybridization between socialized objects and societies rendered more durable through the proliferation of nonhumans. (Latour 1993: 120)

New possibilities inhere not only in the chains these scholars find in the world but also in the analytical connections the Network allows the theorist to make. Network theory is held up as an exponentially more powerful analytical tool:

> More supple than the notion of system, more historical than the notion of structure, more empirical than the notion of complexity, the idea of network is the Ariadne's thread of these interwoven stories. (3)

Like the graph of an equation that represents not just one, two, or ten thousand operations but rather reveals the common equation that accounts for each, the Network, in this approach, is taken as a higher order of analytical process. It cuts across the regions of academic inquiry,[42] at once tracing the commonalities and creating a form that none can recognize or analyze in its totality. As Latour notes: "Is it our fault if the networks are *simultaneously real, like nature, narrated, like discourse, and collective, like society?*" (1993: 6; emphasis in the original).

Why would the Network form have such appeal for modernist social scientists as for networkers in Suva? A preliminary answer may be found in the place of formalism in anthropological reasoning more broadly. William Hanks (1996) has described how the formalism of linguistics effectuates a "break" with the commonsense, or outside, perspective on linguistic practices that are the ethnographer's as much as those of the subjects of study (6). He describes how this "break" then invariably is followed by a "second break"—a turn to "relationality" in which the analyst seeks to collapse the distance effectuated by form and to bring context back in (7). Form, then, serves as a classic device for achieving the distance that makes ethnography effective. The innovation of the Network form is that its formality anticipates this "second break": it claims to take into account both system and heterogeneity, both models and real complexities at once.

Indeed, what is striking from a contemporary vantage point about midcentury social network analysis is the appeal of formalism—of the rigidity of form—where, at the level of argument, the project was precisely intended as a means of bringing the individual and his or her actions back in, after critiques of the rigidity of structural functionalism. One kind of formalism involved the propensity to use language and imagery from mathematics in the presentation. Hypothetical informants took on names such as "alpha" and "beta," for example, while Mitchell, Barnes, and others explicitly modeled images of the kind reproduced in figure 7 on mathematical graph theory.[43] The attraction of formalism lay in the counterpoint it offered to what was understood as the inherent chaos, or informality, of the data (cf. Scott 1991: 20). Having appealed, precisely, to the reality of chaos in abandoning structural functionalism, the network analysts struggled valiantly with this very chaotic quality in attempting to give their analyses coherent form (e.g., Epstein 1969). It was not so much the infinite expansive potential of the Network that most captured the interest of this generation of writers. Indeed, they imagined that there could be both finite and infinite networks of equally interesting research value (e.g., Barnes 1968: 120). Rather, it was the form of the system, and of the heterogeneity of data it organized, that generated the analytical problems and gripped the imagination (e.g., morphological versus interactional features of the network in Mitchell 1973: 288).

By its own reckoning the project faltered in its ability to deliver on its methodological promises.[44] It slowly was abandoned, leaving the questions it raised about how to analyze urban society unanswered. Yet what remained was the appeal of the Network form itself. As Mitchell aptly summarized the Network's output twenty years after the first network study:

> Since the notion of "social networks" was first introduced by Barnes in 1954, perhaps its most striking characteristic has been that it has stimulated much more development and elaboration of the idea itself than empirical field work based upon the idea. (1974: 279; citations omitted)

The Immediacy of Form

Yet if pure form—the Network as an idea at a purposeful distance from the complex social realities it analyzed—was the source of the Network's effectiveness for an earlier generation of network analysts, the present-day networked analyses of cyborgology and actor-network theory represent a change. The power of the Network now inheres in a recursive confluence between the networks observed in the world (cyborgs, NGO networks) and the Network as analytical tool. Network analysis has become a methodology for collapsing the very distance between phenomenon and analysis that rendered the old social network analysis effective. Latour's description of networks, for example, is an exposition of how powerful analytical connections are made. It also is a theory about the "actual" nature of relationships. And it is an argument about the parallel between these two forms of networks: data and persons both are effects of networks, for example (Latour and Woolgar [1979] 1986). What this form enhances, in the course of the exercise, is the scale of analysis.[45] The Network is portrayed, for example, as folding distances through analytical techniques of comparison:

> In a network space, then, proximity isn't metric. And "here" and "there" are not objects or attributes that lie inside or outside a set of boundaries. Proximity has, instead, to do with the identity of the semiotic pattern. It is a question of the network elements and the way they hang together. Places with a *similar set of elements and similar relations between them* are close to one another, and those with different elements or relations are far apart. (Mol and Law 1994: 649; emphasis in the original)

This latest turn is germane to the material of this chapter. For it would be appealing to analyze the "networks" of institutions in Suva by borrowing the network analysts' elaborate methods for determining the constituencies of "cliques," for example. Yet, there is a fundamental difference between the *problem* faced by the Manchester School anthropologists, whose innovation lay in discovering a latent network, and the present case, in which the sociological solution, the Network, is already given in their own networked analysis and explicitly *disclaimed* for the activities anthropologists would label as networks ("what is personal is outside the network"). Ironically, the sociological problem networks pose here is identical to the situation that led Barnes to brand a network analysis of a village as uninteresting: social interactions were too well known there, he said, to be described. Networkers did not elaborate on their personal connections (beyond the careful elaborations of formal Network linkages) precisely because the linkages were given, a precondition of indigenous activity (as well as sociological inquiry), not an artifact thereof. As in the networks of actor-network theory, analysis and phenomenon have become, like Walbiri designs and paths across the land, the "same thing."

The point is not unique to network analysis. Rather, it applies to the broader class of attempts to achieve a reflexive distance from aspects of "modern" life by uncovering systems or structures, underlying patterns or causes, however fluid they might be. Consider, for example, the work of the same period on the rhetoric of social movements whose subject matter also resonates with the material in this chapter (e.g., Simons, Mechling, and Schreier 1984). Inspired by Kenneth Burke's study of political rhetoric (e.g., Burke 1969; 1984), this work sought to answer precisely the question I posed at the outset of this chapter, namely, how and why do movements inspire commitment? Like social network analyses' treatment of relationality, these scholars' close readings of political speech worked from the assumption that social movements existed independently of their own analyses of them. In point of fact, networkers described in this book share more with the analysts of social movement rhetoric than with the social movements these scholars take as their subject: Like these scholars, networkers are fascinated by the way in which language convinces, and they devote considerable time to the close analysis of language and design (chap. 5); like these scholars, moreover, networkers view themselves as sympathetic facilitators of others' activism rather than activists themselves (chap. 6).[46] It is difficult to make of them an outside "subject" for our own analysis, therefore.

Network focal points in Suva would explain the superfluous nature of network analysis differently. They would insist that personal relationships of the kind social network analysts study are not networks because they are not formal. For networkers in Suva, a network was an entity of a particular *form*. To include a person, an institution, or a project in a network was to formalize it and vice versa. The formal structure of the Network mandated that, regardless of what other contacts might exist between parties, the flow of information or funds traveled the path of the Network.[47] Indeed, the definition of information and documents was that which had traveled this path. This formalization of information flow made of the sharing and blocking of information a socially significant activity and also shaped the form that activity took.

One example will illustrate the uses of the device. Once, after a lengthy conversation with a staff member of the DWC concerning the final report of the Technical Support Team (TST), of which she herself had been a member, I requested a copy of the document. "I can't give it to you," she told me, "because officially I don't have it. It still has not been delivered to our office by the secretariat of the TST. We are still waiting," she added angrily, "and the director has written to SPC about it." Of course, the DWC "had" the document in the sense that the document had been drafted by this person herself, who no doubt both had a copy in her possession and had shared it with colleagues in the department. Yet, in formal terms at least, a document that had not traveled the proper network paths did not exist. The "secretariat of the TST" in this case was the Suva office of UNIFEM, and its director at the time was involved in a bitter personal dispute with this staff member's friend and coworker. Resorting to a formal definition of "the document" was a means of pointing to the ineffectiveness of UNIFEM, and hence of its director, as well as a means of blocking information flow to an outsider such as myself (cf. Schwartzman 1989: 80). Had the department "had" the document in official terms, this person would have been pleased to share it with me, as the fact that an outsider requested it would have substantiated its importance and thus the importance of the TST and its work.

Another example of how the network form came into view as a contrast against the background of personal relations concerns the telephone, a piece of equipment, and an ensuing set of relationships that many network theorists would readily include in their analyses (e.g., Callon 1991). Those working in bureaucratic institutions in Suva had numerous means of sharing information at their disposal. They might walk across the street from one office to the next to meet face to face; at lunchtime, they were bound to encounter one another at one of Suva's handful of professional lunch spots. They could send letters, exchange faxes or memoranda, or send their drivers to deliver messages. They also could convene meetings and conferences. Yet the most popular means of day to day communication was the telephone. The telephone was useful precisely because it was regarded as personal (as opposed to institutional), private (in contrast to the collective office spaces in which face to face meetings take place), and informal. As described to me by networkers, as well as observed and practiced on my part, these were lengthy telephone conversations; it was not unusual for people to spend an hour or more on the telephone.

Yet, if an office or a focal point could not exist without a telephone, the telephone was not part of the Network in indigenous terms. In their "opaque kind of referentiality" (Brenneis 1996: 217), the "issues" (subject matter of communication) discussed over the telephone were different. On the telephone, we talked about persons, their disputes, their personal histories, their motivations, and their mistakes. We discussed the perks that flow with a certain job, the differential amounts of per diems offered by various funding bodies for particular conferences, the political situation in Fiji, and the latest rumors about scandals within organizations. We "strategized" for future meetings, so that every issue of formal debate usually had been discussed extensively over the telephone beforehand. Yet, even in the context of such strategizing, we rarely discussed network structure, "women," "issues," projects, or any of the other subjects that captivated attention in formal contexts. We discussed, rather, the personal facet of the problem. Another way of saying that networks are formal, therefore, is to say that they are outside, in a different register than, strategic action, in the conception of the analyst (social scientist or networker). I would offer this as a definition of what I mean by form.

One conclusion one could draw from this small example would be that the work of creating documents, organizing conferences, or producing funding proposals in turn generated a set of personal relations. It drew people together (Latour 1990) and also created divisions of its own. If this observation that networks engender an underbelly of personal relations that criss-cross the gulf of differences that was perceived to exist in Suva has a familiar functionalist ring to it, it is a functionalism that is quite consciously and explicitly embraced by the funding agencies now pouring money into WID projects in Suva. The idea is that by making people work together on the technologies of communication (UN agreements, computer networks, and so on) they actually will communicate with one another and hence will overcome their differences. In this view, the subject of Women, the Environment, or Population is almost a sideline of the real goal of engineering a new web of personal relations.[48]

Yet focal points would also insist that the Network is an artifact of preexisting personal relationships. They would assert at particular moments that networks only give preexisting relations something to do. Indeed, as we saw, personal relationships were an underbelly of network activity, often the very means of achieving network effectiveness, as in the strategizing for meetings by building formal institutional alliances by means of informally acknowledged personal ones. These relationships and conversations were not Network, focal points insisted, because they did not take the network form or concern network issues. In this respect, then, persons and their actions and relations can be understood as an effect of the Network (Simmel [1955] 1964).[49] The oscillation between these two sociological arguments is captured in the frequent ideological statements to the effect that networks are on the one hand revolutionary technologies for social organization and on the other hand simply an enhancement of what ordinary people already do.[50]

Networkers' personal relations, devoid of "culture" or "sociality" and based on an idea of pure individual affect or interest, are liable to strike anthropologists as strangely as does the Network as synthetic civil society. The personal relationships that existed outside the Network, as we saw, were oddly thin and rooted in institutional connections on the one hand and stereotyped notions of difference on the other. Like linkages, they seemed context free, abstract, and, above all, founded on a notion of independent persons and the supremacy of their tastes and experiences (chap. 5). If the Network was simply a product of these relationships, one is left with the question of where these came from in the first place.

The problem is that both of these views impute a level of intentionality to networks on the one hand or their focal points on the other that is out of place here. As in the case of social scientific networks' simultaneous apprehension of "form" and "practice," of the systemic and heterogenous qualities of data, the trick inheres, rather, in the form. We now can understand the networklike sociality of institutional actors in Suva (which, in indigenous terms, is not a network) not as the artifact of networking projects, as in the liberal aspiration—the hope behind the funding of PAWORNET—nor as an artifact of personal relations—the accusations that led to PAWORNET's demise—but as a version of the Network turned inside out.

Drawing upon the character of the network form, we can say that networks and personal relationships are the same form seen twice. It is not that networks "reflect" a form of society, therefore, nor that society creates its artifacts. The inside and the outside of the artifact are not text and context to one another in the modernist sense. Rather, it is all within the recursivity of a form that literally speaks about itself. In the sense of a figure that, seen twice, appears to turn inside out and thus to generate a sense of reality or dimensionality, each serves as the inside or outside of the other. No wonder, then, that the personal identities and differences "outside" the Network seem superficial, just as network linkages outside personal relationships seem to devote an extreme amount of attention to form. The intricacies of the aesthetic are the subject of the chapters that follow.

CHAPTER 3

Infinity within the Brackets

A Layered Form

The *Pacific Platform for Action* (SPC 1994a), a text of some twenty pages plus appendices, enshrines an agreement of Pacific Island governments concerning national, regional, and international development policies toward women. Negotiated at a 1994 intergovernmental conference convened under the auspices of the South Pacific Commission[1] in preparation for the Beijing Conference, the text of the agreement, now printed as a glossy color "document," sits on the shelves of the offices of governmental and nongovernmental organizations throughout the Pacific amid scores of other similar documents. The image on the cover, a carefully composed collage of photographs and text (fig. 9), offers some initial clues as to what lies inside.

At the top of the page is a white band on which is printed the document's title, *Pacific Platform for Action*, while at the bottom a similar band reads South Pacific Commission and displays its emblem. The white background and plain typeface suggest the appearance of the pages of text between the covers, emphasizing visually what the words of the title and institutional affiliation also index: that this document belongs to a set of many similar documents such as the *Asia-Pacific Platform for Action* and the global *Platform for Action*, into which it will be incorporated during successive stages of negotiations. Yet what differentiates the appearance of this document from others of the same genre is that the bands at the extremities of the page rest on a close-up photograph of the weave of mat cloth and the gaps in the weaving of the mats reveal behind them further layers of mats of other weaves. Against this layered background, the white bands appear as simply one more layer of a kind.

In the central part of the image, a close-up photograph of a piece of yet another mat has been torn by hand and mounted upon the layered mats, making it plain that this is not just a fragment of mat but also a fragment of paper containing the photographic image of the mat. On top of this latter layer is yet another torn piece of paper bearing the printed subtitle *Rethinking Sustainable Development for Pacific Women towards the Year 2000.*[2] Superimposed upon the background of mat fabric surrounding this text are the photographs of the delegates who attended the conference and negotiated the document, as well as

Fig. 9. Front cover of the *Pacific Platform for Action*. (From SPC 1995. Reproduced courtesy of the Secretariat of the Pacific Community (SPC). Original artwork by Jipé Lebars.)

photographs of children and decorative flowers, again torn by hand and layered upon the background of photographed mat fabric.

Produced by the "communications officer" at the SPC's Pacific Women's Resource Bureau in Nouméa, a Pacific Islander educated overseas with considerable experience in intergovernmental institutions, this intricate and multileveled image points at the outset to the centrality of form in regional and international agreements such as the *Pacific Platform for Action*. Negotiators of these agreements I knew devoted considerable attention to the aesthetic quality of their work. As we will see, the drafting exercise and the analysis of documents by those who negotiated them emphasized the extent to which language strung together in the proper sequence adhered to a predetermined format and borrowed from other documents while producing its own variations on the standard form. The aim, in other words, was to produce a good specimen of a particular genre. The ethos of the conference demanded an exacting appreciation of the good text, and negotiators largely agreed on what constituted good text when they apprehended it.

The use of mat fabric in the image on the cover of the *Pacific Platform for Action* also illustrates a parallel that I observed among Fijian government officials and NGO leaders between the value they accorded the documents they drafted and negotiated and the value they accorded the mats that Fijians routinely collect, present as exchange objects, and use to cover the floors of their houses or the ground of a ceremonial space. Fijian delegates sometimes made personal gifts of special mats to those with whom they exchanged large numbers of documents, and they displayed both with pride in their offices. Both were pleasant to touch, and one was likely to run one's fingers across them in the course of a conversation or to fix the plaiting of a mat that had come unraveled as one would fold back the dog-eared pages of a document. Shortly before I began fieldwork in Fiji, one of the most experienced veterans of international conferences resolutely abandoned negotiation to found a community center devoted largely to mat-making in what was widely interpreted by colleagues as an indictment of the world of conferences and documents. She refused to make any contribution to the Beijing process other than a donation of mats to an international NGO-sponsored project known as "Women Weaving the World Together," which called for organizations around the world to prepare pieces of "cloth" to be pieced together in Beijing and draped across the Great Wall. Each aspect of mat-making activity could be understood as an alternative to a negative aspect of the conferences, she told me. Whereas people at conferences sat on chairs, at the center people sat on the floor; while only certain people could access the conference floor, here anyone might participate; and while the secular infrastructure of international institutions denied the centrality of the church in Fijian life, the center could work with and within the churches.

In this chapter, I wish to borrow the parallel I observed between the uses Fijian delegates made of documents and mats in order to focus on some dictates of form in international agreements.[3] I wish to consider the way the form of these documents made manifest a reality of levels and levels of realities through a simultaneous and mutual apprehension of the document as pattern and the document as an independent object or unit. I will return at the close of the chapter to the character of this parallel and the implications of my borrowing. I should note at the outset, however, that, although the uses of mats and documents are those of the Fijian delegates, the *comparison* is mine. Indeed, the need to which a comparison of mats and documents responds would seem quite alien to the negotiators: the anthropological problem presented by international legal documents concerns how to make of negotiators' intensive efforts a subject of ethnographic inquiry—how to make their work come into anthropological view, as, for example, the production or exchange of Pacific wealth objects has long held anthropological attention. The problem such documents present for negotiators concerns how to hold multiple levels of action in view at once. This problem of how to take both global and local concerns into account is not wholly unfamiliar to anthropology.

With rare exceptions, the indigenous Fijian and Part-European women who negotiated the Beijing agreement and its subsidiaries did not plait mats. They were urban office workers, and their primary skill lay in the production of documents. As kinswomen, however, they contributed mats for clan presentations at funerals or weddings, and as personal friends and coworkers they also made informal gifts of mats to each other. Each negotiator had her own means of procuring mats to meet these needs, ranging from tribute to barter to purchase at the local market. "I don't know how to make mats, but I know how to judge a good one from a bad one," one leader of a Fijian NGO explained to me, adding, in an idiom reflecting both her institutional position and her rank, "and I know how to instruct others to make them properly." Indeed, the appreciation of mats was a favorite topic for many of these negotiators. Such conversation, and the instruction people took pleasure in giving me in the appreciation of mats, usually centered on the relative differences of form among kinds of mats, the qualities these possessed, and the kinds of mats that should be presented in any given context.

From my academic observer's point of view, the significance of both mats and documents to these negotiators brought to mind a number of similarities between the two artifacts. Both were collective, anonymous, and highly labor intensive exercises that required great attention to detail. Both kinds of production ultimately yielded objects collectively acknowledged as highly valuable and a source of pride to their makers. Like mats in Fijian ceremonial life, moreover, the document provided the concrete form in which collectivities (whether groups of clans, persons, or organizations) were "taken to" another environment. For example, one member of the Pacific NGO Coordinating

Group explained to me how the *Pacific Platform for Action* concretized and carried its aspirations:

> We put together the *Pacific Platform for Action*, which was then taken to Jakarta, and after our issues were inputted that way into the Jakarta document, that document went directly to New York incorporating our Pacific issues of concern.

Both documents and mats also were items of collection (Weiner 1985), elements of sets. Participants at the center that I first mentioned had hoped to exhibit their mats at Fiji's national museum as objects of display. Likewise, although its director had now ceased to attend international conferences, documents still remained highly visible at the center. In the shadow of the daily mat-making activity of the unemployed Suva women whom she had cajoled into joining her program, she carefully stored the documents she had accumulated over the course of twenty years and each week took them out of their boxes to "organize" them. This involved taking a Fijian table (a low table at which one sits cross-legged on mats), stacking it on top of another to create a makeshift filing cabinet, and categorizing the documents one by one. The task evidently was never completed; she used to ask her students for assistance, she said, but she ceased to do so because they did not appreciate the value of the documents and handled them without respect. She displayed the documents in much the same way as she displayed the center's mats and took time to point out particular features of form or to tell the history of each. There was a pleasure about the collection that characterized both documents and mats.

Not all negotiators devoted as much time as she did to their documents, yet all had extensive collections and prized them. During a conference, whether in Suva or at the UN headquarters in New York, documents were rare and delegates sought them avidly. Everyone was continually searching for them; secretaries guarded their copies. NGOs demanded access to versions on computer disk so that they could reproduce them with ease, for if they did not have access to documents, they argued, they in effect were shut out of the proceedings. Each night during the Beijing Conference representatives of Fiji NGOs[4] returned to their hotel rooms to lay out the documents collected during the day with care, sorting them by type, date, size, issue, or region of origin. They evaluated each other's collections and emulated these in their own efforts the following day. At the close of the PrepCom and the Beijing Conference, these delegates returned home with suitcases filled with the drafts they had collected and saved. Upon the delegates' return to Suva, these collections were carefully cataloged and placed in institutions' libraries or on office shelves. All institutions in Suva had extensive libraries of such documents; indeed, a collection of documents was a necessary trapping of any governmental or nongovernmental institution.

In drawing an explicit comparison between mats and documents, the negotiator turned community center director had exploited the parallel presence and significance of the two artifacts in an unusual way. Indeed, it is important to note that documents and mats were *not* analogous from the Fijian negotiators' perspective in the sense that analogy is traditionally defined in anthropology as a device "that 'translates' one group of basic meanings into the other" (Wagner 1981: 9). For negotiators, documents and mats were items of equal importance that often traveled similar paths and that could be appreciated in similar ways but belonged to different worlds and ordinarily did not call for an understanding of one set in terms of the other (cf. Miyazaki 1997). The analogy nevertheless has its analytical uses for outside observers of international conferences, and these uses inhere in the remarkable aesthetics of pattern and counting surrounding the making and exchange of Fijian mats.

Fijian mats are central objects of exchange presented at funerals, weddings, and most ceremonial occasions and also exchanged informally at a person's arrival or departure. Mats are used on a daily basis to make any space into a place of significance, and they are admired for their form, their feel, and the skill involved in their plaiting. Where mats cover the ground or floor to create a ceremonial space, they are layered one on top of the next in the same order so that all but the top layer remain concealed from view except at the fringes or, in the case of large presentations or important ceremonies, from a side view in the thickness of the layering.

The set of patterns and styles of Fijian mats is a finite one. Mats are differentiated by the plaiting (e.g., single or double weave), the presence or absence of a fringe and the kind of fringe, the material used (*voivoi* [pandanus] or *kuta* [sedge]), and the geometric patterns woven into the plaiting by soaking strands of pandanus leaf in mud to give them a dark color (Ewins 1982; Fulmer 1996). These patterns are simple nonrepresentational designs produced in black and white in the weaving of the mat and in multiple colors in the yarn fringe now used in place of parrot feathers for decoration at the extremities. Most women who make mats know only a few patterns and concentrate not on innovation in pattern but on perfecting the treatment and splitting of the pandanus leaf and the plaiting to achieve an even shape and a soft feel. At most, new designs constitute small variations on given patterns, variations that might go unnoticed to the unfamiliarized eye. Creating a mat is a work of repetition—of the careful repetition of simple shapes to form the patterns and of the even repetition of hand gestures in plaiting. The skill involved is one of coordination, evenness, and piece by piece addition rather than transformation such as might be involved, for example, in pottery.

As exchange items, Fijian mats are presented in sets of three or four given kinds, layered one on another and called *vivivi* ('to wrap or bundle'). In the exchanges I observed, and according to Fijian and Part-European informants, it

Fig. 10. Layering mats in a ceremonial space

was appropriate to present a specific number of vivivi at particular occasions—one at the weddings of more distant relatives and two in the case of closer ones, for example. Both sides in the exchange counted vivivi as they were given. The receiving side usually recorded the number of vivivi received in a ledger, while the giver, in assembling the vivivi beforehand, necessarily had counted the kinds of mats it contained.

Yet a vivivi was not a specific number of mats. Rather, it was a number of *kinds* of mats. Thus "two" vivivi on one occasion might actually contain "fewer" mats than one on another occasion. One was never sure at the point of exchange how many mats a vivivi contained, as the number of mats in the vivivi was concealed in the layering of one mat on the next. Although those receiving or redistributing the mats were actually counting, the act of counting was therefore apprehended as an ultimate failure. In it, Fijians came to terms with the potential infinity literally bundled into a vivivi, a device, in short, that defied the specificity of number. Under such circumstances, mats were not individually countable concrete "objects" but an abstract totality.

The Fijians I observed apprehended the totality of the mats that constituted the vivivi in a second sense. Although each mat was concealed by the one that covered it, the mats were layered each on top of the next so that the multicolored fringe of each was left in view (fig. 10). These successive layers of fringe formed a *pattern*, and, where a large presentation of mats was involved, the pat-

Infinity within the Brackets 77

Fig. 11. Women layering mats for the installation of Roko Tui Bau

terned layers of fringe extended over a space as large as a mat. At the moment at which counting stopped, in other words, pattern emerged. The turn to pattern was a distinct turn to the visual, as one kind of apprehension (counting) gave way to another (seeing). Another way of describing this turn to pattern is that the boundaries of the artifact were no longer foregrounded. Instead, when the mats were laid on the floor of a ceremonial space, the viewer suddenly apprehended a pattern that extended from one mat to the next and from the mats to the plaiting of the walls (fig. 11), the arrangement of flowers, or the placing of bodies in a ceremonial context, infinitely inward and outward.

Another crucial aspect of the apprehension of the vivivi was what was—and remained—hidden from view. Before any ceremony I observed, senior-ranking women assembled the mats to be laid out and, watched by junior women, layered these according to vivivi logic whereby mats of each kind must be covered by another kind. After hours of discussion, of trying a mat this way and then the other, they completed the task only to tear up their work and begin again. As a result, all but the top layer and the layers of fringe of this carefully composed artifact remained hidden from view. The pattern was apprehended precisely through the *failure* of apprehension: it came into view in the experience of what was unknowable in concrete terms but that was nonetheless present.

Finally, the pattern of the vivivi always anticipated its own disintegration into concreteness. Later, when the presentation or ceremony had ended, the mats would be redistributed among the recipients, one by one. Vivivi would be taken apart: clanswomen would unceremoniously toss the mats into piles according to type without regard for their origin or participation in a vivivi set and would then carefully record the actual number of mats in a ledger. The mats would be redistributed, and each member of the clan would roll up his or her share and take it home. What each took away was a concrete thing, a singular mat. As clan members sat upon the patterned vivivi during the course of the ceremony, therefore, they knew that the moment would come when the infinity of the pattern would be taken apart, reduced to a finite number of concrete things. Crucially, here, decomposition was not transformation: when one took the vivivi apart one had both nothing (an absence of form) and a collection of concrete things. One form did not emerge out of another.

Negotiation: Working with Pattern

Like mats, intergovernmental agreements such as the *Pacific Platform for Action* partake in a simple nonrepresentational patterning that is replicated again and again within the document, from one document to the next, and in the mechanics of the conference at which documents are negotiated.[5] The UN document's standardized structure of chapters, headings, subheadings, and paragraphs dictates a given progression from the "Preamble" to the "Mission Statement" to the "Global Framework" section and on to the "Institutional Arrangements." On this skeleton hangs a series of self-contained paragraphs. One unit is connected to the next according to a simple and straightforward stylistic logic that encompasses at most two or three paragraphs at a time. It is appropriate, the Austrian diplomat chairing one drafting session of the PrepCom pointed out as delegates argued over the relationship among paragraphs, that a first paragraph list the facts, a second lists the consequences of those facts, and a third makes a proposal for how those consequences might be addressed. This simple structure was as much of an "analytical framework" as I ever heard elaborated in a drafting session. One could negotiate the paragraphs of the global *Platform for Action* in virtually any order, and indeed in the course of negotiations delegates skipped freely from paragraph 31 to paragraph 225 without any of the loss of continuity or cohesion that academics might expect.[6]

Like the given and self-evident geometric patterns of Fijian mats, moreover, the analytical sequence was all on the surface, dictated, and known at the start. The character of the pattern—a simple logic that linked words, paragraphs, documents, or conferences—entailed the collection of a potentially infinite number of concrete and distinct entities (words, paragraphs, conferences) into a straightforward digital[7] sequence of numbers and letters. The document was divided into alphabetically and decimally numbered sections: Strategic Objective F.4—"Strengthen women's economic capacity and commercial networks"—followed Strategic Objective F.3—"Provide business services and access to markets, information and technology to low-income women"—and paragraph 221 followed paragraph 220. This internal digital pattern also was replicated outside the document in the sequencing that related each document to the next. The document had a numerical placement in a series of other documents, where, for instance, document number A/Conf.177/L.2 followed document number A/Conf.177/L.1. Although the system of decimals, letters, and slashes was somewhat detailed and complex, the logic of the system was as simple and transparent as the layering and repetitions in the patterns of a Fijian mat.

Just as the layered mats brought into view a continuity in pattern from one mat to the next, the organizational pattern of the document was repeated in the way documents at each level of negotiation mirrored the others in form and function. Conferences at global, national, regional, and subregional levels all generated their own "platforms for action," which were then "taken to" higher levels of conferences and incorporated into the new documents negotiated there so that succeeding conferences fit together as academics might imagine increasing levels of generality to do. Thus, the Fiji national document was "taken by" the Fijian delegate to the Nouméa conference of Pacific Island governments in 1994 and formed the basis for Fiji's "inputs" into the *Pacific Platform for Action* drafted there. This latter document then was "tabled" at the Asia-Pacific Ministerial Meeting in Jakarta,[8] and so on. At each level, successive drafts were incorporated into preceding ones, first by a "technical team" that produced a draft text and then through a lengthy process of intergovernmental negotiation. The rigid stylistic conventions I have already mentioned ensured that documents replicated one another in structure, organizational logic, language, format, typeface, layout, and even substantive content. As in the mats, although there could be changes in form from one document to the next, emphasis lay not on the innovative details but on the success of the replication of a given pattern from one artifact to the next.

As with mats, then, the skill of the exercise lay in the detail, the degree of familiarity with the aesthetic conventions, and the patience this extremely labor-intensive task demanded, not in the invention of new designs or in the transformation of one form into another. It entailed the wearisome and often highly frustrating detailed work of cutting and pasting, of organizing and collating. One slowly worked the text together, phrase by phrase, heading by heading. The objective was not so much to achieve transparent meaning as to satisfy the aesthetics of logic and language. Commentary, interpretation, or even reflection on the direction of the exercise was beside the point. At the PrepCom, when one state's delegate proposed, "Let's make the language more forceful; let's shorten it," the chair responded, in an impatient tone, "Does the distinguished delegate from Turkey have language he would like to suggest?" A seemingly infinite number of hours of labor by anonymous negotiators, lobbyists, and secretarial staff went into the preparation of the necessary drafts and position papers and the negotiation of each paragraph, and this was made palpable in the conference halls by the sense of collective exhaustion, but also of pride, when the document was displayed at the end.

As negotiators pieced the language together word by word into a document, they also worked with patterns at the levels of word and sentence. These, like the patterns of the mat or the document as a whole, were not strictly representational and were characterized by a high degree of repetition. Certain words fit with others. Language had a shape, a rhythm, a feel, not simply a meaning. Although elsewhere the words—*gender, structural adjustment, violence*—might point only to political conflict, for the moment of the negotiation they pointed more vividly to their own syllables and spelling, to the number of instances in which each word had appeared so far in the document, or to the delegations that wished to see the words included or deleted. For example, if one takes the general subject of this conference as "women," certainly the word *women* appeared frequently enough in the thousands of documents that circulated throughout the meeting. Yet in practice it was hardly clear what this word "meant" at all and how it might be delineated by the scope of other UN conferences on subjects such as development, human rights, population, children, or environment. Instead, attention turned to what should be listed as *elements* in the definition of violence against women, in the list of what birth control technologies should be included in the category of available alternatives, or whether to single out "internally displaced women" as an especially disadvantaged class among "displaced women." By the close of the conference, this subject had not evolved, expanded, come into focus, or been transformed; like the mats hidden from view, it simply was there, underlying the work of the conference.

The work of producing properly patterned language was in the main a sorting exercise in which language was cut, arranged, or inserted to produce appropriate strings of words. The final result was a "clean" text, that is, a completed text without brackets. Negotiators struggled together to generate the right pattern, and, when at last they happened upon the proper phrasing, the collective recognition of the strength or appropriateness of the verbal formulation was appreciated by all. One important element in this effect was the repetition of the language—the extent to which the words resonated through the document as a whole. Delegates actually quantified this repetition by counting the number of times a word appeared in the document. (The word *indigenous* appeared over two hundred times, Fiji delegates noted with satisfaction, although they expressed disappointment that the word *nuclear* was absent from the document). Yet repetition, too, was a matter of aesthetic judgment: the text should be "strong" and "consistent" but not "redundant," delegates said. It should borrow language from other documents, but it could not replicate those documents wholesale. It should be "brief" but also "comprehensive." One had to acquire an ear and an eye for the patterns here.

This orientation toward language can be difficult to grasp. I had to be reminded of it at a national negotiation among government and nongovernmental bodies in Fiji, where delegates reviewed a draft version of the global *Platform for Action* and made suggestions for the Fiji government position. The phrase "universal human rights" was a commonly used one, so that it seemed appropriate that in the patterning of the words *universal* should precede *human rights* and vice versa. However, the phrase had been the subject of intense dispute at a prior stage of negotiations at which some delegations such as that of the Vatican had sought to limit the scope of human rights by adding the word *universal* to the term, thereby effectively reducing the set of recognized "human rights" to those acknowledged as truly "universal," that is, those to which no state could possibly object. The insertion of a seemingly expansive word had the effect of emptying the phrase of representational content by rendering it utterly vacuous. Although one or two Fiji delegates, looking at the effect of the insertion of *universal* in terms of the tactical meaning of each phrase, argued that Fiji should oppose proposed amendments, most of the delegates did not take an interest in this aspect of the text even when, at the urging of the proponents of tactical meaning, I naively sought to explain the argument for removing the word *universal* again and again. For most delegates to the national consultations, *universal* and *human rights* belonged together, sounded right together, and formed a proper pattern.

Pacific academics I knew who came into contact with the UN document-drafting process generally found it confusing, nonsensical, and even counterproductive. They complained that the document artificially separated important Pacific issues and denied connections between them (e.g., by separating "economic development" and "environment" into two separate chapters of the document rather than treating these as a single set of related issues). They bristled at the carelessness with which the "argument" of the document had been assembled. The document should *reflect* the *reality* of women's experience, they also emphasized, and it should have a clear analytical perspective rather than being simply a collection of words on a page. Their efforts to critique the document, as they said, by revealing what lay beneath the surface of the text, struck negotiators as equally counterproductive.[9]

Indeed, one of the most puzzling aspects of intergovernmental documents from an academic point of view[10] is the negotiators' lack of interest in their meaning. The more words negotiators added, the "less" meaning the document seemed to have, as when the addition of the term *universal* to the word *rights* rendered the phrase vacuous. To academics, the string of words in the document consisted of a jumble of words and paragraphs that seemingly pointed nowhere.

It is difficult to imagine meaning as anything other than paramount, for anthropologists have long understood that what makes others as human as ourselves is their capacity to hold signification dear. Indeed, the elucidation of other's implicit meanings has long been one of the anthropologists' principal tasks. Knowledge, in this understanding, is the artifact of the transformation of one set of meanings into the next.[11] This understanding may capture the character of academic analysis, but in its transformative element it is utterly unlike the documents described here, for which all patterns are given at the start.

Brackets: Infinity Within

If the generation of meaning through the transformative power of analysis is not the objective of negotiation, how does this institutional knowledge achieve its effects and what effects does it achieve? As we will see, the document's principal aesthetic device involves an alternation between concreteness—the document as object—and abstraction—the document as pattern. We can understand the elicitation of this double view, that is, the alternation between object and pattern, as negotiators' principal endeavor; it is the *work* of producing the document. There are two central devices through which this effect is achieved. The first is the bracket.

For the most part, the layered collage on the cover of the *Pacific Platform for Action* (fig. 9) consists of representational images; the photographs of negotiators and the text in the title point to particular people or things. Yet in the case of the mats photographed in the image the magnitude of detail is such that it is impossible to identify with any degree of certitude the kind of mats shown in the photograph or their place of origin. As one progresses toward the upper layers of the composition to the mat fabric directly beneath the title's words, the camera zooms in so closely that the shape of the mat is lost altogether, leaving only an abstract pattern of shapes and colors. In the eye of the close-up lens, representation fades into pattern as the camera moves from one scale to the next.

Just as the background of the image on the *Pacific Platform for Action* cover of layers of mat and paper made visible through their gaps evokes the sense of levels behind levels, behind every institutional arrangements section, behind every use of the phrase "universal rights," and, indeed, behind every document and conference, delegates knew, lay countless others of the same genre, artifacts of activity at other levels. Although negotiators always "knew" this, from time to time the apprehension that each document, survey, or position paper was layered upon countless others overtook them. They commented on the number of people, the amount of time, the amount of paper at stake in preparations to this point. For a moment, at least, the apprehension of the seemingly infinite number of texts or amount of labor that text or labor concealed imbued the events with a weightiness that was almost overwhelming.

Bringing such levels of action into view was a paramount concern. On returning from the Beijing Conference, for example, the leader of the Fiji delegation argued vehemently in a major speech to community groups that the ultimate purpose of the great expenditure of time and public funds had been "to make an impact as a region, not as a country." Documents made a region or level "visible" at the next level of negotiation, and Pacific delegates spoke with pride of the newfound "visibility" of the Pacific "at the regional level." The national preparatory conferences held in Fiji explicitly sought to replicate all of the UN processes "at the national level" by organizing plenaries, working groups, and main committees, by tabling working papers, and by producing agendas in standardized form. The aesthetic may have puzzled national delegates who had never witnessed a UN meeting, for the organizers took no interest in adapting "global" procedures to "local" circumstances or understandings, nor did they attempt to give local meaning to global activities. The objective was rather to bring to the collective attention a formally ideal national "level" of preparatory activity. In this sense, we also might understand why a regional map of the Pacific, with imaginary geographical boundaries marked with a bold black line, appears on the back cover of the *Pacific Platform for Action*. It is the mirror image of the layered mats and documents on the front cover, what is visible when the document is complete.

Like mats layered one upon the next in ceremonial contexts, therefore, documents were entities that at key periods of time faded into patterns replicable at seemingly infinite levels. The documents were valuable collection items when delegates took them home in their suitcases to place on library shelves, and they were concrete objects that delegates carried from one level of negotiation to the next in the same way that they physically displaced themselves from Nouméa to Beijing. Yet the documents emerged as such objects only after the fact, when the negotiation was complete. During the negotiations, the documents did not exist as physical entities, nor did they capture the imagination, for at that point the negotiator's attention was turned only to language and pattern. The following day, after the secretariat had keyed the changes into the word processor and produced hundreds of copies, the draft appeared in boxes in the office for collection. Indeed, at the PrepCom, something called a "document" did not appear at all until the final moments of the conference, when the secretariat presented the results of the conference to a first "outside" audience—a gathering of the press.

During the negotiations, then, a document was better imagined as an orientation of thought and action, a state of being, than as a reified object. In essence, one lived through the patterns of the document. Sessions defied any distinction between writing and conversation (Brenneis 1994). The chair proceeded through the paragraphs one by one, calling out their numbers, and delegates held up their nameplates to indicate that they wished to make "inter-

223. [The World Conference on Human Rights and the
International Conference on Population and Development
[which did not create any human rights] reaffirm [all
aspects of the [universal] human rights of women, including]
women's reproductive rights [as defined in the Programme of
Action of the International Conference on Population and
Development, taking into consideration the reservations to
the Programme of Action] and the right to development.]
Bearing in mind the definitions given in chapter II, chapter
VII, paragraph 7.2, and on the recognition of the basic
right of all couples and individuals to decide freely and
responsibly the number, spacing and timing of their children
and to have the information and means to do so, and the
right to attain the highest standard of sexual and
reproductive health. It also includes their right to make
decisions concerning reproduction free of discrimination,
coercion and violence, as expressed in human rights
documents. [Therefore, the unique reproductive and
productive roles of women [and men] must be recognized and
valued.] [Changes in both men's and women's consciousness,
attitudes and behaviour are necessary conditions for
achieving harmonious partnerships between women and men. It
is essential to improve communication between women and men
on issues of shared responsibility, including sexuality and
reproductive health, so that women and men are equal
partners in public and private life. Special efforts are
needed to emphasize men's shared responsibility and promote
their active involvement in responsible parenthood and
sexual and reproductive behaviour.]

Fig. 12. Paragraph 223 of the *Draft Platform for Action*, 15 May 1995 version (Future A/Conf. 177/L.1). This paragraph is taken from the last draft version of the document, and therefore the brackets already have been consolidated considerably.

ventions." When called on, they read out proposed language, then scribbled it out and handed it to the secretary sitting at the podium. "So European Union, you have no objection to [the role of women and girls] but you would like to keep [the gender dimension], is that right?" the chair called out. Life proceeded at dictation speed, and it was not unusual to spend several hours on a single paragraph as delegates agreed to add a clause, delete another, or eliminate three alternative formulations for a certain phrase but to keep two others in brackets for further negotiation. The document at that stage was not an entity of its own but a collective patterning of intention.

This work was performed by assembling all proposed "language" into "brackets" (fig. 12). Bracketed text gathered together every possible alternative formulation into a messy and very lengthy document. Negotiators then worked for hours in word by word negotiations to whittle away at the brackets until they achieved the "cleanest" (nonbracketed) version possible. "Consensus" among states was manifest in a specific form, that is, in the form of the "clean" and "tight" text, the text without brackets, the text that had not been watered down but made strong, precise statements. If the parties reached consensus, the brackets were removed, to the satisfaction and pleasure of all. If any one state refused to agree, however, the brackets remained and people said that the text was "unreadable." The chair used every power of persuasion at her disposal to cajole, bully, or beg delegates to eliminate the brackets or at least to pare down the number of words within the brackets by consolidating one line of text with another. Delegates' references to "lifting" the brackets, "freeing" the bracketed text, and "liberating the paragraph" evoked the normative nature of their common task. If the parties formally confronted each other as adversaries, they also were collaborators in what they experienced as the truly challenging task of producing a complete physical document in proper form in time for its adoption at the closing ceremony.

These brackets were visual phenomena. Fijian negotiators noted in conversation that they preferred some versions of the *Draft Global Platform for Action* because the brackets were in bold type, making each instantly noticeable on the page. At Fiji's national consultation, delegates carefully and laboriously marked the brackets with bright highlighter pen on their copies so that they stood out in fluorescent yellow against the remainder of the black type. Moving through the text involved focusing on one bracket after another rather than proceeding evenly from one line to the next (as in ordinary reading). For these Fijian delegates, the bracket was more than a representational marker of the lack of consensus among states. It was also a self-representational graphic entity, and the project of removing brackets engendered a commitment that was independent of their commitment to the conference's substantive political goals. For negotiators brackets were not asides, pauses, or explanatory devices but focal points to which attention was immediately drawn. The argument happened within the brackets.

More difficult to appreciate is the fact that the bracket was also a point of potentially infinite internal expansion. The rule of such negotiations is that, although one cannot alter the text outside the brackets, within the brackets a state can add as much as it wishes. Theoretically, at least, a delegation could therefore propose within the scope of any one bracket an entirely new text that would overtake and engulf the whole. Yet this potential infinity of text within the brackets is contained within the concrete graphic parameters of the bracket on the page.

The bracket is an expansive moment in at least one other sense. When negotiators focused their attention on the bracket, when they peered into its infinite potential, what was visible were the layers and levels of language, other documents, and alternative possibilities out of which the text had been created, as proposed amendments were taken largely from documents produced at other levels. As noted earlier, these successive layers of previous debates, previous interventions, or previous drafts and amendments all partook of a similar patterning of words, phrases, paragraphs, and sections. Text within brackets had the potential for endless internal fragmentation. For example, at Fiji's national consultation, debate over the resolution of a single bracket among the delegates with whom I worked decomposed into a conversation about the languages in which chemicals are labeled in Fiji, the programming on national television, the recent death of one of their members, and the impending privatization of the hospital, for to focus on the bracket is to tumble into a rabbit hole of seemingly endless concrete instances. This device is precisely the reverse of the conventions of academic reading and writing. For negotiators, the world does not encompass the bracketed text or the document, as context does for academic text, but rather is contained *within* it.[12] And, unlike the additive quality of the academic's context, this layered reality is as much a gap or vacuum as a thinglike entity.

Finally, in keeping with the aesthetic of counting and digital sequence linking paragraphs or documents, a great deal of effort was devoted to quantifying the number of brackets and the amount of bracketed text within the draft document. At the Beijing Conference and the PrepCom, the secretariat kept a running tally of the percentage of the total text that remained in brackets as an indicator of the progress of negotiations, and delegates checked this statistic frequently as a marker of their collective progress—60 percent of the text was in brackets at one point, then 40, then 20, they learned. At the close of the PrepCom, NGO newsletters again and again mentioned the fact that "60% of text is in brackets" as a marker of the failure of the meeting. Yet such quantification, people knew, could not take into account the infinite expansion possible within any single bracket, for, as we have seen, one bracket might expand to equal the totality of the nonbracketed text in length. This counting mechanism, then, ultimately rehearses the point at which counting *fails*. Negotiators apprehend the infinity within the brackets, we might say, by encountering the limit of number.

I noted earlier that negotiators only grasped the levels of their activity (global, national, and so on) at particular moments, and I might add that these were the moments at which they were drawn into the bracket. It was both a thrilling and a deeply troubling effect. On the one hand, there was a weightiness and sense of awe about the endless levels of activity and artifact. Yet this black hole of meaning within the bracket also had to be backgrounded, made stable, held at bay. To fail to resolve the brackets into language would mean aesthetic failure, for a document with brackets is not a finished document but "unreadable" confusion, they repeatedly told themselves.

Quotation: The Text Solidifies

Negotiators seeking to mask the infinity within the brackets found what from an academic point of view seems like an improbable ally in language and, in particular, in the second principal device of their aesthetic activity, the quotation. In negotiations, the chair directed participants' attention to a particular bracket, and, as they turned their attention away from the text as a whole to the specific bracket, gaps among proposed versions of the language collected within the bracket came into view. For example, in paragraph 223 (fig. 12), the chair might direct negotiators' attention to the distance between the two final bracketed phrases ("[Therefore, the unique reproductive . . .]" and "[Changes in both men's and women's consciousness . . .]"). Inside the bracket itself, therefore, the same pattern of gaps that characterized the bracket's relationship to the main text reemerged. "Could any delegation suggest language that might bridge this gap?" the chair asked. And negotiators began to "bring in language" to attempt to close it. At this stage, as one of the Pacific's most skilled negotiators explained to the NGOs, everything but language and politics was left behind—women, the Pacific, the issues. What NGOs should do, she instructed them, was to propose language that would "bridge the gaps" among the texts suggested by the major delegations, for this was the only way to participate effectively.

Proposing language to bridge the gaps was not a process of thinking of an evocative phrase or of putting meaning into words. Indeed, as the paragraph in figure 12 illustrates, negotiated language often fails to conform to what academics would consider standards of proper grammar let alone elegant form. Rather, delegates know that there are certain words they would like to see included in the bracket and others they cannot allow. Bridging the gap is a matter of "bringing in" words that will satisfy all, as one might bring in pieces of equipment, and of finding a way to string these words together so that the language will conform to stylistic conventions.

In several senses, this language, as the "things" delegates bring in, was the antonym of, as well as the antidote to, the infinity within the bracket. First, language was the opposite of the logic of counting that characterized the brackets. In counting paragraphs or sections or brackets, one moved through the text vertically, from top to bottom, following an outline structure, and one did not need to take notice of any particular sentences or words. Language, in contrast, was a horizontal weave. It existed entirely independently of the logic of the numbers, although it was built across the vertical skeleton that the numerical outline set for it—for, as I have mentioned, the paragraphs and even the sentences were virtually self-contained. One could move across the two-dimensional surface of the text either way, according to number or words.

More importantly, as we saw in the previous section, counting revealed levels, for in counting one apprehended the point at which counting failed, the point of infinite expansion within the bracket. Language, in contrast, masked these levels. Negotiators were only momentarily overwhelmed by the spectacular sense of levels in their work because most of the time their focus on language represented a turn away from the world at any level. Their work was neither national, nor regional, nor global, but "technical," as they said; it foregrounded its own activity. For example, during the conference the Fiji delegates never mentioned life in Fiji or in the Pacific or even referred to "Fiji" or "the Pacific" as ideas. Rather, their interest was absorbed by which copies to use, similarities and differences between alternative texts, with what language it was easiest to work, which word was stronger or weaker, or which word was used at the previous conference in a similar paragraph. Like the form of the document, the activity of drafting was self-contained.

The ideal form of language, according to negotiators, is the quotation, and they revered the encyclopedic knowledge of phrases from other documents that was necessary to produce the appropriate quotation at the opportune moment in the negotiations. The text of every document made frequent mention of language negotiated at other conferences or set out in other instruments, and a deadlock in negotiations was often resolved by a proposal to quote directly from language already agreed upon at a previous conference. These quotations reaffirmed the strength of the language negotiated earlier and also provided firm grounding for the claims of the new text. In the document, however, these quotations were unacknowledged borrowings and were incorporated seamlessly into the text. The notion that documents linked to one another as were paragraphs engendered a rule of procedure: the chair would not allow delegates to bracket language taken verbatim from previous UN conferences.

The visual apprehension of the quotation was precisely the opposite of the bracket. While the bracket was a focal point, the quotation faded into the text without so much as the quotation marks that academics use to indicate textual borrowing. Anyone other than a connoisseur of such documents would fail to note the quotation at all. Even more powerfully than ordinary language, therefore, the quotation concealed the layers, for in borrowing from one conference or document to the next without so much as a citation the quotation collapsed all levels of conferences or documents into a single text. Negotiators apprehended this as a great feat, a sign of progress, the creation of a solid linguistic regime.

Likewise, we saw earlier that the bracket was an abstract form (infinity, the pattern of levels) contained within a concrete form (the visual markings of the bracket on the page). As the substance that hides the bracket, language, in contrast, was at once both abstract and concrete. It was abstract in the way it was apprehended primarily as patterned sequences of words, quotations, or paragraphs. As with the infinite levels within the bracket, the pattern lay in the repetition of forms, and, as we have seen, delegates carefully counted the number of times words such as *nuclear* or *gender* appeared in the document in the same way that they counted the brackets. The objective was form and quantity, not the way words stood for analytical positions or contained images.

Language in this context was also abstract in that it never pointed to a particular instance of anything. In order to participate in the drafting process, one had to amass an astounding number of small pieces of information. This included statistics about nutrition, rising sea levels, or rates of increase in gynecologically related deaths; knowledge about what was happening in each committee meeting or about how far each drafting group had proceeded; knowledge about procedures and compromises reached at other UN meetings and about the workings of the UN bureaucracy; or information about the positions of the parties on each of dozens of issues. Just as people collected documents, they spent much time collecting information. Unlike the information about the time and place of meetings, however, the information included in the document as *language* was never specific. Pacific delegates needed specific information about rising sea levels to argue for the inclusion of a proposed paragraph that mentioned rising sea levels, for example, yet in their proposed amendment those sea levels were rising everywhere and nowhere. During the conference, the difference between the specificity of the facts outside the document and the generality of the facts within the document defined a distance between the inside of the text and the inside of the coffee bar where delegates gathered to talk about their amendments.

Unlike the patterns of levels within the brackets, therefore, the language that bridged the gaps within the brackets held firm and did not reveal other layers. It was opaque in its masking of the potentially infinite layers of language, even as it was presented as absolutely transparent in the sense of holding a singular and self-evident meaning.[13] The quotation epitomized this concreteness of language in the way it could be taken from one conference to another, like the physical displacement of the document or the negotiator. One Fiji delegate explained to me that "our platform solidified" through the process of transposing language from one document into another through quotation. The concreteness of the language, when woven into a proper pattern, constituted the concreteness of the document that emerged at the end.[14]

Finally, like participants in a Fijian ceremony seated on the pattern of layered mats, delegates knew that, once assembled into a concrete document, language would be taken apart again. The document did not exist to be "read" in the academic sense of the term. Rather, after the close of the conference, governments and NGOs would *use* the document by dividing sentences into categories and reshuffling the text into material for quotation in further documents of their own. The carefully crafted patterns of the artifact, delegates knew, would be decomposed into their myriad composite parts.

A Figure Seen Twice

I have described a double view. First, just as the pattern of the *vivivi* emerged from the layering of one mat onto the next, we saw that the apprehension of the global *Platform for Action* entailed a failure of representation—at the point at which the counting of brackets, like the counting of mats, failed—and that this failure also enabled the realization of "the pattern which connects" (Bateson 1980: 8) one level (of documents, conferences, text) to the next. In this apprehension of pattern, the difference of scale that separated the negotiator from the document or the global from the local was no longer foregrounded.

There were also points at which the document, as an object, was distinct from the patterns of conference procedure and the patterns in delegates' minds. Such moments were also those at which only one level of language was accessible, while others were (temporarily) closed. The concrete document was an encapsulation of the infinity of pattern within something that stood on its own, just as the vivivi could be rolled up and taken away. The possibility of the further extension of the pattern always remained: a copy of the document could always be reproduced an infinite number of times. Yet for infinity to emerge anew would require some intentional reactivation. One needed a typist, a printer, or a photocopier to make it happen, for example (see Latour and Woolgar [1979] 1986).

From this vantage point, however, a problem emerges concerning the cultural specificity of what I have described. Whose patterns are these? Is this a Fijian phenomenon, something "global," or something "in between?"[15] Perhaps one of the initially most surprising ethnographic observations to be made about the negotiations described in this chapter was negotiators' collective failure to problematize what anthropologists describe under the rubric of global-local relations during the course of their work.

This returns us to the cover design of the *Pacific Platform for Action*. As in the cover design, mats often served as symbols of the Pacific, and especially of Pacific women, in documents, newsletters, and promotional videotapes produced by Pacific governments and NGOs. Such depictions of generically "Pacific mats," and of "the Pacific," might raise precisely the concerns about cultural specificity noted above. Note the way in which the representation emerged here. It is the great detail of the close-up lens, the scale of the image, that renders the mats in the photographs unidentifiable and thus engenders the loss of precisely the cultural detail that interests anthropologists. In this foreclosure of representation, the loss that brings pattern into view, the image also brings into being a visual representation of another kind—one of regionalism and scale change itself.

We might take this image as a particularly graphic example of a phenomenon described throughout this chapter: the generation of the perspectival experience of local, regional, or global levels. I have endeavored to show that far from being contexts *outside* the document, the local and global are brought into view through the aesthetic devices described in the previous pages. This material would then draw attention to the importance of aesthetics in the imagination and experience of global and local. It would also imply that the relationship of global to local cannot provide the analytical framework for such documents—that one cannot understand the experience of these documents in terms of contextual shifts—because such a perspective is overdetermined by the material itself. That is to say, the very contexts or perspectives of global and local are artifacts of the practices we wish to understand.

In *Resisting Representation,* Elaine Scarry examines how the language of the English novel is able to accommodate subjects that seem either too abstract or too concrete for representation—subjects such as truth, on the one hand, or pain on the other. Her answer turns not to the well-chosen image or the evocative phrase but to similarities within the novel between "grammatical structures and narrative structures"—that is, "between small and large patches of language." Such repetitions in the pattern of language in turn engender "the 'extendibility' of language the coherent way it can be steadily elaborated and unfolded. Once opened and elaborated, it can be contracted again" (1994: 3–4). In the same way, what the patterns in the language of the global *Platform for Action* ultimately represented, what we might understand as its meaning, was precisely the "levels" (global, national, regional, and so on) that the designers of UN procedures so desperately sought to bring together. The twentieth-century problem of international institutions has been one of how to grasp these levels at one and the same time, how to bring them into a single encompassing view. The aesthetics described in this chapter—a figure seen twice—provides a means of representing precisely what resists representation. One outcome of these aesthetics is that the fixed and self-contained form of analysis of international negotiation deprives the academic observer and reader of the familiar ethnographic journey through transformations of meaning from concrete apprehensions of facts to abstract analyses. Yet, as I have endeavored to make clear, documents such as the global *Platform for Action* cannot be analyzed— at least in academic terms. That is, any attempt to transform the material from concrete to abstract would fail to achieve the effect we expect of our analyses in the first place and would simply sit like one more layer, one further replication, one convention upon a series of other conventions. The achievement of the document is that the levels of analysis—from global to local or national to regional—are revealed from the start.

CHAPTER 4

Division within the Boundaries

In "The Net and the Self," Manuel Castells has proclaimed a "structural transformation" of the world around a new raw material, information (1996: 15–16). He terms the "new society" the "network society":

> our societies are fundamentally made of flows exchanged through networks of organizations and institutions. By "flows" I understand purposeful, repetitive, programmable sequences of exchange and interaction between physically disjointed positions held by social actors in organizations and institutions of society. . . . Networks organize the positions of actors, organizations and institutions in societies and economies. The social relevance of any social unit is thus conditioned by its presence or absence in specific networks. Absence of a dominant network leads to structural irrelevance. (28–29)

There is a certain excitement surrounding the claim. Castells's discovery that patterns of social and institutional organization depend on access to information neatly literalizes the midcentury uses of the Network to draw correspondences between knowledge and social organization explored in chapter 2. Moreover, as capital did for an earlier generation, "information" gives academics of all orientations and disciplines a shared purpose. When we can agree on little else, we share an interest in information, its patterning, and its distribution. Anthropologists may find themselves as seduced and enchained by information and its forms as were the delegates to the PrepCom described in the previous chapter, as we wrestle with matters from free speech to intellectual property rights to the latest Internet browser or departmental assessment exercise.

Nevertheless, what another scholar has called a "mode of information" (Poster 1990) is difficult for this former materialist to accept: "If my hypothesis is correct, then we have lost the direct linkage between the structure of social organization in terms of identifiable material interests and the logic of social mobilization" (Castells 1996: 33). The problem, then, is that the notion of "material interests" no longer functions as an explanatory device. This is the essence of the metaphor of information "flows" borrowed from the way capital is described as flowing about the globe in a way that resists and evades efforts to manage or analyze it. On the one hand, flows are by definition beyond our explanatory powers. On the other the displacement of capital by information is confirmed in the very theft of the metaphor. In asserting that this claim is a function of changed conditions, Castells is typical of many contemporary social theorists who throw away sociological skepticism and take people's statements at face value to reproduce the informational networks' own self-descriptions as empirical reality.[1]

It has become commonplace to assert that information has come to rival and in some cases displace capital as the fundamental basis of life (Bell 1973, 1979; Giddens 1990: 2; Lyotard 1984: 5; Poster 1990). The statement deserves attention by virtue of its implications for the character of academic work. Capital was a powerful organizing device in twentieth-century social science, and if it is now understood to have been replaced, this is an indicia of changes in the character of analysis. In the past, capital was an analytical tool that applied everywhere, that was analytically prior even to social relations. In practice, however, there was little discussion of what capital actually was. The power of capital, as an analytical tool, rather inhered in its own opacity; its ability to point beyond itself. The point, rather, was what others did with it and the social consequences that flowed from its distribution. The mode of analysis, in a world in which capital served as grounding, was critique.

As the latter day analog to captial, information shares this opaque aesthetic. Like capital, information does not *in itself* merit ethnographic attention; what matters, rather, is how it flows and what social consequences follow. It is a means, not an end, of knowledge, one of the given universals whose diverse uses generate the pluralism (the "modernities" in the plural [Comaroff and Comaroff 1992: xi; Faubion 1988, 1993: 9]) that anthropological analysis uncovers. The popular treatment of information as a commodity in the global economy (e.g., Gore 1991) furthers the notion that the only issues are its availability, what people do with it, and whose control it should be under—hence the constant references at the Beijing Conference to differences between the "information rich" and the "information poor." As the economic characterization of information as a "public good"[2] succinctly denotes, more information is always assumed to be better than less. Like globalization, its infinite horizons are taken as a given condition of contemporary life.

By way of contrast, I now turn to an entity whose horizons are known from the start—a Part-European clan for whom "kinship" is a question not of networked flows but of dividing in spatial and legal terms. From the point of view of clan members living in Kasavu, on the northern island of Vanua Levu, the parcels of freehold land that the Whippys of Kasavu have divided in each successive generation are finite, bounded entities capable of infinite internal partition, albeit according to a singular form. The corollary of the given and concretely delimited nature of the facts about land and kin is that for the Kasavu

Whippys, knowledge is a question not of gathering or managing disparate pieces of information, but of dividing in spatial and numerical terms.

It may seem odd that a chapter devoted to globalization and the "mode of information" would concern the patterned divisions of a very limited parcel of land in one very out of the way place. At first glance, life in Kasavu might constitute the very antithesis of globalization. Yet as it turns out, Kasavu offers an apt comparison to the extent that it is imagined that in a globalized world information has superseded capital. Where social scientists might take land as the classic instantiation of capital, people in Kasavu see not relations of value but numerical relations—literal correspondences between particular quantities of feet and chains. Indeed, the divided parcels of land that are the principal ethnographic subject of this chapter might be better translated into the Euro-American kinship vocabulary as biological facts, that is, as information prior to the social construction. If anthropologists find this hard to believe, they might ask themselves why they so easily accept a similar claim about the character of information in their own globalized world.

One could imagine a critique of the social scientist's discovery of a mode of information that would emphasize the way in which information, like capital, does not exist a priori but is the product of social relations. That is not the objective of this chapter. As we will see, for people in Kasavu, land, as a set of numerical correspondences, is indeed independent of and beyond social relations in the sense Castells and others imagine. Rather, my point is to query the particular understanding of information that characterizes late modern social science in general and the literature on globalization and the mode of information in particular—the notion that information is potentially infinite but in actuality scarce. As Marilyn Strathern (1991) has noted, assumptions about the quantity of information in turn imply a notion of perspective: modernist perspective is always partial because there is always more information than it is possible to take into account. For contemporary social scientists, to switch perspectives therefore means to gain new information only at the expense of information "loss" in another sense. To put the point in the language I have used in this book, to see the gaps in the figure is also to lose sight of the image of the figure itself.

As Strathern notes, the provisionality of perspective is managed by the device of context. One's context defines one's perspective or worldview. However, the proliferation of contexts associated with global capitalism has also meant a proliferation of perspectives. Hence the endless and infinite quality of information "flows": the apprehension that there is no limiting device on what there is to know, the sense of being overwhelmed by all there is to discover but also of constant loss associated with switching from one perspective to another. In Kasavu, in contrast, what there is to know—the numerical correspondences of land—is determined and bounded prior to knowledge itself.

The experiment of this chapter, then, builds on a contrast between two kinds of informational infinity. On the one hand, there is the infinity associated with the mode of information—the possibility of infinite extension. On the other, there is the infinite potential for the internal division of a given form—an infinity already encapsulated by a given set of correspondences, as in the case of the mathematical expression of infinity as a number in a given number set.

As it happens, the parallels to the materials of the previous chapters are concretized for the outside observer in the centrality of documents for Part-Europeans as devices and artifacts of their divisions (cf. Maurer 1997: 167–226). Clan leaders maintain collections of documents, including wills, land titles, historical records concerning their land, and photocopied pages from Fijian history books, that refer to the exploits of their ancestors as early settlers. More recently, these timeworn collections have been complemented among a younger generation by a new documentary genre—legal documents concerning a dispute over the ownership of Whippy land. As we will see, this collection of documents evidences a new kind of knowledge that negates the very logic of closure at stake in the divisions described below.

My initial interest in Part-European kinship, however, lay not in land or documents but in the nature of change. Urban Whippys routinely lamented the changes in the rural way of life brought on by the fact that land had "gone small" as a result of generations of partition. They chastised their "family in the country" for failing to find new ways of making their land productive such as forming agricultural cooperatives, mortgaging their land for development purposes, introducing tourism to Kasavu, and educating their children for employment in the wage economy, in short, for failing to find a strategy for survival in a changed world. In Kasavu, however, the Whippys repeatedly asserted that "nothing changes" or "nothing has happened." When confronted with questions concerning how the school, church, or land had changed in his lifetime, for example, John Whippy, a man in his fifties and the head of the household in which I stayed, seemed puzzled and finally responded that nothing that he could think of really had changed. On the face of it, the claim seemed absurd: surely an increase in number, or a decrease in size with respect to clan members and shares of land should constitute a change in his view. In Kasavu, however, the Whippys showed a stubborn lack of interest in, or anxiety about, such "real changes," dismissing the promise of new hybrid forms of coconuts offered by overseas development programs just as they dismissed the consequences of drastic reductions in the world price for their copra. Conversation among men and women gathered around the kava bowl in the evening turned instead to events fifty or one hundred years earlier—to an ancestor's exploits or a marriage several generations ago—recounted as effortlessly as if they had happened the week before, as if nothing had been *lost* of those events in the intervening time.

To understand how things fail to change in Kasavu requires an inquiry into how things are measured—into the nature of what the networks take as information, in other words. As we will see, the disjuncture between conceptions of kin, land, and their uses among urban and rural Whippys ultimately rests on a difference in understandings of the character of what exists prior to knowledge—of what is knowable before it is known—and of its social effects. If the infinity and ease of circulation of information are often taken as the material condition of globilization, then the question of how things fail to change in Kasavu may provide a vantage point from which to query the reach of the claim.

Within the Boundaries

Part-Europeans are the "mixed race" descendants of Europeans who settled in Fiji from the early nineteenth century (cf. Stoler 1995). At the last government census (1996), there were 11,685 Part-Europeans in Fiji, that is, approximately 1.5 percent of the total national population. They speak both English and Fijian with varying degrees of fluency, although both languages are patois of grammatical and vocabulary borrowings. Since the second generation, the "old families" (those whose presence in Fiji dates to the mid–nineteenth century) have largely intermarried with other Part-Europeans, and continue to do so to this day, although in the last twenty years Part-Europeans have intermarried considerably with Fijians.[3] Over half of all Part-Europeans live on scattered freehold estates[4] settled by their ancestors on the island of Ovalau, in the Rewa and Savusavu regions, as well as in Bua, Serua, and Ra. For the most part, they cut and dry copra there, as they have done for generations (cf. Whippy 1977; Kelly 1966; Parry 1989).

Over the last fifty years, however, the decline in the economic viability of planting has pushed many Part-Europeans into Suva, Lautoka, and other urban areas, so that at the time of my research, close to half of all Part-Europeans lived in the towns. During this same period, newcomer Part-European families who established themselves from the start in commerce or the trades rather than as planters have formed a distinct and increasingly prosperous Part-European class. Educated through secondary school and often at university, or even schooled overseas, and less than fluent in the Fijian language, they earn their living entirely in the cash economy in business, professional, administrative, service, or tourism-related professions. These newcomers (descendants of European and Chinese immigrants to Fiji in this century rather than the last) are related through kinship ties to the older Part-European clans and also, to a lesser extent, to Fijian clans.[5]

The members of the Whippy clan are descendants of David Whippy, an American seaman from Nantucket, Massachusetts, who arrived in Fiji around 1822 (Brown 1886). As urban clan members routinely remarked with pride, the Whippy clan is one of the largest in Fiji, and counts over one thousand living kin. Clan members spoke of themselves as a "clan" or "family" (using the English words and never Fijian kinship terms) headed by "uncles" or "leaders" who make decisions concerning the allocation of land and who represent the clan in negotiations with the government and in ceremonial contexts. The Whippy clan is internally subdivided into four subclans (also referred to as "clans"), which take their names from each of David Whippy senior's sons.[6]

From the point of view of people in Kasavu I knew, the Whippys living in Suva were marginal figures. Many were women now married into other urban families. Many had shown little interest in the clan until recently, as they oriented themselves more toward their professions or their personal connections in Suva and overseas. Most importantly, all were landless—they had no rights to a share of the scattered plots of land acquired by their founding ancestor throughout Fiji—although some now sought to acquire shares of this land through purchase from landed relations. Contact between rural and urban Whippys was confined primarily to contributions and attendance in ceremonial contexts such as funerals and weddings. Some clan members in the cities contributed money, kerosene, or other store-bought items for mortuary rites, fundraisers for the Kasavu school, or presentations to Fijian chiefs with whom the clan maintained special ties. Funds were collected and relayed through several city persons, known as the "doors" to Kasavu, who visited Kasavu once or twice a year. Urban clan members talked of their rural kin with a mixture of reverence for their perpetuation of dying family ways and pity for their lowly economic status.[7]

Kinship within the Boundaries

The settlement of Kasavu is located on a rectangular plot of freehold land once owned by their ancestor and known as Lovonisikeci, two miles by one mile in area and bordering the sea (fig. 13).[8] Each of the Whippy subclans also owned a portion of *Yadali,* a tract of 13,262 acres of mountainous land covered in hardwood forest bordering the Wainunu coast, in the western portion of the island of Vanua Levu four hours west of Kasavu by truck. Although that estate had been partitioned many times since its acquisition, the land had remained largely "empty." In formal speeches and casual conversations around the kava bowl, men and women of all ages talked at length about the land, recounting how it was acquired and how it had been divided, and in private conversations they whispered about the many conflicts concerning its division. This talk often addressed divisions among kin but also emphasized the form of the place—its shape and boundaries and its internal partition—as people made their points concerning these divisions by tracing the partitions in the rectangular shape of Kasavu in the sand.

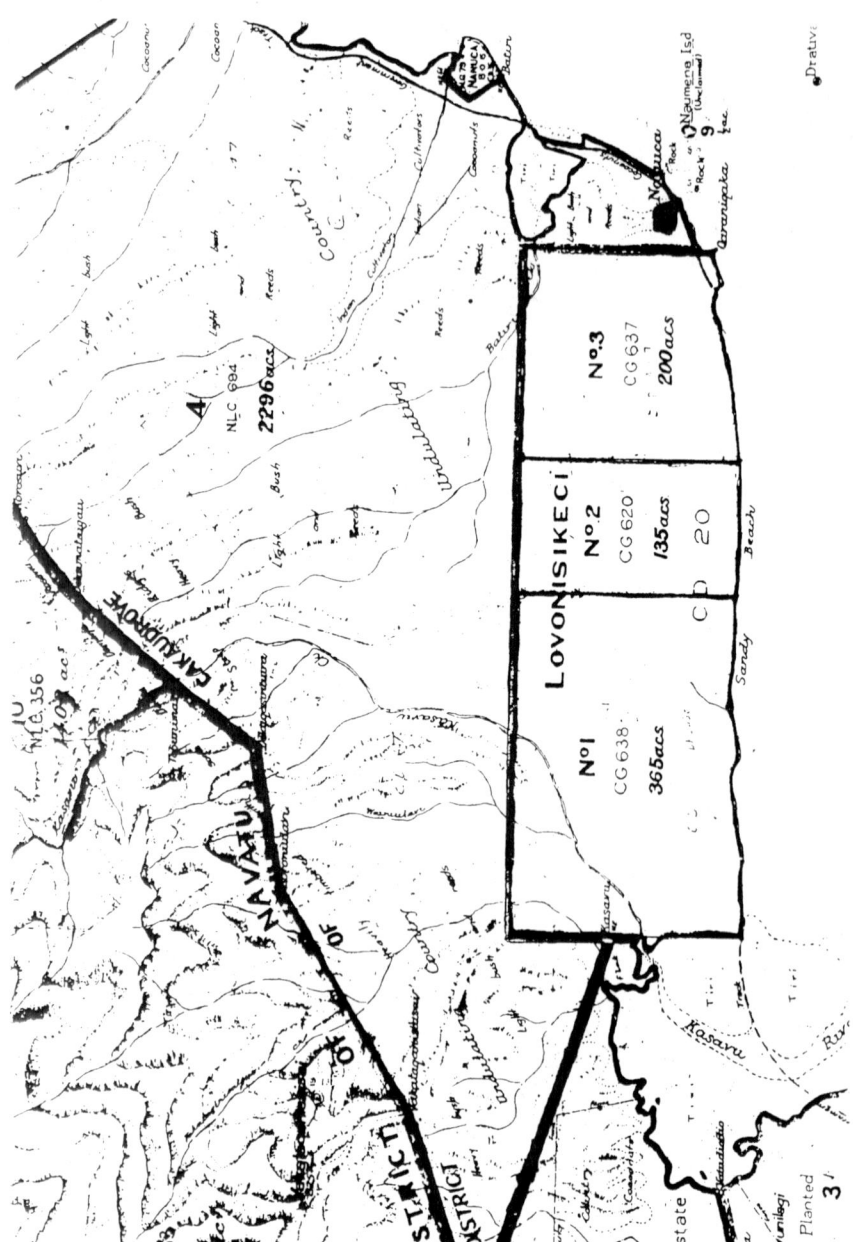

Fig. 13. Early survey map of Lovonisikeci estate, Cakaudrove Province, Vanua Levu. (Reproduced courtesy of the Director of Lands and Surveyor General.)

In marriage, the rural Whippys repeated a given and inward-looking pattern. To think of the Whippys was to think also of the Simpsons, as a Whippy joked whenever he or she encountered a Simpson, "if no Whippy, no Simpson," prompting the invariable retort "if no Simpson, no Whippy!" The relationship traces back to a commercial partnership between apical ancestors[9] when David Whippy and his friend William Simpson, a carpenter and shipbuilder from Poplar, England, jointly engaged in a plethora of small business ventures ranging from sugar mills to cargo. There are many stories about the friends' common exploits and the complementary relations each maintained with alternative Fijian chieftainships.[10] Each clan constitutes the most likely source of marriage partners for the other.[11] Simpsons and Whippys call one another by the Fijian term *tavale*,[12] indicating that they are closely related and ideal marriage partners, and the joking, teasing character of the relationship between any Whippy and Simpson is similar to the *tavale* relationship among Fijians.[13] Some phrased the relationship between clans in terms of "a *tabu* against marrying outside the family," while others simply said that it "closes the circle," or "renews the link," or "blood looks for its own." As one clan "leader" explained it to me:

> Those two families, they complete each other. They always intermarry. You always see a Simpson and a Whippy together. It's best to marry *tavale*. It's good. I meet a married couple, and I'm related to both of them that way.

People in Kasavu did not speak of this relationship in an idiom of exchange or reciprocity, however, as did their Fijian neighbors. Marriages, likewise, were not marked by any imperative exchange of mats or whale's teeth. There was no pattern of exchange to the marriages beyond a prohibition against marriage within the Whippy clan. Despite the attention given to generational differences between kin,[14] for example, a relatively high number of marriages were cross-generational.[15] Although marriages were arranged in a minority of cases, an arranged marriage denoted the weakness of a man who could not "talk to a girl properly" rather than an opportunity for expanding relationships between clans. If "blood finds its own," then blood did not serve as a particularly salient idiom for elaborating group relationships. Indeed, by Fijian standards, the Whippy and Simpson clans were hardly clans at all, for they had no ritual obligations toward one another and did not constitute salient groupings for the purpose of exchange (cf. Hocart 1952).[16]

Rather than a medium for connections, marriage between Whippys and Simpsons was most often discussed as a matter of the division of land (fig. 14). The two actions that were said to have founded the Whippy and Simpson clans—a partition of estates among David Whippy and William Simpson, and

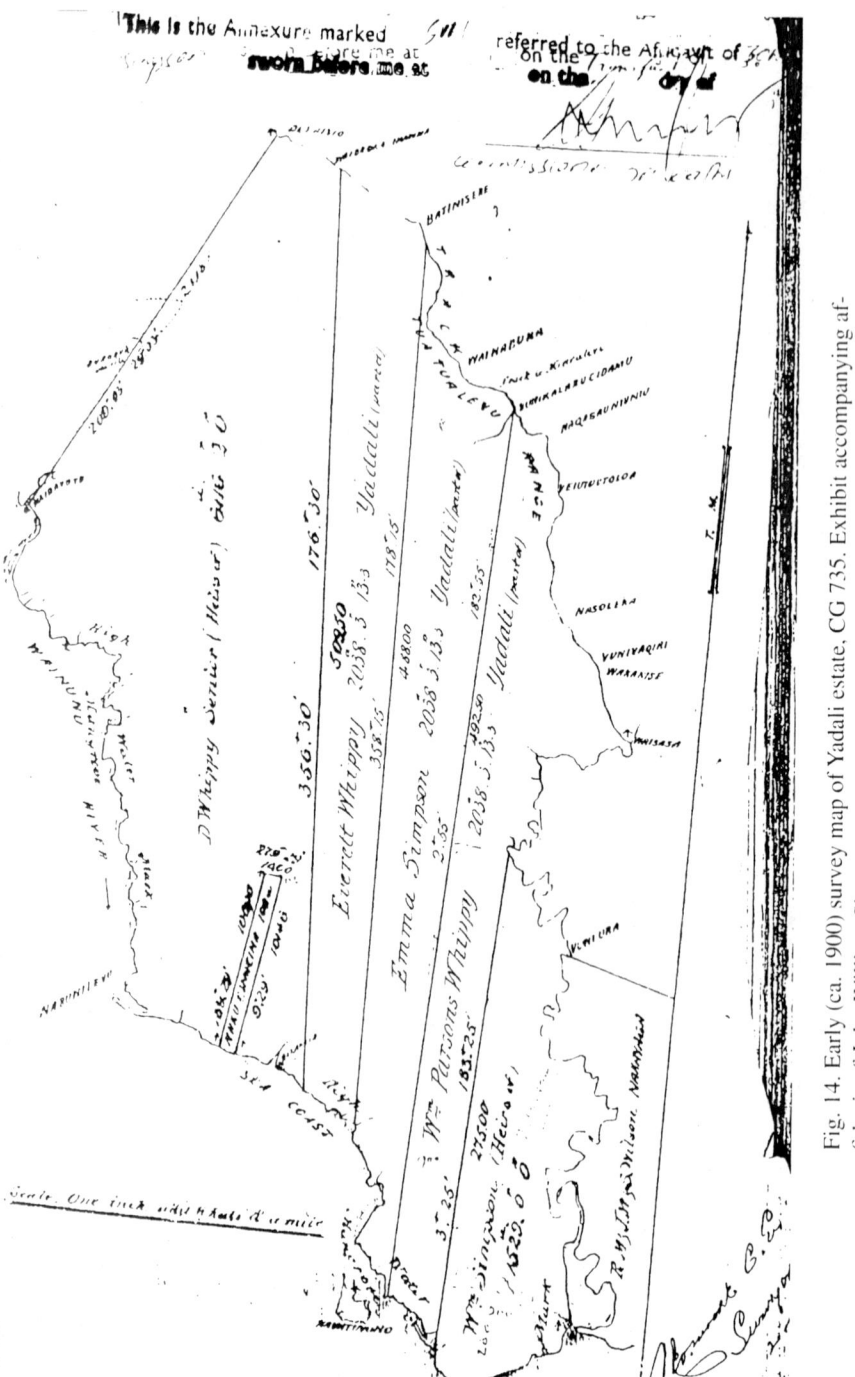

Fig. 14. Early (ca. 1900) survey map of Yadali estate, CG 735. Exhibit accompanying affidavit of John William Simpson. "In the matter of Jacob Andrews and William Chang" (Action no. HPP054/94S). 18 May 1995. (Reproduced courtesy of the Director of Lands and Surveyor General.)

the marriage of David Whippy's daughters to William Simpson's sons—were conceptualized in singular terms, as both land and people divided according to a shared logic. During his lifetime, David Whippy informally transferred the southeastern corner of the Yadali estate to William Simpson. Since then, the logic of inheritance that links land to people has followed the same pattern or form (cf. Crocombe and Marsters 1987).

For example, the marriage of William Simpson's oldest recognized son, Matthew, to David Whippy's eldest daughter, Emma, brought together two divided portions of the Yadali estate. Emma Whippy inherited from her father a strip of 2,038 acres in the central portion of the estate, while Matthew Simpson inherited 1,529 acres of the southeastern corner owned by his father. Matthew and his wife's brother, William Parsons Whippy, then each divided their land, and Matthew acquired a portion of William's, adjoining his wife's, in exchange for a portion of his own. In so doing, however, he spatially divided his own holdings between the Whippy and Simpson lots. Even at this stage, the geometry of Yadali presented an image of staggered partitions of Whippy and Simpson land. William's land, comprising both "Whippy" and "Simpson" pieces spatially divided, was further divided among his eight children. Four of these children married Whippys, thereby further partitioning among their children spatially divided partitions of the estate. Emma Whippy's share was not legally partitioned among her children and remains undivided communal land today.

The history of Lovonisikeci, likewise, might be described as a pattern of division legally performed, and the passing of generations was etched in the divisions marked out in the land. Originally, the Whippys emphasized, Lovonisikeci was a square block of land two miles by two miles, later halved by the colonial government into a rectangular plot of two miles by one mile (Fiji Land Claims Commission 1880). The brothers Samuel and Peter Whippy and Jacob Andrews (described alternatively as David Whippy's adopted son or his grantee) divided the land into three rectangular shares, each fronting on the sea and stretching inland toward the bush (fig. 13). Samuel took the "bottom end," Peter took the "upper end," and Jacob was given the middle portion.

In each successive generation, the land was divided by tracing lines parallel to those the brothers drew in the first act of partition.[17] These divisions created a series of parallel plots of an even length and of successively decreasing widths so that at the time of my fieldwork each plot constituted only a long thin strip of land not much wider than the dirt road that cut through Kasavu but stretching a mile from the beach to the bush the width of the original estate

---

Fig. 15. (*Following pages*) Survey map of a portion of Lovonisikeci estate. CT 4321, lots 1–4, property of John, Walter, Bertie, and Eric Whippy. (Reproduced courtesy of the Director of Lands and Surveyor General.)

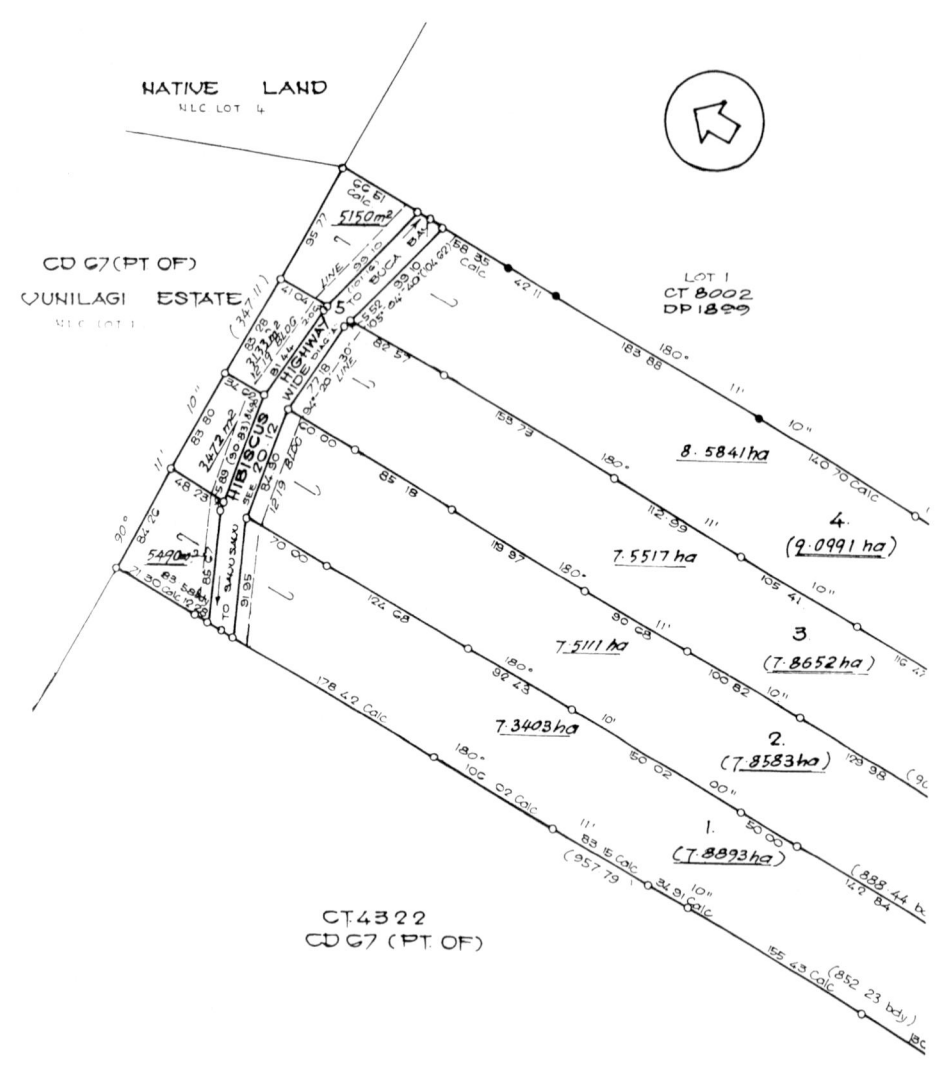

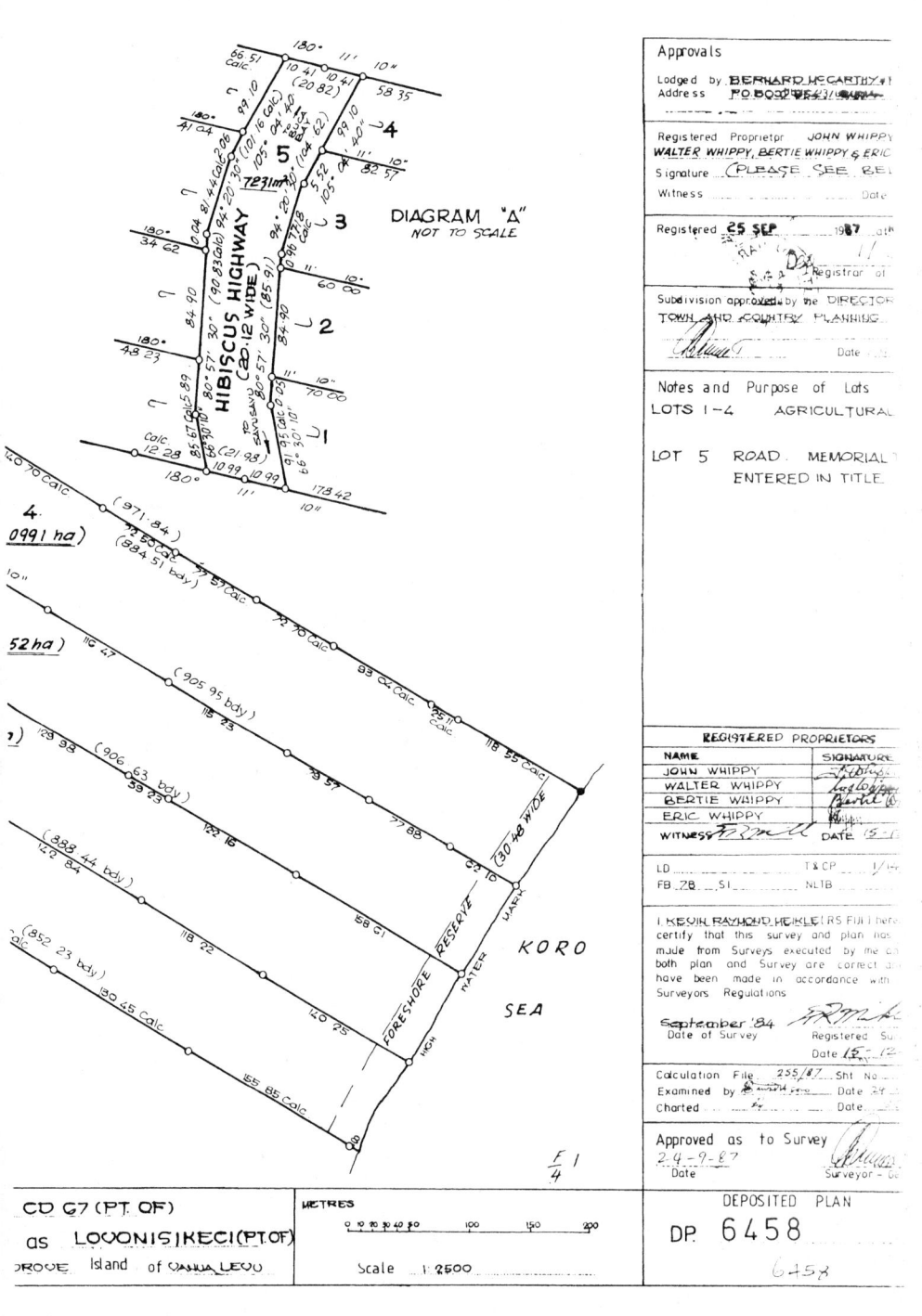

(fig. 15).[18] The width and arrangement of parallel plots reflected the number of generations since the first act of partition and also the relationship among landholders, since categorical brothers held proximate plots, while those belonging to separate subclans owned plots in separate parts of the original estate. This pattern of division was an unchallenged and irreversible generational process. People took my suggestion that the partition of land might proceed according to some other logic—a horizontal or diagonal partitioning of plots, for example—or that the thin strips might be recombined through purchase or some collective arrangement as absurd.

The rural Whippys, then, shared a geometry dictated by a series of divided parcels acquired by their ancestor. That marriage, for example, should be conceptualized as a spatial quality of land is reflected in the following account, given to me by one elder, of how Part-Europeans acquired their land:

> In those days, a Part-European would steal his wife from a Fijian chief. He couldn't just come calling at the chief's house, or he would get a hell of a hiding. And when the chief would finally hear that his daughter was safe and had been taken as a wife and would be cared for, he would say, "*vinaka!*" [good] and "from here, to here, to there." And that land would be given, for the future generations of children they would produce.

Those living on a parcel of land pooled their resources to engage a surveyor to chart the division according to legal specifications and then sent a representative to Suva to file the necessary documents with the Register of Title. In the case of inheritance, division proceeded according to the dictates laid out in the deceased's will, duly filed with the Probate Office together with a map delineating the necessary partitions. The titular registration of these divisions was only achieved with considerable hardship. A group of siblings might work their land in common for an entire generation before saving enough money from their copra sales to pay the surveyor's fee, and the magnitude of such fees eclipsed the amount of funds accumulated for funerals, marriages, fund-raising for the church or school, or the construction of new houses.

The legal documents provided the graphic images of Lovonisikeci and Yadali and of the numerical measurements that so permeated life on these estates. This was made palpable in constant references to Certificates of Title (CT) numbers in daily discourse. When I proved unable to keep up with the chain of characters in a family story, for example, my hosts obliged me with schematic tree-shaped diagrams listing those who had inherited a share of the land, the amount of their acreage, and "their" CT number. In Suva, where many of the younger generation of Whippys had found employment, clan members met to discuss family affairs and to *soli* (collect funds) under the groupings of "block A," "block B," and so on, according to the label assigned to each block of Yadali land by the Register of Title in the course of titular division. If in the previous chapter we considered the document as a form of patterned interaction that preceded the actual production of a "document" in concrete and physical form, here one might speak of land as a similar documentary entity. The document's graphic representation of the geometric shape and boundaries of the land existed for the Whippys not simply in the physical document but as a lived pattern of interaction.

The mathematical calculation of fractions of land was a commonplace element of conversational rhetoric. Everyone knew the number of feet and chains of each parcel and divided fractions of past or present quantities with lightening speed. The reference numbers of each Certificate of Title, likewise, were known to all, and at times the owners and the land merged in conversation into references to these numbers alone.

The division of quantities of land in Kasavu was also a division of quantities of money. Before brothers could muster the necessary costs of legal division, they took turns cutting the copra from the land, sharing equally in its returns.[19] Copra is a crop to which humans add very little. Palms planted many generations ago bear fruit virtually without tending, and one only collects the nuts from the ground once they have fallen. The quantity of nuts harvested is not a function of the addition of human energy or ingenuity, and it is largely uniform from one month to the next. The only element of human influence on the yield of the crops mentioned to me was that the palms must be evenly spaced eight feet apart. Yet even this was a matter in which the present generation took no additional action, for like the initial divisions of land the even rows had been laid out generations before.

This uniformity in turn was what made division intelligible. The limited but standard cash income that copra planting from these divided parcels yielded was, in its monetary form, a divisible and measurable quantity that correlated with the divisions in the land. Little wonder, then, that the Whippys treated new varieties of coconut, or government admonitions to switch to more lucrative cash crops aimed at increasing their yield, with disinterest and even suspicion. The few who attempted to produce a variable quantity of wealth by planting profitable kava plants for sale in the market, for example, became the victims of sorcery or awoke to find their plants dug up from the soil. Any effort to accumulate resources of food or money would immediately be met with requests that could not be refused (*kerekere*), and people went to considerable lengths to convince others that they had no such resources to share.

The leadership of the Whippy clan was a matter of constant contest and uncertainty, and clan members often pointed to the absence of a given source of authority among brothers as a fundamental difference between themselves and their Fijian neighbors.[20] The only clear differences in rank were generational, where generations were evidenced in past or future acts of division. The constant disputes among brothers over perceived inequalities in status or resources were repeated, I was told, in each generation and were understood as inevitable until land could be formally divided. In all the cases I observed the disputants were persons arranged side by side as equals by virtue of past or future acts of division. Whatever conflicts there were, however, occurred within fixed parameters. The source of such conflicts was always the same. Most of all, it was inconceivable that such disputes might alter the form or pattern of generational division. The latter was utterly beyond these disputes, not available for contest.

This was because there was no given truth in Kasavu, no fixed point in daily conflicts, but the boundaries of the land. The conflicts among those placed side by side within the finite and bounded land were never available as sources or arbiters of collective truth because all positions were equal, and coexisted within the boundaries. Unlike societies in which some distinguish themselves through discursive prowess, for example, in Kasavu it was impossible to win a dispute, that is, to change the discursive landscape, by convincing others of the truth of one's claim and the falsity of their own. Even the Christian church offered no outside source of truth that might stop interpretations (Miyazaki 1997).[21]

In contrast to the fluidity of the truth in daily conflicts, the divisions of land and the outcomes these produced were concrete and preordained. The boundaries of the land existed independent of the perceptual faculties of any person (Gell 1985), and these served as their own points of reference so that space had a definite shape irrespective of the persons located there. People in Kasavu did not, for example, imagine their spatial world as forming outwardly extending concentric circles around the self (e.g., Munn 1996: 453–54), nor did they show any particular interest in the orientation of persons relative to these divisions (e.g., Danziger 1996). Division was understood as fixed in outside arbiters such as government registers of land titles rather than in human experience.

Yet, although division emerged—for myself as I sought the truth about Kasavu as much as for those living there—as a solution to the endless succession of alternative truths, it was not an *outcome* of that contest. Rather, division was an inevitable generational repetition independent of the identity and ambitions of those living on the land. This grounding of space in its own parameters rather than in an image of society would seem to contradict a common anthropological assumption that "people in all societies, order space into different spheres which convey a moral focus for acts and things associated with them" (Beidelman 1986: 49). Spatial organization did not express or reflect (e.g., Durkheim [1915] 1957) social realities. The divisions did not, for example, correspond to parts of a cosmology, nor did space serve as a "metaphor" for personal or social relations (Beidelman 1986: 54). Division was not so much a shared basis of egalitarian politics as a given set of independent and outside principles, an exercise in the internal relational possibilities of a limited set of numerical and arithmetical rules that correlated with and verified the reproduction of generations. Division paralleled social life, just as each plot of divided land lay parallel to the next.

This fixed relationship of quantification is most palpable in the Whippys' constitution of "truth" or "reality." One day Matthew Whippy suggested that he show me something "real." We walked along the beach until we reached a rocky point known as Qaraniqaka at the end of the Lovonisikeci estate. Matthew struggled onto the rock and then, standing solemnly, announced this to be the place where Tui Cakau, the high chief, had sailed along the coast and from his cutter had pointed out the boundaries of Lovonisikeci to his ancestor. Raising his arm to emulate the chief, he pointed them out once again: "From Qaraniqaka to the mouth of the Kasavu river, and two miles inland. So you see, this is *real* (*dina*). There's no question about it."

I asked how he knew the story to be true. As it turned out, Matthew had learned this story twenty years earlier when he had visited the National Archives in Suva and obtained a copy of the Land Claims Commission records concerning Lovonisikeci. The story was included in the record of evidence presented by his ancestors to the commission. In reading the documented account, Matthew recognized its veracity, for it retraced the shape of the land that was so familiar to him and mentioned the name of the rock that he had known all his life.

The "real" for Matthew was manifest in the identity of the physical and documentary geometry of the land, in the relational verification of fixed correspondences. It was something quite different from the real as outside grounding, whose vanishing has been widely celebrated and lamented (cf. Baudrillard [1972] 1981; Strathern 1992a). In Kasavu, one could not hold on to one's interpretations of disputes in the face of the equally true claims of equally situated kin in exactly the same way as one could not accumulate or hold onto wealth in the face of the demands of categorical brothers because there was no outside grounding for either kind of claim. Instead, reality was encountered in the quotidian reconfirmation of what was already known. Each official land survey performed in the course of division reconfirmed the true dimensions of the whole through the remeasurement of the part. Even when, as in Matthew's case, facts were obtained from sources outside of Kasavu, the truth was found not in the discovery or management of additional information that shifted one's point of view but in its correlation with and reconfirmation of what was given from the start.[22] In this sense, division is an exercise in verification, a rehearsal of the given truth, as much as a principle of kinship or ownership.

We now might better understand the Whippys' insistence that things do not change in Kasavu. On the one hand, disputes did not change things because they could not be won, that is, they could not change what knowledge was already given. On the other hand, although the passing of time was marked by division, nothing was added or taken away, in the endless repetition of this process, from the prefigured whole. Division, rather, verified what was always given and completely known. Everything was a fraction of a whole that existed in the past and still existed in the past-in-the-present because nothing had been taken away. The past and the present were a singular form not only in the metaphorical terms of memory (Munn 1995), therefore, but in the spatial form of areas of land in turn locked into a fixed numerical relationship of identity to the replication of generations. Although one could not "go back" in time to the point at which the Whippy clan was one estate and one ancestral figure, it was not necessary to do so, for the entire estate was still there, in the same field. In both the divisions of land and the disputes among those who took the resulting shares, therefore, no new perspective, no changed position, could be individually or collectively attained.

One to One

It now will be clear that despite the parallels to modern sociology's "mode of information" land as information in Kasavu had very different properties. One might describe this as a difference between the fixity of information and information "flows." Or one might say that in Kasavu information took a concrete form. In claiming that information was concrete, I mean that it did not point to a further, greater, more complex reality beyond itself, as metaphors do (Wagner 1986). Land was not of a different order of magnitude than knowledge about land as, for the Suva Whippys, for example, clan genealogy was of a different order from the family tree. As a result, land did not reflect any particular perspective (cf. Strathern 1991). The apparent irrationality of these divisions from the point of view of urban clan members, then, might be understood as an exercise in the preservation of concreteness. What difference does it make that the "facts" in Kasavu are fractions of chains of land rather than a given and closed cosmology, for example (Harrison 1989)? Since academic analysis calls for outside interpretation rather than division, I will violate the logic described to this point with an addition.

The first formal definition of number is attributed to the nineteenth-century German mathematician Gottlob Frege. In Frege's view, although number did not have a spatial location, nor could it even be imagined, it nevertheless was not simply an attribute of other objects but an independent object of its own ([1884] 1983: 134). If number was an *object*, Frege argued, it was also a special *relationship*, one of equivalence between entities that "fall under" that number. Equinumerosity, he noted, was a one-to-one correlation among elements in a set: a waiter who wished to place as many knives as plates on a table could ensure that this was done by placing one knife to the right of each plate such that plates and knives correlated in a one-to-one positional relationship (141). Crucial to Frege's definition was the understanding that the *form* of such a numerical relationship remained constant throughout: if the waiter were to begin in midcourse to place a knife to both the right and left of the plate, it would no longer be possible to speak of a singular number of plates and knives. As real objects, Frege also argued, arithmetic truths existed a priori (159) even though they were also the objects of analysis. Number in this view, then, might be understood as a relationality which takes a concrete, objectified form.

In the twentieth century, the discovery of new kinds of number altogether led to an abandonment of Frege's conception of number as relational object in favor of an understanding of number as representation. In its old-fashioned quality, therefore, Frege's conception aptly captures the logic of the curious practice of division in Kasavu that results in strips of land no wider than a road but a mile in length. In the product of parallel instances of a singular form, what the Whippys generated was pure commensurability,[23] what Frege called number, that is, a literal analytical relationship that exists a priori even though it is also the object of their knowledge practices. Like Frege's conception of number, division worked, as an analytical device, only because Lovonisikeci was an object whose boundaries were concretely defined. It would be impossible, for example, to divide a "society" or a group in this way, for the rules of arithmetic would not apply to something that is not prefigured as a finite quantity with its own given rules of analysis.

The relationship of each part to each whole in Kasavu, in other words, could be known perfectly (not simply modeled) in numerical form—as a quantity of acres, a number of chains—and that relationship is an "object," something a priori and fixed. Division was an a priori analytical form that proceeded according to a series of one-to-one correlations (boundaries) and was deductive (rather than additive) in character since the raw materials of information (quantity) and the method of analysis (arithmetical division) were given. Divided land was a finite object, not a resource for further growth. It could not transform itself into wealth despite the urgings of urban kin. It did not increase over time but rather was partitioned away while also remaining concretely whole. It was inconceivable, for example, that the Whippys collectively might "amount" to more (or less) land, wealth, or prestige in present-day Fiji than did their ancestor David Whippy individually 150 years ago.

The Disappearance of Title and the Emergence of the Family Tree

Yet at the time of my research something was about to change for the Kasavu Whippys: they feared that they might soon lose their land at Yadali altogether.

In 1994, members of the Andrews and Simpson clans living in Suva and overseas individually brought suit to have themselves declared the rightful trustees of the 2,110-acre portion still held in common by the heirs of Samuel Whippy.

As far as anyone could remember, the division of land among Whippys, Simpsons, and Andrews had always proceeded without legal contest. Yet the recent construction of a government road through the mountainous area of Wainunu for the first time provided vehicular access to the land in question, thus attracting the attention of logging companies seeking to purchase virgin hardwood. Logging is a very different activity than copra cutting, for the large-scale investment in equipment necessary to render the operation profitable demands an agglomeration rather than a division of interests. This kind of exploitation introduced a new problem of scale: until recently, the Whippys had looked upon Yadali as a place capable of endless generational division. Yet now that information had become capital, Yadali had become a limited resource.

This had brought change not only to the land but also to the documents: although the flurry of court affidavits, pleadings, and submissions of evidence included many of the same Certificates of Title considered previously, these documents had become instruments, means to a social end (ownership) defined in terms beyond the documents, rather than arbiters of referential truth.

This new collectivizing activity coincided with a change in thinking among the Whippys living in town. In 1993, together with relations living in Australia and New Zealand, some prominent Whippys working in Suva organized the first "Descendants of David Whippy Reunion" aimed at "discovering connections" among unacquainted kin. The discovery of these connections meant an acquisition of new knowledge for the organizers; it represented a change. Albert, the chairman of the reunion organizing committee, was a well-known journalist and public relations consultant in Suva. Albert's children lived and worked in Sydney, where they were married to foreigners. Although he was personally close to many of his father's kin, he said, he knew little about the Whippy clan and its history and never thought much about being a Whippy. It was only at the first family reunion that he discovered that so many of the people whom he *already* knew by other means in town "were related."[24]

The objective was to extend personal networks, conceptualized in an idiom of genealogy. In the follow-up reunion planned for December 1996, organizers even hoped to attract "our white relatives," descendants of their original ancestor's kin from Nantucket, Massachusetts, who since the early 1800s had had no contact with the Fijian Whippys but whom the organizers insisted were "related." Although the reunion project was principally a hobby for organizers and participants, the new knowledge it generated could also generate pecuniary benefits. As one prominent Whippy put it to me, "I know the connections. I make it my business to know." He went on to describe how, on the basis of his superior genealogical knowledge, he was able to demonstrate to a business associate that the associate should call him "uncle," thus asserting a privilege of generational rank. For their part, most of the Whippys in Kasavu refused to attend the reunion. If the purpose of the event made little sense to them, their confusion found expression in their vehement insistence that the event was literally misplaced: the Whippys were not from Suva but from Levuka, where David Whippy first landed and married, and from Wainunu, where he died and was buried, the "uncles" of the Kasavu Whippy clans insisted. Any Whippy gathering would have to take place in one of those locations.

A principal focus of the reunion was a collective effort to produce a complete Whippy family tree.[25] The Whippys, like other members of the old families living in Suva, devoted great efforts to the creation of bilaterally reckoned genealogies for their clan. The Whippy family tree was kept at the home of a woman born in Kasavu who had left at a young age. When she proudly unrolled the graph paper covered with the names of husbands, wives, and their children in tiny script, it stretched from one end of her living room to the other. The idea, she explained, was that each person who visited her might know a different piece of the family history and might add it to the chart. The family tree conferred a sense of cumulative accomplishment upon its makers, as they congratulated themselves for collecting this information before it was "lost" with the passing of the older generation.

In the family tree, therefore, information was collective and cumulative: each person brought new information, based on his or her own position in the family and life experience, and could literally fill in a different gap in the tree. There was a *desire* to know the connections both present and past, a newfound curiosity about this project that paralleled some urban Whippys' desire to own their own piece of the family land. Any singular point or name on the family tree entailed the possibility of seemingly infinite expansion through the addition of generations of ancestors and descendants. The quantity of information known, therefore, was a matter of productivity, not something given at the outset. It was also, if only implicitly, an outcome of choices made concerning which lines to research and which names to include—choices that in turn were experienced in the way they made all the more evident the gaps in what was known.

The logic of assembling and reassembling that characterized both the battles for control of Yadali and the new collective interests in genealogy also introduced a new sense of perspective. In contrast to the literal correspondences in Kasavu that were anchored in the land, not in its inhabitants, and were therefore aperspectival, these projects assumed the particularity of each person's point of view and aimed to satisfy the desire of each person to know or own a totality that forever remained beyond their grasp by piecing knowledge and land together rather than dividing. Knowledge now floated free, anchored only to persons, just as land ownership also attached to persons and groups that claimed legal rights. No longer was it possible to speak of a one-to-one correspondence among document and land. That personal nexus of knowledge would mean an end to the literally local quality of Whippy knowledge was made particularly palpable by current plans for a family excursion to Nantucket, Massachusetts, to visit the place where their ancestor once lived in order to recapture the Whippys' American roots.

These information-gathering activities—the expansive possibilities and also the limiting choices they demanded—have a certain familiarity for social scientists, who have taken the discovery and management of selective facts, from among the infinite depth and breadth of potential information, as a fundamental aspect of human experience. The genealogical model employed by urban Part-Europeans has been a standard tool of such management in anthropologists' own work. Indeed, the notion that potential information—the raw material of social knowledge—is infinite, and thus cumulatively gained or lost, is one of the implicit universals that render our conception of human differences meaningful (e.g., Kant 1952).

From this point of view, the literal conception of space and kinship in Kasavu is bound to provoke a sense of incredulity among late modern social scientists not unlike the exasperation expressed by the Suva Whippys over the Kasavu Whippys' irrational and self-defeating practices. The fixity of life in Kasavu is difficult to reconcile with the contributions of twentieth-century ethnographies of space to the deconstruction of the assumption "[t]hat space is static and to be contrasted with the dynamism of time; that spatial boundaries are always fixed, relatively enduring forms marked off on the ground" (Munn 1996: 465).[26] Likewise, kinship, in this case, would seem to make too literal the kinds of divisions or categorizations that anthropologists use only as models, tools for imposing limits on what is understood as a potentially infinite field of data. Anthropologists by now are accustomed to meeting such "cartographic" modeling practices with the realist critique that such categories are only artifacts of one particular perspective, only "a way of *looking at things*" (Hobart [citing Salmond 1982] 1995: 52; emphasis in the original).

This reminder as to the indeterminacy of the real world behind the models is a standard analytical move where, as in the mode of information, there is an endless amount to know. The inherent expansiveness of potential genealogical "ties" for the Suva Whippys was depicted, for example, in the visual image of the genealogical tree (Bouquet 1996) whose possible lines extended outward indefinitely into ever more numerous and distant connections.[27] The faith in the infinite complexity of the realities out of which anthropologists and their subjects make models in turn always anticipates the decomposition of such models into complexity. As such, kinship, the paradigmatic set of anthropological models, is routinely subjected to such a critique (e.g., Schneider 1984). The limits of models are as fixed and given in this view as the boundaries of land in Kasavu.

The aim of this account, then, has been, first, to offer a counterpoint to the notion that as far as actual phenomena in the world are concerned, the loss of a singularity of perspective that we identify with globalization and that is exemplified by the transnational network of Whippy kin represents a replacement of capital with information. As we saw, the emergence of this network coincided precisely with the introduction of a notion of scarcity and of capital to the division of land.

Conversely, the example of Kasavu as a case of a "mode of information" may challenge the assumption that the primacy of information in social life renders knowledge and social relations infinitely extendable. What is difficult for late modern academics to appreciate is that the very artifacts we imagine as being at the heart of "information flows" may not partake in the aesthetic of flow at all. Like the Whippys of Kasavu, for whom history and sociality were as given and bounded as information itself, the networks described in chapter 2 preferred to imagine themselves as a limited circle rather than an outreaching star. Likewise, as we saw in chapter 3, the apprehension of infinity that defined the experience of being a global actor at a global conference was only possible because of the way pattern was contained and repeated with the limitations of the brackets.

But what interests me most about the academic discovery of a "mode of information" is its consequences for academic work. For social scientists, capital was an analytical category; it was a framework that could be applied to conditions in the world, not a condition in and of itself. A mode of analysis grounded in a notion of capital, then, made analytical connections between phenomena that were not apparent prior to analysis. This is what we meant by critique. In contrast, information is understood to be a thing in the world. To point to information as an explanatory device is not to reveal a hidden explanation, therefore—it is not critique. In this respect, the transition to a "mode of information" is indeed disorienting: the academic response to information is not class analysis, not even network analysis, but networking (cf. Wagner 1995: 60).[28] Academic analysis has become an instantiation, a making evident, of academic networks.[29]

CHAPTER 5

Designing the Facts

Monday, 3 April 1995, The Asia-Pacific Caucus Meeting, UN Fourth World Conference on Women PrepCom, UN Headquarters. The Caucus, a meeting of representatives of NGOs from the Asia-Pacific region, is to decide on a set of "issues" and slogans for an upcoming press conference.

C: You're not supposed to demonstrate at the UN.
A: Of course you can! You can stand with placards, but not scandal mongering.
B: Yes, you can stand with placards silently.
. . .

B: Excuse me, can we answer the question, would we demonstrate? What are the issues?
. . .

A: But along with this will we also have placards?
C: We should get a number of people together with placards, how many of us are there—15–20 of us? It would look very miserable if there are just a small group. Can we have enough people and if so what is the thing we are going to put on? And everybody should be saying one thing.
"The common issues are accessibility."
"No going back."
"Yeah, no going back."
"No going back to what?"
B: Whatever room they give us it'll be a very small room, so whatever you are carrying or wearing it's supposed to be something which is small and you can see it. I don't think you can carry a placard because placards means carrying a banner and that's a lot of space, so that's my concern, that in a jam-packed space, how can you get a placard in?
. . .

114

E: I think what we can write on the placard is "make a commitment in Beijing."
A: That placard is going to take space and that place is very crowded, and I suppose . . .
B: We could hold it above our heads.
C: That is what has been done and it's been very visible and it should be done. The small things we stick on . . .
Chair: This kind of paper . . .
[*Everyone is now shouting at once.*]
A: This morning also they took up those big bits of paper.
B: And we can choose a bright color like yellow or green.
"Red, red . . . florescent yellow."
"Somebody takes charge?"
[*Laughter, giggles, numerous conversations*]
X: Not only some. Something else, more than some.
Chair: More common. Common demands.
F: One word: equality.
Chair: No! That doesn't say much.
A: "No going back"; "governments commit yourself." Commitment from the governments.
B: We need commitment in Beijing. What are the heads of our delegation going to come, just to show their faces at each other.
D: Power to endure.
"What? To What? No, No."
B: No, No, No. We want commitment in Beijing.
F: Do you want just one word? Forward!
"What?"

If it were held in Fiji rather than at the UN headquarters, a meeting of this kind would have taken on a different character and tone. Yet what would not have differed is the way the presentation of information stirred collective passions and drew participants into a seemingly interminable conversation. What would be "their" issues? What word or words would capture those issues? Should they use posters, placards, or sheets of paper? What kind of lettering should be used? To whom should the statement be distributed? What engaged attention, commitment, and anger for participants, in other words, was the form of information—its selection, framing, and display.

In chapter 2, we saw that for institutional actors in Suva the passion for "networks" and "networking" had much to do with what they perceived as the "formal" nature of networked interaction. I argue that networkers deploy the optical effect of Network form as a "fulcrum or lever" (Scarry [1985] 1987:

307) that generates alternative inverted forms of sociality by projecting an image of each—Network and "personal" relations—from the point of view of the other. Although form is a central concern in all aspects of network activity, the networkers I knew took a particularly avid interest in visual depictions of network form. "Look at the chart: it gives the links," I often was told in response to queries about the nature of particular organizations. At a glance, people took in such visual presentations. Like focal points, they instantly absorbed the structure of the Network, gathering it into themselves without further verbal or textual explanation.

Networkers in Suva or at UN conferences are not alone in their appreciation of the Network's possibilities for visual representation. The midcentury social anthropologist Clyde Mitchell, for example, noted the "immediate visual appeal" of the network diagram and its ability "to convey a statement about the social relationships eloquently and succinctly" such that there was a danger that "the diagram *may take on greater reality than it really merits*" (1974: 292; emphasis added). Indeed, midcentury network analyses produced some of the most heavily illustrated genres of anthropological literature, so that the authors sometimes even felt compelled to include explicit disavowals of matters of artistic creativity and taste.[1] As we will see, however, this explicit turn away from aesthetics as "art" toward the technical by no means constitutes a rejection of the possibilities of form.

To appreciate the aesthetic significance of these artifacts requires giving what to an academic mind may seem like fairly trivial objects the close attention they receive within networks. The discussion that follows concentrates on two of the most significant network artifacts—newsletters and network diagrams. However, the principles of form described here apply to many aspects of network activity, in the broadest sense in which I have used it, and whether of a visual nature or not. In aesthetic (as well as informational) terms, there is little difference between a document, a newsletter, a conference, and a network, and it is this self-similarity that networks "work" as they produce the effect of sociality described in chapter 2.

Networks concentrated critical attention on two broad genres of visual artifacts. The first were items intended for circulation outside the Network. The prototypical artifact of this genre was the newsletter, although networks also produced banners, films, demonstrations, and special forms of documents for public consumption. The second genre consisted of items intended for circulation within the Network (or among similarly situated institutions and networks) and included project proposals, funding applications, meeting minutes, forms and form letters, directories, project reports, and evaluations.[2] Although both genres of artifacts demanded inordinate amounts of time, energy, commitment, and expense to produce, each involved a distinct style of self-presentation and criticism.[3]

The Evocation of Heterogeneity

I begin by comparing an example of each genre produced by a skilled designer of network artifacts, Lili King, the Fiji focal point for the Asia-Pacific Women in Politics Network (APWIP) and the vice president of the Fiji National Council of Women (FNCW). The FNCW "links together" affiliate organizations ranging from village clubs to religious groups to organizations of women market vendors in the cities. Housed in a one-room office in the YWCA building in downtown Suva, the FNCW had two computers, a photocopy machine, and a fax machine as well as an extensive collection of newsletters and other publications at its disposal for producing its own newsletters. The FNCW had no professional staff, although Lili voluntarily staffed the office in addition to her duties as Fiji focal point for APWIP. The FNCW distributed NCW FIJI WIN to each of these affiliates—imagined by FNCW board members as "grassroots organizations"—as well as to anyone else who might have an interest in the FNCW or its activities. The pages reprinted in figure 16 are excerpted from the "post-Beijing issue" of the NCW FIJI WIN, which, as the banner at the top of the page indicates, stands for "National Council of Women, Women's Information Network." In a particularly explicit example of the way in which the network and its artifacts are a singular entity, *network* here refers only to the newsletter, there is no Women's Information Network other than the newsletter itself.

During the course of our work together preparing the newsletter, I learned to appreciate Lili's commitment to matters of form and presentation. This presentation would have a message more important than the "news," she often reminded me. "We want affiliates to know what was decided in Beijing and what we're going to do about it here," she said. Certain aspects of the newsletter were given. For example, in each issue of NCW FIJI WIN a collection of smiling women of different races ran at the top of the first page as a framing device that graphically signaled the uniformity of the newsletter series even as it emphasized the heterogeneous character of FNCW membership. Likewise, each issue included the logo of the UN Decade for Women (1975–85), which had provided the impetus for the founding of the FNCW and other NCW chapters (referred to as "national machineries") worldwide.

Lili's interest lay in the design of the global *Platform for Action*, in both structural and informational terms. She noted that the principal portion of the platform consisted of twelve sections, each devoted to an "issue"—health, the environment, or the girl child, for example. Her newsletter would replicate the structure of the *Platform for Action* by devoting one page to each issue. Within the page, the pattern would be replicated again by including a textual quotation from the *Platform for Action*, by showcasing one affiliate of the FNCW working on the issue in question, and by describing one project that implemented the

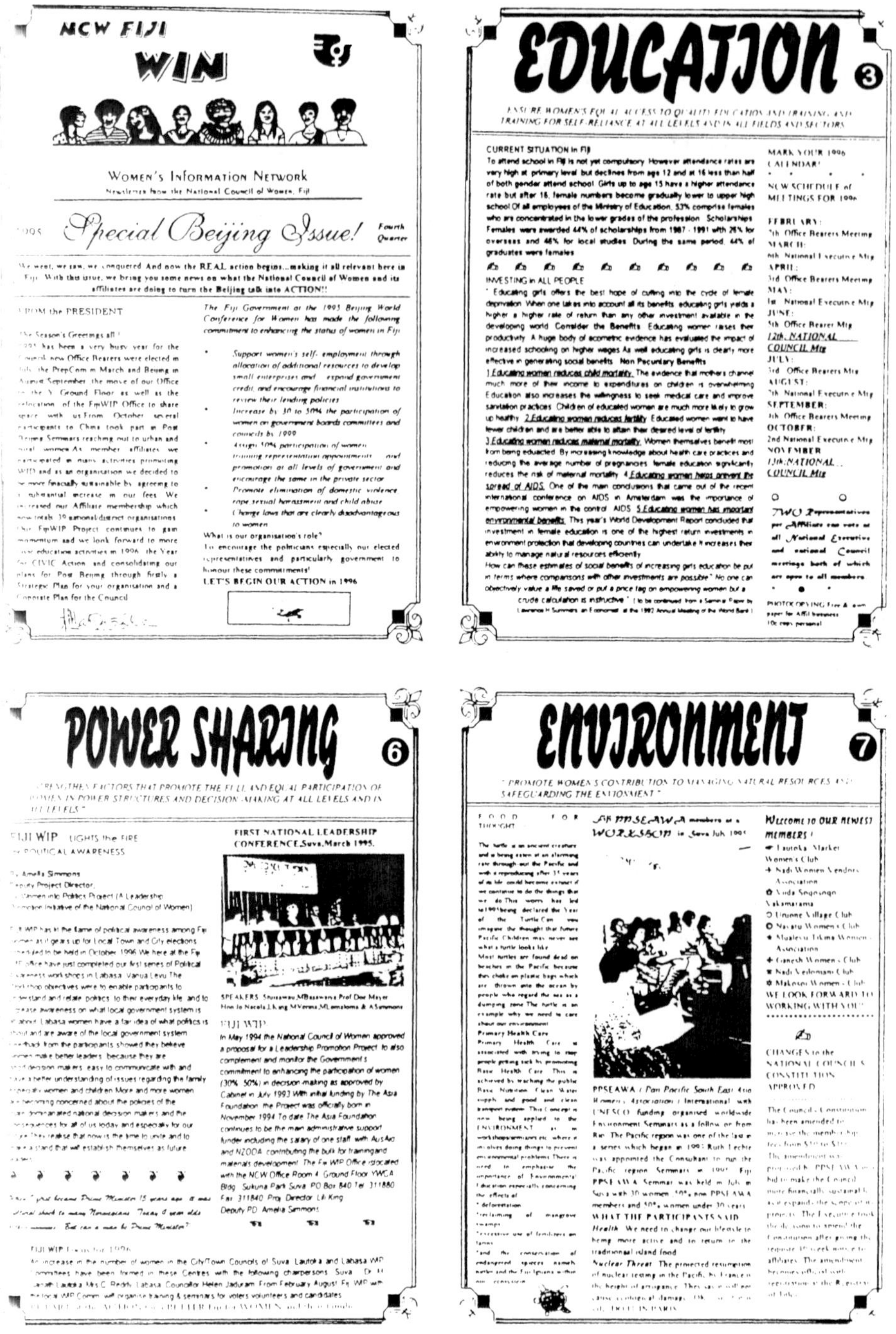

NCW FIJI

WIN

WOMEN'S INFORMATION NETWORK

Newsletter from the National Council of Women, Fiji

1995 Special Beijing Issue! Fourth Quarter

We went, we saw, we conquered. And now the REAL action begins...making it all relevant here in Fiji. With this issue, we bring you some news on what the National Council of Women and its affiliates are doing to turn the Beijing talk into ACTION!!

FROM the PRESIDENT

The Fiji Government at the 1995 Beijing World Conference for Women has made the following commitment to enhancing the status of women in Fiji:

LET'S BEGIN OUR ACTION in 1996

EDUCATION 3

ENSURE WOMEN'S EQUAL ACCESS TO QUALITY EDUCATION AND TRAINING, AND TRAINING FOR SELF-RELIANCE AT ALL LEVELS AND IN ALL FIELDS AND SECTORS

CURRENT SITUATION in Fiji

INVESTING in ALL PEOPLE

MARK YOUR 1996 CALENDAR!

NEW SCHEDULE of MEETINGS FOR 1996

POWER SHARING 6

FIJI WIP LIGHTS the FIRE of POLITICAL AWARENESS

FIRST NATIONAL LEADERSHIP CONFERENCE, Suva, March 1995.

ENVIRONMENT 7

"PROMOTE WOMEN'S CONTRIBUTION TO MANAGING NATURAL RESOURCES AND SAFEGUARDING THE ENVIRONMENT"

FOOD FOR THOUGHT

FIJI PPSEAWA members at a WORKSHOP in Suva July 1995

WELCOME TO OUR NEWEST MEMBERS!

WE LOOK FORWARD TO WORKING WITH YOU!

CHANGES to the NATIONAL COUNCIL'S CONSTITUTION APPROVED

Fig. 16. Pages from *Women's Information Network*, the newsletter of the National Council of Women, Fiji (fourth quarter, 1995): 1, 3, 6–7. (Reproduced courtesy of the National Council of Women, Fiji.)

spirit or letter of the text. The design of the newsletter, then, elucidated a graphic connection between the Beijing Conference and activities in Suva by demonstrating that an internal pattern within the document could be extended and replicated within the FNCW network in Fiji. Issues of graphics and layout in this context were inseparable from issues of informational content.

One of the reasons for this newsletter's success, people who commented on it said, was the variety of both "information" and "graphics." The newsletter brought together many different stories, produced in different typefaces and demarcated with borders made with different symbols. The verbal text drew the reader in with words in capitals, exclamation points, and bold or italic fonts. However, Lili carefully balanced the "exciting" effect of this heterogeneity of messages with repetition at the level of composition. What looked like heterogeneity at one glance could be viewed as replication at the next. For example, in an effort to satisfy Lili's desire for variety, I had used different type faces for each of the page headings. However, Lili chose to render these uniform in a move that emulated the uniformity of the print styles of the *Platform for Action*. Yet having done so, she then added an elaborate border to each page, something clearly out of the scope of the technical UN document style, thus bringing the "catchiness" of visual heterogeneity in at another level of framing, and subverting the clear connection to the UN document that she had worked to create.

These issues of composition sometimes even became subjects of conferences of their own. At an SPC regional meeting devoted to networking and communication (Fourth Regional Conference of Pacific Women held in Suva on 17–23 September 1988), for example, representations of Pacific NGOs openly debated the ideal characteristics of the newsletter genre. One portion of the program, led by the regional administrator of the Canadian International Development Agency (CIDA), focused on developing participants' skills in creating newsletters, posters, and radio programs. Distributed materials in the poster-making session listed what constituted a good poster:

> It is attractive.
> Uses bright and strong colors.
> Emphasizes only one main idea.
> Uses a short but clear message.
> Uses big bright letters so that it can be clearly seen from a distance.
> Uses a variety of sizes of letters with the main message the biggest.
> Has some interesting drawings to attract attention.
> (Goodwillie 1988)

The discussion leader emphasized that one should "use strong pictures" and a variety of lettering techniques and that one should stress the positive rather than the negative aspects of an issue. One should place important information at the center of attention and use colors, arrows, or circles. The leader also emphasized the "appropriateness" of drawings. "Don't use blue-eyed blond children or houses with modern 'automatic kitchens' or fruits and vegetables from overseas," participants were told. Likewise, one should "use appropriate scale and perspective," "for example, use orange for pawpaw, not brown or green." The course on radio programs at the same conference likewise emphasized the use of simple language (participants practiced taking written sentences and simplifying them), repetition, brevity, and defining a simple "point" that one wished to communicate.

This aesthetic of controlled heterogeneity surfaced in multiple genres of networking activity. The nongovernmental portion of the Beijing Conference consisted of hundreds of panel discussions explicitly celebrated as a diversity of viewpoints so extreme that it bordered on chaos. Crucial to this composition was the understanding that organizers had not orchestrated or constrained the content of the panels and workshops in any way but rather had allowed a diversity of feminist (and nonfeminist) viewpoints to be expressed on any subject by anyone. As the convenor of the NGO Forum put it,

> Women from women's organisations, networks, coalitions and community based organisations are welcome.... In this strategy the space is there for all women's organisations.... Everybody has a voice and will be heard.... The organisers will do everything to hear the women who are rarely heard.... They should feel safe and respected with us. (IWDA 1995: 1)

This celebration was achieved, however, by framing the heterogeneity of "issues" or "groups" within an extremely rigid organizational form. Every viewpoint, no matter how unusual, could be indexed within the program guide under one of a set of predetermined topics, then listed in the program in a box of the same size, under the name of a particular organization or group, and with a title or subject matter classification for easy comparison. At the conference site, this great diversity was presented within a physical space of identical booths, logically numbered and arranged on a map distributed to participants. For participants, who each morning flipped through the dozens of pages of workshop listings in their program guide on the bus from their hotels to the forum site or who searched the endless tents and classrooms for the workshop of their choice, the effect truly was one of bewildering heterogeneity. Yet the production of this foregrounded effect demanded an extreme rigidity of the composition or frame.

Lili did not verbalize these questions of balance, however, beyond describing the general theme of the composition and voicing her desire to make people notice the FNCW and its post-Beijing activities. Rather, people collectively acknowledged a common pleasure in good work when, for example, a negotiator happened upon the right word, or a newsletter produced the correct appeal. A good, correct example of the genre was self-evident; it did not require elucidation or explanation but simply solicited collective recognition. In this respect, the collective pleasure in Network aesthetics differed from both the explicitly articulated descriptions of the formal network structure and the personal conversation outside of networks described in chapter 2.

The Elucidation of System

Now consider "Communication Line," the network diagram reproduced in figure 17. Created by Lili for a FIJI WIP funding proposal, this diagram describes the place and functions of the project's components in the institutional and political geography of Fiji. The diagram's intended audience consisted of FNCW board members, FIJI WIP board members, international aid agency project evaluators, focal points in the APWIP network, and members of the government and political parties. Lili viewed "Communication Line" as an example of a set professional genre, a way of communicating that illustrated that the project was expert and serious.

The diagram presents a universe of relevant entities in Fijian politics; unlike the newsletter, it is the limitation rather than the proliferation of information, the selection of facts, that generates the diagram's systemic form. In the diagram, only certain acts of communication are relevant: "Government" communicates with the "FIJI WIP secretariat" in the diagram but does not communicate with either the "FIJI WIP board" or the "political parties." In the absence of scale or perspective, the diagram gives no information about the distinction between the political parties or the FIJI WIP board. All that is explained is the analytical relationship between entities: Both communicate with the FIJI WIP secretariat but do not communicate with one another or with the government. In this treatment, all of these points are entities of the same genre. We might imagine the equivalencies the diagram engenders as a graphic version of the equivalencies of number, described in chapter 4.[4]

We might call this an aesthetics of system: "Communication Line" encourages the viewer to think of Fijian politics as a set of integrated components, and to consider what difference the addition of a new component might make to the workings of the system as a whole. The system's formality, that is, the reduction of Fijian politics to the contours of a network form, leaves open the question of the diagram's claims about its relationship to the reality it represents. Does the diagram claim to present an accurate representation of the state of Fijian politics? we might ask, for example. Does it suggest a vision of what

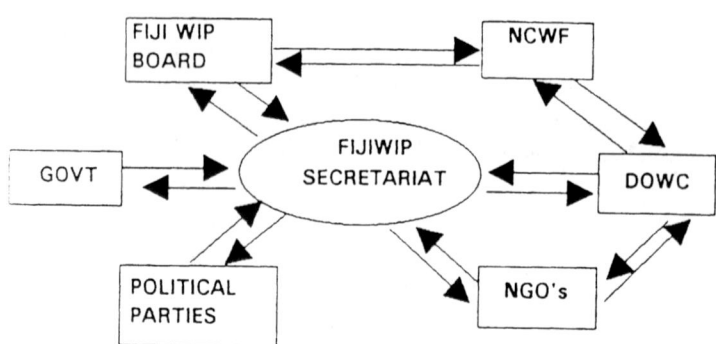

Fig. 17. "Communication Line," a schematic depiction of the Fiji WIP network. (From Fiji WIP project proposal, August 1994, 10. Reproduced courtesy of Fiji Women in Politics.)

Fijian politics might look like once the FIJI WIP program gets fully under way? Does it make a normative statement about what politics should be like in Fiji? These possibilities collapse into one another implicitly as the diagram hedges the question of its own truth value.

This stark, dramatic, no-nonsense drawing signals a very different presentation from the newsletter's visual aids and eye-catching symbols. The labeling of forms in a uniform standardized script recalls the genre of technical drawings and lends an impression of maplike completeness that the newsletter does not claim. The pure symmetry of the image elegantly manages the chaos of multidirectional communication that it represents. Where the newsletter foregrounds the heterogeneity, complexity, and abundance of information gathered within the Network, the diagram emphasizes the simplicity and internal coherence of network form. Where the newsletter is primarily representational, the diagram is highly abstract. The newsletter self-consciously reaches out to the imagined viewer and projects a tone of excitement as it invites observation at a fast tempo. The diagram, in contrast, is a cool image that invites dispassionate observation like the calm tone of the negotiations described in chapter 3.

The effect of the diagram is no less dramatic than that of the newsletter, however. The central position of the FIJI WIP box, framed by other organizations, its enlarged circular shape a contrast to the smaller square boxes that represent other institutional forms, conveys a sense of novelty and difference about the project. This was Lili's intention. "We want them to stand up and take notice!" she said. The strong arrows emphasize movement, what the newsletter refers to in words as "action" (cf. Kress and van Leeuwen 1996: 44, 52). If the form is simple and clean, the movement of information it describes is as chaotic and heterogeneous as the newsletter composition.

Despite overt differences, then, both genres share a strong emphasis on the patterned quality of communication and analysis. If the newsletter replicates the internal divisions of the global *Platform for Action* in its own internal divisions, demonstrating that a pattern in one document can be replicated in another, the network diagrams take their form from the patterned arrangement of a series of identically shaped and sized boxes and vectors. The PAWORNET diagrams reproduced in figure 5 made this repetition of pattern particularly explicit by demonstrating graphically that the same shape literally replicates itself at the regional and national levels.

These artifacts demonstrate pattern in the informational assemblages or collections they produce. The emphasis is on the way things that are attenuated come to be next to each other in the Network's acts of analytical reorganization. For example, consider the ubiquitous network acronyms that gave focal points such pleasure. The significance of acronyms is illustrated in the way that even words with representational "meanings" could be made into acronyms. For example, a "network" of "indigenous healers" organized by the ECOWOMAN project was known as Wainimate, the Fijian word for "medicine." A focal point of the network insisted that the name was not a word but an acronym: "The word *Wainimate* is derived from the Women's Natural Medicinal Therapy Association, W-N-M-T, so we just fit in the vowels, so it formed WAINIMATE," she explained. These acronyms are collections of words and concepts brought together in the same way that the Network brought together the elements enumerated in the acronym term. They enact the aesthetic of collection in the form of the acronym itself.

This aesthetic is not limited to visual artifacts. For example, the Women's Information Network for Asia and the Pacific (WINAP) conference on the "technical processing of information" asked network focal points to send a collection of individuals to the conference as participants and requested these to prepare a collection of papers for presentation. The parallel requirements for participants and documents[5] formed an internally patterned collection of persons and information provided.

One principal device for creating patterned collections is the convention of textual and visual borrowing from one network or artifact to the next. Every network document typically includes at least one page, section, or graphic borrowed from another document. A meeting agenda, likewise, typically might include a graphic image from one newsletter, a page from a second government document, and a memorandum produced by a focal point assembled together under a single cover sheet. This circulation of artifacts foregrounded the networked division of labor at issue in their production (cf. Palmer 1996).

This collation of text also figured prominently in the international negotiations described in chapter 3. One of the great innovations and achievements of the PrepCom, from delegates' point of view, was the creation of a new chapter on the subject of "the girl child." Negotiators produced the text of this chapter by combing the entire existing document for paragraphs on subjects related to young women, infants, and girls and stringing those paragraphs together to form a text of its own.

This borrowing and collation of information and design was the subject of careful aesthetic judgment. In creating the WACC-Pacific *Pacific Handbook*, (WACC 1995), its editor borrowed text and graphics from a wide variety of institutions and publications. She emphasized that her contribution lay in the judgments she made about what to collect. "There's so much information out there and the same information in every publication. I don't want to repeat. I want to pick and choose from a particular perspective," she said of her "graphics." A newsletter that borrowed too many or too few images from other newsletters was considered a failure.

A good example of the aesthetic of collection and its implications for multiple acts of image borrowing is "Network!" the graphic image reproduced in figure 18. This image is clearly of the newsletter rather than the internal technical genre. Instead of a collection of focal points connected by lines to signify the Network, we have a representational drawing of a collection of women of different cultures marching in a line, one fist raised in the air, as if with a common cause despite their superficial differences. As the image implies, "Network!" can be a collection of different persons, assembled and lined up as if in a singular vector, as much as it is a device for crossing distances.

In their dress and stance, the figures seem to encourage certain stereotypical assumptions about their identities—perhaps the first is a Caribbean activist, the second a Latin American, the third a European or North American, and so on. Their collective attitude also appears to draw upon certain further stereotypes concerning the spirit and tenor of women's activism. Yet all that we know about the substance of their collective cause is that the women depicted here stand for the indeterminate idea of networking in a double sense. In the image, therefore, networking is elevated to a political cause; it is no longer simply a means to another activist end. This is achieved, however, through a collection of cartoonlike stereotypes of difference that come together in the network image and in so doing draw the viewer into a series of assumptions about the pattern as a whole.

This image was a particular favorite in Suva. Lili reproduced it at the bottom of the FIJI WIP letterhead, removing the word *Network* in the process of photocopying and adding a Fijian woman to the line, thus adding a figure to the collection as she added a level of borrowing. This illustrated letterhead elicited general critical praise among Lili's cohorts in Suva and further confirmed her

Fig. 18. "Network!" (From *Tribune*, no. 53 [July 1995]: 29. Reproduced courtesy of the International Women's Tribune Centre.)

reputation as an achiever among government and NGO institutional actors. The letterhead conveyed the feeling Lili wanted to convey, one officer of the DWC told me. It said "Action!"

Technical Work

Focal points regarded the production of both genres of network artifacts as a matter of "technical skill." They emphasized the professional, practical aspect of their work, and they took pleasure in its functional form. Some were more skilled than others at the word games and layouts; some knew how to operate a computer to produce graphics and others did not. Design was technical work, then, in its emphasis on the skill of its producers[6] rather than on a conception of "beauty" (Gell 1992). The notion of communication as "technical" information processing, for example, had tremendous appeal. Even Fiji delegates to the Beijing Conference who took little interest in the purposes or processes of the conference picked up the specialized UN vocabulary with ease and reproduced it with pleasure.

Newsletters were almost always in English despite the fact that it was the mother tongue of very few network participants. The language of the colonial and postcolonial bureaucracy, English is the lingua franca of contemporary multiculturalism in Fiji, and it also has strong connotations of specialization, professionalization, and elite education. The English of network communications, whether oral or written, was replete with acronyms, nominalizations, and document titles strung together as if to form a network of their own. Focal points referred to this language as a "technical vocabulary," and they enjoyed using it. Many Fijians did not like talking about their projects in Fijian; they found it difficult, as they did not have the "technical vocabulary," they said. When they translated their statements for a Fijian audience, they usually did so in an abruptly summarized form. Networking did not work in Fijian because, in the way that language foregrounded its own patterns as much as its meanings, English was like a network diagram, a design of its own.[7]

This conception of design as technical work highlighted a specialized relationship of human labor to technology in the Network. The producer of network images was the Network, a collection of persons, institutions, models, and machines, not any particular author or designer. The shapes and stark contrasts of "Communication Line" render the image particularly easy to reproduce, for it is designed to be cut out, photocopied, and repasted in further documents. In its form and uses, then, the diagram foregrounds its own production by one machine or project officer with future ones in mind, while the newsletter signals the same mechanical reproduction in more subtle, backgrounded terms. In this sense, the newsletter and the diagram are inside out views of one another. Although the diagram is internally coherent and cannot be decomposed into separate components, it is designed to be abstracted and included effortlessly in further documents. The newsletter is also an artifact of mechanical reproduction, yet the reproduction takes place at a different level in the production process. Although the newsletter is a composition of individual pieces that will be used many times (the banner heading, the logos, the photographs), it is transacted as a totality that is not cut up and reproduced.

Yet it is important to understand that in the case of both kinds of artifacts, the "technical" work of reproduction and shared authorship is enabled by the artifact's adherence to formal standards of production. It is the formal standards of data entry that enable the productive use of directory data bases, for example, or the standard size of the paper that enables its easy reproduction.[8] Form, in other words, is what machines and humans both understand. In its high degree of formality, the "technical" is a cross-actant aesthetic, therefore (Callon 1986; Latour and Woolgar [1979] 1986; Law 1994).

Yet if network aesthetics provided a vehicle through which human and nonhuman focal points can process and transmit one another's information, this formality excluded another entity referred to as "Women." In conversations among networkers, one often heard references to "the Women," "the needs of Women," and especially a demand by "the Women" for a particular program. Women, as a concept, served as an outside "grounding" (Strathern 1992a) for network analysis, a subject that, although never investigated or analyzed, provided the basis for the analyses of network structures and programs. In the lived form of network analysis, this grounding was dramatized in post-Beijing presentations given for the most part in an English language replete with acronyms and other jargon, opaque to any outsider, to groups of assembled "women" in a format in which panelists sat "above" and the audience sat "below"[9] and rarely asked questions. At several such presentations I attended, many of the women who made up the intended audience spent the duration of the presentation in the kitchen preparing the meal that was to follow for their guests. The audience provided a raison d'être for the presentation, however. The same passive image of "women" ("that woman in Naitasiri")—the image of the faceless, helpless, uneducated victim of discrimination and receiver of assistance programs—often surfaced in descriptions given by those working in women in development institutions. These imagined actants were defined precisely as those who lacked the technical skills of formal information processing. Female focal points were not "women" in this sense, just as personal gossip was not the Network. One communicated with "women," instead, using the nontechnical pictures of newsletters, and one simplified and translated before doing so. In the aesthetic of the Network, then, the human/nonhuman distinction that has been the subject of much Science Studies Scholarship was replaced with a new divide (cf. Star 1991). That the analytical grounding here happens to be an entity familiar to feminist theory draws attention to the way analysis can become its own form of harm.

The relationship of Network aesthetics to technology is illustrated in "What you need," an IWTC graphic reproduced in a Beijing flier of the Association for Progressive Communication (APC 1994), an NGO devoted to establishing computer linkages among NGOs worldwide (fig. 19).[10] The image brings together the two genres of Network artifacts considered above. On the left side is a cartoonlike illustration of the newsletter genre but drawn in a slightly less engaging style (the woman at the computer looks away from the viewer, the computer does not display any particular message, and the woman fades into a map of the globe more evocative of the abstraction of graphs than cartoons). On the right side of the image is a network of the "technical" diagram kind but drawn in a slightly more cartoonlike style (the details of network structure and identity of focal points are left out in favor of the image of a Network rather than of any particular network). The two kinds of images are connected, first, by technology (what we need)—a modem, a telephone, a phone jack—all carefully labeled, in the style of technical drawings. The representational and abstract facets of the image also are connected by a line, however—a telephone line—but also something more abstract, like the linkages that connect the local network to the international regional networks.

The two images come together in two female symbols positioned at the top of the image so that the narrative shape of the line linking the abstract and representational versions of this network rises to a climax at that point. In the

Fig. 19. "What you need....," leaflet distributed at the NGO Forum, Beijing '95. (From International Women's Tribune Centre computer newsnote, 1995. Reproduced courtesy of the Association for Progressive Communications.)

symbols, the image appears to convert from a network as a collection of things to a network as pattern. The technology—the telephone lines, modem, and computer—are not the only technical items we "need" to network, therefore. It seems we also "need" feminist symbols.

The odd aspect of these particular symbols, however, is that they are labeled as "telephone lines," thus betraying expectations about the symbol's prima facie meaning. In this small detail, the image presents a recursive play on the concreteness of representation and the abstraction of symbol, number, or pattern. For while this particular symbol, unlike many others, has a plain, even literal meaning—Women—in this case, the image makes use of the shape of the form to signify something completely different—the telephone equipment that connects a material rather than a symbolic network. It would be impossible to speak of symbolism and technology as disparate entities here. More importantly, the image's own self-reflexive approach to its literalization of imagery serves as a focal point, a dramatic puzzle that draws the viewer in.

This image recalls the statement of the POPIN focal point in the previous chapter that "the technology is the catchy part, not the information." The network linkage is a mechanical image, a formalized substitute for personal relationships made unidimensional so as to extend beyond their natural scope. In the imagination of the Network as a mechanical entity, an addition in distance comes with a sacrifice in depth or complexity, so that linkages are singular, numerical relationships of equivalence and direction. The image of the FNCW network as "national machinery" imputes to that network the powerful image of the collectivity as machine.

There is evidence that the aesthetics described here are increasingly common in a variety of transnational institutional contexts. In a recent study of Aboriginal film producers and the criteria relevant to the evaluation of their work, Faye Ginsburg opposes evaluations based on "questions of narrative or visual form" to evaluations of the work "as a form of social action" (1994: 368). The argument becomes relevant to the present material when, in the final portion of the piece, Ginsburg describes the participation of indigenous filmmakers in what she calls "global cultural flows" (376). In response to the absence of explicit discussion of questions of artistic form at the international meetings of such filmmakers, Ginsburg concludes that the "aesthetic innovation" is not "in the text itself" but in the new kinds of "relations of production and reception" that shape the work (377).

Ginsburg's principal example of the artists' lack of interest in form concerns an international meeting of indigenous filmmakers interested in founding a "transnational indigenous network." She cites as evidence of the absence of attention to aesthetic matters the following "statement of aims" produced at the close of the meeting. As a document produced out of the deliberations of an international conference, it is an artifact of a now familiar genre:

a. to raise awareness of First Nations issues
b. to establish a film and video communication network
c. to ensure that traditional lands, language, and culture are protected
d. to implement work and training exchanges
e. to establish a world conference
f. to ensure environmental protection and management
g. to promote our teachings of history and culture
h. to distribute and market our own films (1994: 377).

In light of the materials presented in this chapter, we might interpret this list as an artifact of great aesthetic significance, albeit of an internal networked genre. We might notice, for example, how well the list conforms to the rigid requirements of conference documents and how, like similar documents considered above, it sets into motion an internal network between each of the points "linked" by the pure and symbolically empty lettering system that connects each point to the next. Like the networks that engendered it, the network of the list here literally enacts itself—its endpoints are a network of another scale—by pointing to actions to be taken, which in turn enable further networks, documents, and conferences, as the list makes plain.

Aesthetic Activism

To return to the visual elements of the Network diagram, however, we note that, as in the case of the symbols in "What you need," the diagrams make clever use of visual focal points to draw the viewer in. The focal point might be a person, a piece of technology, a symbol, or all of these. What defines the focal point, however, is, as one networker put it, "the catchy part"—the aesthetic attraction, the desire to captivate that it evidences. Yet each image does more than focus attention. The bold arrows of "Communication Line," for example, direct the gaze, guiding the viewer's thought process in the same way that it traces the Network's own processes of analysis.[11]

Experienced delegates to international conferences viewed this question of how to capture and channel attention as the essence of the game, and, indeed, capturing attention was no simple task. Lili told me that she always traveled to conferences with a map of the Pacific in hand. She was accustomed to meeting people who had never heard of her country, and she found that if she could point to Fiji in visual terms others became more receptive to learning about her projects. Once she had succeeded in capturing audience attention, she said, she found that describing her project as a "grassroots organizing experience," together with having a vibrant and funny presentation, kept the audience's attention. The success of this technique bore fruit for her in Beijing, she said: "I had quite a lot of women coming to ask me questions about where is Fiji and what could they do to help because they were interested in the angle that I took." We might think of network aesthetics as aesthetic activation, then—as a matter of how graphics, layout, and form of all kinds capture the imagination and guide analysis.

The interrelationship of aesthetics and informational content, and in particular the power of design to transmit information across national and cultural differences to effectuate action, is a classic modernist theme. Most often associated with the Russian constructivists of the 1920s and their socialist counterparts in Europe, the ambition of aesthetically inspired international activism proceeded from a hope that design might speed the efficient functioning of communication. In the call for form to follow function, an object's "beauty" depended upon its appropriateness to its (communicative) purpose (Palmer 1996: 110). Ideal communication had a "scientific" character, confirmed in genres of lettering or layout that subtly conformed to an imagined scientific ideal (Kinross 1989: 139).[12] The objective was to render the object's meaning as transparent as possible, thus enabling the truth value of the design and its message to reach the individual at a level of subjective experience that cut across differences of culture, nationality, or ideology.

Consider, for example, the isotype figures, the generic figures now used as signs in public parks, corporations, and institutions around the world, which in their formalized design style are evocative of the images that circulate in the networks described in this chapter. The invention of positivist philosopher and social scientist Otto Neurath in the 1920s, these now ubiquitous drawings sought to create a "universally readable language of vision" (Lupton 1989: 145) that would "eclipse interpretation with perception" (148) and thus serve as a pure factual basis for international communication by means of an appeal to the universal neural aspects of visual perception. Where parallel attempts at linguistic commonality such as Esperanto have failed, the isotype figures have been widely successful. Yet the ambition of transparent cross-cultural informational transfers behind the project has been so devastated in the wake of cultural relativist critiques on the one hand and deconstructionist ones on the other that it almost takes on a certain nostalgic quaintness today.

The project seems oddly resuscitated in the Network's aesthetic actions. In Suva, it often seemed that design had displaced the "project" as the most pervasive medium of First World influence. For example, Beneath Paradise, the most heavily funded of all Beijing-related nongovernmental projects in the Pacific, effectuated precisely this shift from project to network and design. A project of the International Women's Development Agency (IWDA), an Australian NGO, Beneath Paradise assembled a collection of representatives of "grassroots organizations" into a new "network"; brought in Australian design consultants who trained them in writing poetry, producing posters, "telling their stories," and other forms of "documentation"; and displayed the "documents" that resulted as "grassroots women's voices" in a booth at the NGO Forum.[13]

Like the earlier modernist tradition of aesthetic activism, then, the patterns of networks and network designs are explicitly cross-cultural forms of communication, albeit in this case forms that postdate cultural relativist critiques. Consider, for example, the International Women's Tribune Centre, whose graphics appeared in the office of every focal point I encountered. An NGO founded in the wake of the first UN women's conference in 1975, IWTC describes itself in publicity materials as

> a clearinghouse of information on women and development. . . . As a producer of education and information resources, IWTC seeks to translate research findings and policy mandates into information materials that bridge the gap between policy and action. (IWTC 1995a)

The center's most influential project is its newsletter, the *Tribune*, aimed specifically at "women" in developing countries. The newsletter consists of a series of cheerful, uplifting images of feminism and feminist activism that aim to counteract negative stereotypes of the women's movement and to inspire women in the developing world to activism of their own. It contains little text and few specifics; the principal contribution is the images.

The assumption of the newsletter, and indeed of all the visual forms described above, is that visual images touch people, regardless of the superficial differences among them, in a way that statements do not. Empathy toward pattern in this view is a matter of personal and therefore universalizable experience; it is not culture bound. For example, Lili learned some of her design techniques on an Asia Foundation (TAF) "study tour" of American political campaigns. TAF's ambition here was to change institutions in Fiji by engendering particular kinds of personal experiences that changed individuals first. The experience made her want to "do something" in Fiji, she repeatedly said. With great excitement, she described the lessons she had learned from visiting the offices of other "leaders" overseas. She told me, "Their offices were covered with signs, and posters, and pictures, and they had plans and lists on this wall and on that wall, and it made me think about how dull our campaigns are here."

In a sense that recalls the personal underbelly of the Network explored in chapter 2, however, this interest was a personal one. Lili did not expect other networkers in Fiji who had not had the privilege of this experience to share the insight. One also might take note of less intentional mechanisms of aesthetic influence. The typefaces, figures, and drawings that appeared in Lili's newsletter were preprogrammed by her Microsoft wordprocessing software, thus offering her the same aesthetic choices as millions of other Microsoft users around the world.

Designing the Facts 133

If one takes as a standard the simple appeal of these images, the activism of aesthetics has proven vastly effective. A biographical note will illustrate the nature of the success. As it happens, the IWTC's executive director began her career as cofounder of the Fiji YWCA in the 1960s, and it was in her early years in Suva that she first experimented with the power of graphics. "We had never seen anything like those pictures before. It was completely new here," one person recalled. "It was so exciting." Through her pictures, the director succeeded in creating an image of activism as cheerful, friendly, fun, and feminine that persists in such graphics today.

Of course, today the activist educational agenda of the YWCA would seem like an untenable exportation of First World liberal views. Indeed, on the occasion of the second UN women's conference in Copenhagen in 1980, after the director had left Fiji to found the IWTC, two Fiji delegates brought into the global feminist movement largely through their early association with the YWCA pointedly confronted her about the interference of "white women" in others' affairs. An era clearly was over. The suspicion that turned on the institutional project never fell upon the designs, however. On the contrary, these blossomed into one of the most visible beacons of the global feminist movement in the developing world. At the Beijing Conference, as Pacific delegates prepared to demonstrate against French nuclear testing in the Pacific, the division of labor in the preparation of banners and posters evoked the early days of the YWCA. As one Fijian participant stated, the former director "drew, and we colored her drawings in."

Yet it is not just that network designs transcend culture, as was the ambition of modernist design. They also make use of "culture" as components in their compositions. We saw how the image "Network!" brought together a collection of persons of different cultures to illustrate the network effect. One could understand the NGO Forum in Beijing, in its celebration of cultural diversity, with each region and nationality on exposition under its own tent, as a cultural collection of the same genre. At the forum, "Women" became a network of its own, an abstract design that could accommodate endless representations of difference under a single pattern and render these differences pleasurable. At the Beneath Paradise booth, the appeal of the Pacific women's "voices" on display was palpable. "It's beautiful!" visitors said, smiling at the Pacific women working at the booth as if they had grasped something fundamental in the two or three minutes that they had perused the display, "wonderful!" The Pacific women, partly aiming to please and partly aiming to relieve their boredom, responded to this praise with further performances in the same genre. "You can look at our pictures, but don't take them away because that's like taking our soul," one told a sympathetic viewer. "For many of us, telling these stories is like giving part of ourselves away to you."

Barbara Kirshenblatt-Gimblett has written of the Los Angeles Festival, an avant-garde festival of arts and performance of the Pacific Rim, which like the NGO Forum is a gathering of heterogeneous aesthetic experiences into one framing "event," that a random collection of cultural performances, purposely devoid of ethnographic explanation, generates a "multiplicity of foci" such that each viewer must make his or her own experience (1995: 250), thus "locat[ing] authenticity in a moment of aesthetic reception" and privileging aesthetic experience over artifact (251). Yet was the viewer's perusal of the Beneath Paradise booth "experience"? Did the Pacific women's accommodation of their viewers privilege the authenticity of those viewers and their aesthetic reception? And did the form in that case convey information, or meaning in the modernist sense, avant-garde or otherwise?

Recall that the starting puzzle of network sociality presented in chapter 2 was that focal points showed very little interest in the extension of their knowledge or relationships. Whatever pleasure they took from "Network!" and related images, therefore, did not require imagining the Network or its extensions as a model for their own sociality. Networks were not machines for enabling prosthetic extensions but images, simulations of machines; everyone knew that the FNCW was not actually a "national machinery," for example. The Network was not personal relationships extended and amplified through information transfer, but personal relationships made technical.

As keen appreciators of network aesthetics, focal points showed a greater interest in pattern than in meaning; "action" for them inhered in the design pattern rather than in something outside or beyond the artifact. When I visited one focal point's office, she often pulled out a roll of butcher paper and taped large sheets across each of the walls. We worked at identifying issues and then turning them into slogans. For example, once she had determined that it was necessary to identify participants for a particular project, she would design a campaign entitled "Have You Got What It Takes?" These plans and campaigns hardly ever took place; a week or so would pass until it was time to plan again, and without any further discussion of the previous plan we would reconvene to map out further objectives.

We might understand the appreciation of these artifacts literally on their own terms as a literalization (cf. Strathern: 1992a) of the modernist-activist aesthetics described above. The poststructuralist critique of modernist design, centered in an effort to demonstrate the impossibility of "pure" information untainted by rhetorical, cultural, or political content (e.g., Kinross 1989) misses the point here. For the character of the information—whether pure and untainted or ideologically or culturally biased—ultimately mattered little to focal points in Suva.

A good example of this literalization of activist aesthetics concerns the interpretation of "Anatomy of the *Platform for Action*," the IWTC diagram reproduced in figure 20. This diagram depicts the chapters and sections of the Bei-

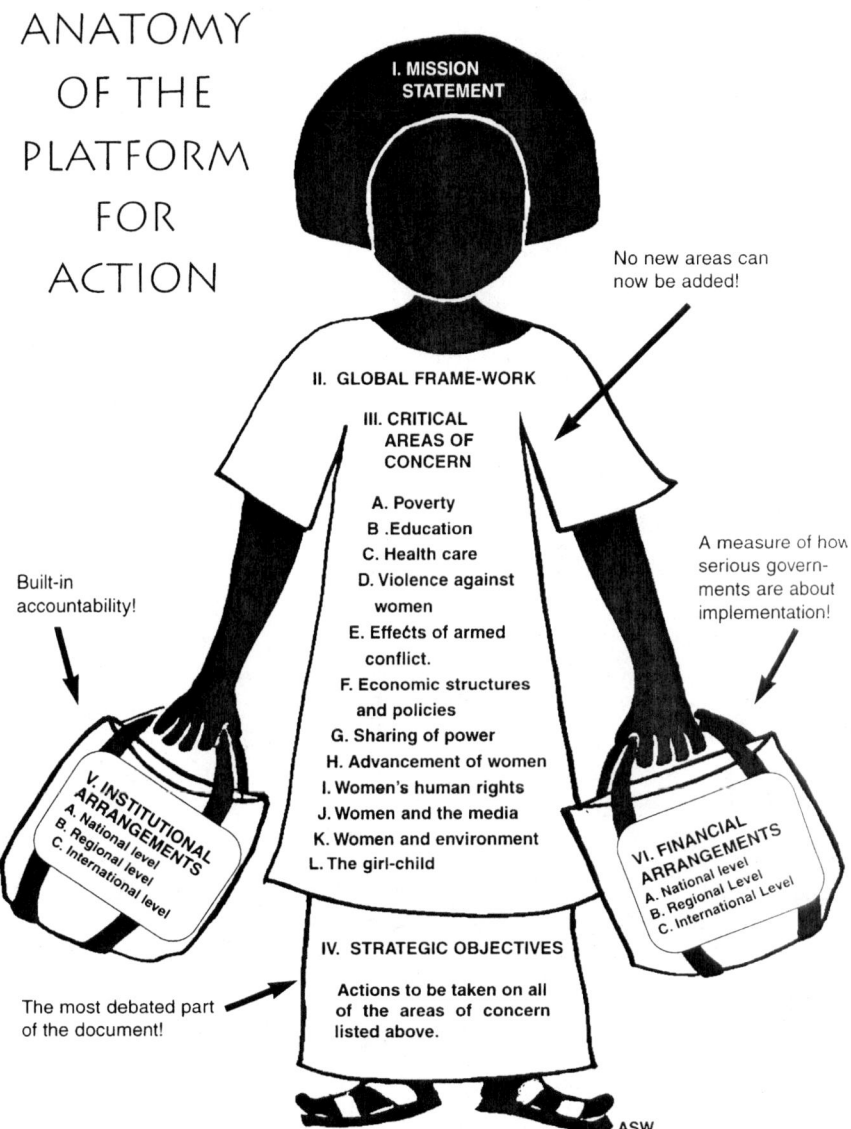

Fig. 20. "Anatomy of the *Platform for Action.*" (From *Tribune,* no. 54 [August 1995]: 12. Reproduced courtesy of the International Women's Tribune Centre.)

jing document. The "meaning" of this diagram, as noted in the text accompanying the image, is that the document has a series of sections with different contents of relative importance. The medium through which this is communicated is a metaphorical relationship between the designer's dissection of the document and a classical anatomical drawing.

This diagram again was a great favorite in Suva. One reason lay in the fact that in her appearance the cartoon silhouette of the woman depicted here resembles a Fijian woman, as its artist, the IWTC director and former director of the Fiji YWCA would have known well. Yet the connection Fiji's participants in the Beijing Conference drew between the document and the figure turned the intended thought sequence of the piece inside out. "Poverty is the face of a woman," one speaker repeatedly told audiences as she held up the diagram, which made no explicit reference to the subject of poverty. The analogy of sections of the document to sections of the body had failed to inspire. Yet in a more literal sense the diagram had done its work, for the display of the image elicited a statement, a slogan from Beijing, which in its form was a verbal counterpart of the sloganlike image. Like Lili's newsletter, which sought to continue the pattern of the *Platform for Action* into a document in Fiji, one form elicited another of the same genre.[14]

To literalize is precisely to show empathy toward network pattern, for, as we saw, the network as an organizational form literally is analysis and organization in one. The emphasis on pattern, in other words, entails a fine appreciation of the self-similarity of network genres as the very nature of the network multiplied. Where literalization is the network's own artifact, however, to read network actions literally would be to make a profound mistake of interpretation.

The Aesthetics of Fact

In chapter 1, I alluded to Gregory Bateson's definition of *aesthetics* as empathy toward pattern. In his analyses of "primitive art," Bateson described two such patterns. "Digital" patterns, such as numbers and language, foregrounded arbitrary sequencing, he noted, while "iconic" patterns foregrounded the way sequencing generated form. Bateson's interest concerned how a digital code in his terms could be "iconic" at another aesthetic level. For example, we might say that the "digital" quality of the Network's informational linkages also generates an "iconic" image of the Network and of communication as Network in the numerical equivalencies of image and analysis that the graph proclaims.[15]

One might reframe this insight for the networks presented here as a question of the relationship between the inside and outside of analysis. As we saw, the two principal genres of network artifacts, the newsletter and the network diagram, were differentiated according to their imagined circulation inside or outside the Network, and from that initial difference a series of patterned contrasts ensued. Each genre of artifact foregrounded what was backgrounded in the other—the same "system" represented in the diagram served as a principle of composition in the newsletter, for example—so that according to principles of perspectival drawing, each was the other turned inside out.

Yet the notion of something outside the Network, a place beyond where newsletters could circulate, was also an effect of the design since in practice these newsletters traveled within rather than without. The FNCW newsletter, for example, circulated to the FNCW network's own focal points, albeit imagined by the FNCW board as "grassroots organizations." That the same affiliates had representatives on the board simply meant that at another moment they might be imagined as insiders. The same was true of other graphics meant for "outside" distribution. In practice, as we saw, the Network was much more of a circular than a star-shaped form; there was no outside space in which to expand. Yet this did not stop focal points from orienting themselves differently to newsletters than to network diagrams, evaluating the former as if they were an audience of grassroots women.

The contrast between a newsletter and a diagram was not a difference between two kinds, then. Rather, the two figures were more a single, flat image given three-dimensional perspective in the way that it was seen twice (chap. 2).[16] If the newsletter at times physically framed the diagram, the abstraction of the diagram also framed the simulated representationality of the newsletter, which only produced "news," as it produced a grassroots readership, as a device for producing information as form, for example.

This aesthetic also recalls the text and brackets explored in chapter 3. As we saw, the bracket and the quotation were substances of the same kind that framed one another, as the bracket delimited a space for quotation and the quotation papered across the divides opened up by the bracket. The infinity within the brackets, we might say, was language turned inside out. In the same way that a set of documents might be imagined alternatively as quantity or pattern, likewise, "Network!" was a collection of women seen a second time as a visual pattern that inhered in "Network!" Or, again, one might think of the systemic aspects of the Network as an opportunity to reflect on analysis as an integrated material totality (Bateson 1987b); yet one might equally turn the system inside out to focus on the linkages and hybrids between networked elements (Latour 1993; Haraway 1995). Although NGOs in Fiji ultimately made greatest use of the circle rather than the star, the image gains its depth precisely from the internal accessibility of its own outside.

The most important contrast with an earlier era of modernist aesthetic activism, therefore, is that this networked form of "action" makes no appeal to a "reality" outside the artifact, be it the artifact's interpretive context or the viewer and his or her aesthetic experience. Consider once more the "Women" so often referred to in meetings or imagined by focal points as the viewers of network artifacts. If one thinks of "reality" as what lies outside of analysis and grounds it, then reality is an effect of the Network here.

If the question of network aesthetics concerns how information engages, or how the Network's patterns tap into the patterns of the "mind" to capture attention and stimulate the Network to action, therefore, this aesthetic effectiveness is simply a matter of the way in which, like Walbiri designs, each lived pattern is literally "the same thing" as the next. As with the newsletter's call to "Action!" or the marked directionality of the diagram's vectors, the pattern creates action within the Network by producing designs for action without and vice versa. In this context, "action"—the aesthetic agency of information[17]—consists in the figure seen twice.

There is an element of utopianism to an artifact as organizational form in which design and reality are one and the same. Yet what the Network ultimately effectuates is not reality, then. The cartoonlike figures of the newsletter and even the thousands of identity performances of the NGO Forum did not "pretend" to be real. If the activists in "Network!" had been realistically drawn, the image no longer would work, for not all viewers might agree with their cause and the "real" differences that now divide feminists might come into view. To critique these as mere artifice therefore would miss the point. Rather, one might consider how controlled heterogeneity generated the desired effect, as the Beneath Paradise performances generated "the Pacific" as an element of their design. In the postcoup climate of Fiji, for example, the performance of racial stereotypes generates a powerful effect indeed.

In chapter 4, I considered how the information that is often taken as the foundation of a new and global information society is imagined to exist in infinite quantities, and queried the necessity of such claims. The same could be said of the designs in this chapter: if one thinks of a network as a representation of chaos, that is, of the retrospective path, one can see in the way that one random connection leads to another, the Network turned inside out is an equally effective image for a systemic world already known from the start, the circle rather than the star (chap. 2; cf. Poovey 1998). We are now in a position to understand better how the popular understanding of information that dominates discussions of globalization is generated in the first place. For if, as I have tried to demonstrate in this chapter, the aesthetic of system is grounded in a play on the inside and outside of analysis, then this aesthetic of system has implications for the character of the information it systematizes—for what we might call the aesthetics of fact.

To talk of an aesthetics of fact may at first bring on confusion: discussions of fact proceed, rather, under the rubric of epistemology and in the mode of critique. The fact has come under considerable attack in recent years, as sociologists have demonstrated that its social construction enables its sociological deconstruction (e.g., Latour and Woolgar [1979] 1986: 107).[18] Some have interpreted the opacity of facts under the rubric of ideology, that is, as statements that mask the true complexity of information and the reality of political contention. For example, one feminist planner has written of the kinds of practices described in the preceding pages:

> Images, verbal modes, abstracted forms, symbols, documents, are not a direct reflection of everyday experiences but are produced for us by experts, academics, intellectuals, media people and so on. Those who produce this ideological material are part of the apparatus of ruling and their work is part of the ruling relations of capitalism. (Walker 1986: 19)

She proposes instead "[s]tarting outside the professional framework, taking the standpoint of women and listening to what women have to say." Indeed, some of the most powerful applications of sociological analysis to contemporary institutions have involved demonstrations of the politics behind the construction of facts. In the context of documents, for example, the sociologist Dorothy Smith argues that

> the investigation of the text-reader relation must preserve the movement and sequence of the social relation. Analytic strategies that begin in document time, treating the text as an internally determined structure of meaning, will not serve this purpose, semiotic and structural analyses being for this reason generally inappropriate. (Smith 1984: 72)

"The text does not appear from nowhere," she adds. Yet it would be incorrect, for example, to describe the Whippy family tree as an outcome of a political contest over the nature of historical truth, as Latour and Woolgar describe scientific facts to be in the laboratory in which they conducted research. The politics lay elsewhere altogether—in the conflict between urban and rural Whippys over which form, the land or the family tree, should have predominance, for example. The material in this chapter draws attention to how the fact is collected, selected, and patterned as much as to how it is created or adjudicated.

The fact is an aesthetic of units, and these often take a numerical, quantifiable, collectible form. The amount or quantity of names on the Whippy family tree was noticed, and it mattered from the point of view of the makers and critics. We saw in chapter 3, likewise, how words such as *structural adjustment* or *indigenous rights* were quantifiable units, known by the number of times each appeared in the document. This numerical form is the inside out version of the Network's aesthetic of collection, the aesthetic of connection among units imagined as "in the same category."

Most importantly, as their critics have noted, facts are opaque entities; they shield interpretation and close off *interest* in further questions and answers.[19] The desire associated with the family tree, for example, concerned the collection of facts taken at face value, not an inquiry into what lay behind them.[20] What is not always appreciated in such critiques is that it is this opacity, the fact's very resistance to analysis in itself, that enables the Network's collectivizing quality, that evokes system. In network designs, for example, the opacity of focal point subjectivity deflected attention from the focal points onto the systemic relationships of the Network and thereby brought the Network form into view. In chapter 3, likewise, we encountered the precedence of form and pattern over meaning in the "language" negotiators battled to "bring in" to the document. It was this characteristic of the language that enabled it to paper across the infinite levels of alternative text within the brackets and produce a document.[21]

It was also this very opaque quality of the fact—a function of the fact's inclusion as a composition in the Network's systemic designs but also a constitutive element of those designs' systemic quality—that accounted for the fact's appeal. Consider, for example, the appeal of statistics of various kinds. One of the "strategic objectives" of the *Platform for Action* is to "generate and disseminate gender-disaggregated data and information for planning and evaluation" (UNFWCW 1995a: 198). Among the messages, movements, experiences, political causes, and contacts that the Beijing Conference and NGO Forum were designed to serve up to participants, statistics most powerfully captured the attention of participants from Fiji. Again and again, they commented on the official tally of the number of participants or the number of AIDS cases worldwide. "Wow! That's more people than in all of Fiji! Can you imagine?" my roommate at the Beijing Conference told me excitedly of European unemployment statistics upon returning from a workshop. Like the names collected in the urban Whippys' family tree, most of these statistics centered around the sheer size of the numbers at issue. They attested to the appeal of collecting.

The *Pacific Platform for Action* (SPC 1994a) included an extensive statistical preface to the negotiated text labeled "Overview on the Status of South Pacific Women." The "overview" was prepared by a Samoan anthropologist and development consultant hired with Australian funding to perform this task, and it provides "data" in a series of categories preordained by the secretariat of the FWCW. These include the "principal physical and economic features" of each country (11), the "percentage of labor force engaged in agriculture by gender" (34), and the "composition of established public service by gender and level" (39). The consultant "compiled" the data in this report from reports produced by other experts serving as consultants to their governments "at the national level," as mandated by the FWCW. In Fiji, for example, the DWC hired a University of the South Pacific lecturer in population studies to assemble the statistics and produce its "national report" (DWC 1994). This task consisted primarily in reshuffling existing data on poverty, education, and demography into new matrices and flow charts and writing additional summary descriptions of the physical, economic, political, and social features of the country. The overview in turn was to be incorporated into yet another study produced by the same consultant for the Asia-Pacific region as a whole and then forwarded to the Beijing Conference secretariat in New York for incorporation into a final statistical report (United Nations Secretary-General 1995). This collection of facts proceeded along the same trajectory of successive levels of inclusion and incorporation as did the negotiated document, although in this case the problems of assimilating multiple versions, emphasized visually in intergovernmental negotiations in the form of the bracket, were largely shielded from view.

In presenting her findings at the Nouméa Conference at which the *Pacific Platform for Action* was negotiated, the consultant who produced the overview

> highlighted the need for Pacific women to present a united view to this world conference and to seek regional commonalities rather than highlighting differences between sub-regions or countries. She also drew attention to the difficulty of finding reliable statistics that could be compared across the region and to the need for better gender-disaggregated data to be collected in the future. (SPC 1994b: 5)

The question of "the status of South Pacific women," in other words, was subordinated to such questions as common negotiating positions or the comparability of different statistical studies. As in the case of the language of negotiated texts (chap. 3), the question of the "meaning" of the statistics was also deferred. I never heard the meaning of such statistical reports discussed among DWC staff or NGOs in Fiji, although the *fact* that a report had been completed was often noted as an accomplishment—a gap that had been filled—while the lateness of a report was grounds for private criticism of the bureau or consultant involved.

Fiji's "national paper," then, represented a literally accurate reflection of the "status of women" in Fiji only because the "status of women" was a "technical" term, internally defined precisely by its place in such reports. Yet, if the hedging procedures surrounding the preparation of such reports were acknowledged by all, the form of the fact went undebated. I learned this point through my own mistakes. At the Beijing Conference, I was asked to represent Fiji in a negotiation concerning language that called for governments to account for women's "unpaid labor" in GNP "satellite accounts." In what proved to be a short career in applied anthropology, I raised the question of cultural bias in the constitution of "women's contribution" and the supposed benefit to women that would flow from being counted. When I reported this to members of the

Fiji delegation, they were dismayed. The notion that there was some "cultural" problem with counting the monetary value of women's contribution to the production of exchange items, for example, struck them as politically and technically backward. What I had done was to confuse my own uses of social science as an analytical tool with negotiators' uses of social science as design.

From this vantage point, we now can understand the fact of the kind that is taken as the building block of the new global information society as an element in the network composition, and one that shares all of its aesthetic features, including its play on the relationship of the inside and outside of analysis and on the relationship of system to chaos. Like the Network diagrams described previously, statistics limit information to what can be related in a series of direct one-to-one correlations, all in the guise of adding information through collection; they are designs that point to interrelations and do no more.[22]

The nature of the "reality" imagined to lie behind the statistics, and indeed the character of the relationship between the numbers and the worldview they represent, is a question outside the numbers, something shielded by the opacity of the fact and always open to debate at a *later stage*. The form is purposely two dimensional; it fails to reveal what is beyond itself.[23] The anxieties that surround questions of access to information in the information age, then—in particular, the notion that information is potentially infinite but in practice scarce and the endless oscillation between a utopian understanding of information as pieces of a complex system and information as the source of contemporary chaos—are the ultimate three-dimensional rendering of the design's flirtation with what lies beyond and outside its own form.

This returns us to PAWORNET, the case of network collapse presented at the outset of chapter 2. From this point of view, the conversion of network resources into personal ones, a common and implicitly accepted (if always explicitly denounced) aspect of many network activities, simply replicates the pattern that translates overseas funds into action within and without the image. Yet it points to an aesthetic problem inherent in the device, that of keeping the inside and outside of analysis separate enough to generate the effect of a shift from one to the other. To give up the distinction would be to give up the optical illusion and to collapse the organizational form into a two-dimensional design.

CHAPTER 6

Filling in the Action

Inherent in the design's effectuation of global reality, however, is a problem of form. The difficulty, shared by international aid agencies, negotiators, and NGOs alike, concerns how to turn funds into documents, documents into action, or action into further funds—in other words, how to manage the distance between inside and outside that is internal to the design. I hope to demonstrate, in the context of artifacts that anthropologists might imagine as of a different scale than the diagrams and newsletters considered so far, that it is this problem of design, not the "issues" nor the large amounts of funds now donated from overseas in their support, that constitutes the "real," the substance, the politics, and the "meaning" for those encountered here.

A Space for the Real: Three Articulations of Desire

I noted in chapter 5 that, unlike the designs of an earlier modernist era of international activism, Network designs make no appeal to a reality outside and beyond themselves. Nevertheless, the Real, that which lay beyond the design, had a recurring and powerful appeal for those involved in networks, negotiations, and their funding. At frequent intervals, negotiators, staff members of international aid agencies, government workers, and networkers stopped to invoke a notion of the "real world" or "the reality of women" or simply what was "real." The Real was understood as outside but also somehow contingent on the formal activities of negotiation and networking, and such an invocation evoked an aching awareness of a distance between the Network and the Real, an emptiness, a self-critical apprehension of lack. This view of the Real in turn gave rise to an impetus to put the real world back "into" the documentation projects, to find the missing funds, or to reveal one's activist credentials. It stimulated an urgent need for "Action."

This sense of lack has certain parallels in anthropological analysis. One might imagine, for example, a line of critique that would find in the previous chapter's focus on form a lack of attention to politics, economics, practice, power, substance, or a variety of other entities, which at different periods have filled the quadrant of the Real in anthropological analysis. Whatever its substance, the Real, in this view, is what lies outside analytical form. For anthropologists, as for these institutional actors, this outside always remains internal to the analysis, so that if the anthropologist's analysis fails to appeal to a reality "outside," the lack is imagined to inhere in the analysis, not in the reality. One of the themes of this chapter is that this empty space or "lack" is an artifact of the design itself, like the self-styled sociology of the Network. In such a situation, this line of critique and the preemptory response it generates are not so much "outside" analysis as a replication of the work already indigenously done.

The relationship between networkers' hope for real action and the frustrating stillness of analytical forms was elaborated clearly at a national consultation on the Beijing Conference held in Suva in January 1995. On the first day of the meeting, a government minister asked to deliver a keynote address took a critical posture against the entire Beijing Conference in the name of "action." Asked to speak about his experience at the Cairo Conference, he chose instead to tell the story of a woman washing laundry in the river he had passed on his way to the conference site. Would the conference amount to anything in that woman's life, he asked? Probably not, he surmised; in the main, it was all talk and no action.

On the second day of the conference, the Asia-Pacific NGO focal point for the Beijing Conference was scheduled to give a presentation about "the road to Beijing." Before beginning her presentation, however, she recalled this anecdote and the skepticism it entailed:

> I want to go back to what the minister alluded to yesterday in his remarks, when he was telling us the story of the woman in the river and the question raised . . . what does this conference mean to those women who are washing in the river. I think the minister answered that question well later on in his remarks by saying "irrespective of what happens if there is no reasonable political will or if politicians are not involved those women continue to wash in the river." . . . That is why, I believe, Beijing is quite significant because it is at the political policy level that water supply in the remotest islands of Fiji gets to be done not through, as some has suggested, that these conferences are hyperroutinized international conferences and so forth and that it doesn't really affect your ordinary Fijian women. I think it is an outright lie because we all know, as I said earlier and as the minister said yesterday, in order for safe water to happen to the community political will and politicians have to be involved.[1]

The argument at first blush is nonsensical: in order for there to be action and real outcomes (a reliable water supply in the remotest islands) one must have inaction and form (hyperroutinized international conferences). If the problem is simply political will, for example, one could imagine generating it by less elaborate means. Yet such seemingly circular arguments about action abound in most every document, newsletter, and conference speech. The global *Platform for Action*, for example, listed over two hundred separate "actions" to be taken by governments, international bodies, and NGOs. As the secretary-general of the Beijing Conference stated in the closing words of her address to the delegates at the preparatory meeting for the Beijing Conference described in chapter 3: "[T]his is the mission in Beijing: not further analysis, but a deeper level of action" (Mongella 1995a).

For the subjects of this book, Action was a matter of how to energize the forms described in the previous chapters—how to spark the commitment of the focal point, how to captivate the attention of the newsletter reader, how to turn the figure inside out, to see the other possibility in their forms. Action was "real" because it was the underlying purpose, and also the desired outcome of all other forms and activities, albeit also explicitly opposed to the "analysis" of documents and conferences. Why people periodically robbed their own efforts of "realism" in this self-critical stance, and why the stance took the form of gaps for the Real known as Action, will require further consideration of matters of design. Before doing so, however, it may prove useful to review some exemplary articulations of Action as distance from the Real.

Translation: A Desire for Meaning

One of the ubiquitous and indispensable enabling technologies of any UN conference is simultaneous translation, a sideline "technical" occupation that aims to replicate the conversation in alternative linguistic forms. Translators also produce documents of their own—translations of conference documents in each of the six official UN languages—so that one can follow a particular phrase as it is discussed from any one of six versions. As participants following the proceedings on their headsets know well, however, simultaneous translation is something of an illusion. The texts always bear the mark of translation, for, although grammatically perfect and literally identical, the prose of each version is never quite coherent. There were frequent disputes during the course of all the negotiations I attended about differences in meaning from one translation to the next (cf. Tabory 1980).

At the PrepCom, one such dispute—a question about the "meaning" of the word *gender*—threatened to bring the entire negotiation to a halt when several states demanded that each of the hundreds of references to "gender" in the global *Platform for Action* (GPFA) be placed in brackets due to the indeterminacy of its meaning when translated into other languages (cf. Baden and Goetz 1997). According to members of the Fijian delegation, who lobbied some of the delegations seeking to bracket the word to drop their objections, delegations from non-English-speaking states in Africa and Latin America had been influenced by fliers placed on each delegate's desk by conservative North American groups. The fliers asserted that in English the term carried the connotation of "five genders instead of two" and that these additional "genders" included "homosexuality" and "trans-sexuality."[2] The leaflet strategy proved to be one of the most skilled exploitations of the primacy of the English language and the limitations of translation in UN practices.

At the PrepCom, opposition to the bracketing of "gender" mobilized and united NGOs. NGO delegates sat in the balcony of the main conference hall holding up signs that read "gender" and "gendre" in English and French, and Bella Abzug, the cochair of the Women's Environment and Development Organization (WEDO), read an impassioned statement that referred to the common social scientific meaning of *gender* as socially constructed relations between men and women, to the thunderous applause and cheers of NGO participants. To a social scientific observer, it was a moment in which the self-referentiality of analysis came home to roost, as the very terms coined by an objectivist social science were reclaimed as political slogans because of their scientific objectivity.

The dispute was resolved only when a special contact group of member states met over a period of several weeks to "determine" the "meaning" of the term. Although the contact group's findings were claimed by feminist NGOs as a victory in that the group found no reason to refrain from using the term, its findings also might be viewed as a demonstration of the elusiveness of meaning in its ultimate abdication of definition altogether. After a simple introductory paragraph, the group's statement read only:

> 2. Having considered the issue thoroughly, the contact group noted that: (1) the word "gender" had been commonly used and understood in its ordinary, generally accepted usage in numerous other United Nations forums and conferences; (2) there was no indication that any new meaning or connotation of the term, different from accepted prior usage, was intended in the Platform for Action.
>
> 3. Accordingly, the contact group reaffirmed that the word "gender" as used in the Platform for Action of the Fourth World Conference on Women was intended to be interpreted and understood as it was in ordinary, generally accepted usage. (Mongella 1995b)

The Beijing Conference witnessed many other kinds of translation. As the delegates pieced together a text one line at a time, the press, the NGO lobbyists, the UN staff, and the delegates reformulated the text as issues, points, or accomplishments, transforming and replicating the text in internal daily news bulletins, "fact sheets," daily briefings, interviews, demonstrations, songs, political banners, radio and television programs, and newspaper articles (Riles

1999). The unifying trait of these translations, in stark contrast to negotiation, was the way each raised questions of the "meaning" of the document.

Consider, for example, negotiations at the PrepCom over the drafting of the Beijing Declaration, a short statement signed by governments to introduce the GPFA. The declaration aimed to serve as the document's translation of itself; those drafting it reminded themselves that "this declaration is not just for the UN or for the press but for the women." As one participant put it: "We recognize that at the end of the day what the media will read, what the women will read, will be not the platform but the declaration." If this translation had a different audience (or more accurately, unlike the negotiated text, if it was drafted with an audience in mind), the style of the proposed text also was almost symmetrically opposed to the style of the GPFA. Negotiators insisted that the text be "short and concise" and even considered abandoning the style of UN documents altogether, as one delegate put it, to "finish with urgency—ACTION NOW!"

The explicit purpose of the exercise was to give meaning to the "abstractions" of the document. One negotiator suggested that

> in the first sentence, we should have the key word, *women*; we should have very simple sentences. We should say what we mean in simple language. Even *empowerment* is abstract. We should use layman's language, not technical language . . . concrete language rather than abstract ideas.

In contrast to the previous emphasis on "language," negotiators now aimed to define "issues" and "cross-cutting themes." As another put it:

> I'm approaching it in answer to the question "what was Beijing about?" We have had twenty years of conferences, so it's "where have we come and what have we learned?"

This, in turn, generated for the first time a problem of meaning:

> This is very difficult—we have been using all these words like *sustainable development* and *mainstreaming*. But what do they mean?

And this question of meaning for the first time also brought into the foreground the personal involvement and commitment of the negotiators:

> I mean, fifty years ago I couldn't have opened a bank account in my own name. That's what I mean!

Like these negotiators, government and NGO representatives considered the "translation" of the *Platform for Action* a task of paramount importance, for, as they stated again and again, it was through "translation" that the document became "real." One of the leading members of the Fiji delegation, speaking on "the meaning of Beijing" at a public gathering in Suva, noted:

> A lot of us believe that the greatest challenge is putting those statements, those hopes to action, back here, in our own community where it matters the most.... And this document the governments worked on has also identified significant parties who would also contribute towards the advancement of women. Parties such as nongovernmental organizations, women's groups, research bodies, statistical offices, the media—all these parties have been identified as playing a very important role. I think one of the major things that women have to do is at least translate those materials, translate what happened in the World Conference in Beijing for the advancement of women. Because each of us here have a part to play.[3]

In a technicalization of this figurative task of translation, many NGO members in Fiji spoke of literally translating the *Platform for Action* into "the local vernacular" (a term commonly used among women's NGOs, "Fijian" or "*Vosa Vaka Viti*" or "Hindi") as their first post-Beijing task. Yet if, as in the case of the definition of *gender*, the meaning of the words proved elusive even to their negotiators, there was no guarantee that the "meaning of Beijing" or the "Action" would emerge when the document was "simplified" or translated into Fijian or Hindi or broken down into the parts that each group had to play. In the elusive task of translation, therefore, participants repeatedly made themselves collectively aware of a distance between their work and the Real. Desire by definition remained eternally unfulfilled.

Activism: A Desire for Commitment

A second articulation of the desire for the Real was the periodic enactment of "activism" by persons who more regularly presented themselves as "professionals" in Fiji. On the second day of the inaugural meeting of the Omomo Melen Pacific network, a network of women for the Pacific Colonies, for example, the journalists and UN employees who attended as observers shed their formal Fijian dresses, suit jackets, and fans for T-shirts bearing political slogans, sandals, and strings of beads, abandoning the language of "delegates" and "agendas" to refer to one another as "sisters" and to discuss their role in "the struggle." The staff of donor institutions, likewise, often thought of themselves as covert activists working within the system and even at times against their own institutions to bring about the very objectives that NGOs publicly espoused. Privately, staff members even criticized their NGO donees for their lack of activist commitment. One representative of a donor agency expressed to me her disgust with the "hierarchy among women" within Fiji's NGO community and went on to lament the lack of true interest in feminism among those involved in WID activities. Likewise, the representative of another major donor expressed to me her despair at the fact that "so many of the women in this area just have no integrity and don't even have a gender perspective."

Often the turn to a register of activism coincided with press conferences, interviews, and other presentations imagined to reach the outside world. In May 1995, several months before the Beijing Conference, the UN secretary-general briefly visited Fiji on his way home from a state visit to Australia. A controversy had been brewing for several months among NGOs around the world concerning the decision of the Chinese government to separate the governmental and nongovernmental portions of the Beijing Conference and to relegate the NGO portion to a small undeveloped site one hour from the city center. After their request to meet with the secretary-general to discuss the issue was denied, the focal points of several Pacific networks[4] staged a press conference to publicize their "demands." The press conference began by presenting those assembled as "women" joined in a worldwide struggle for justice. Laying out the background, the speakers noted:

> We have joined the global lobby. Right now we have what we believe is a golden opportunity of the UN secretary-general being here, which other women in other parts of the world will not have.

Emphasizing that it was only worth participating in a conference if participation was "meaningful" and noting that they did not want to suffer "discrimination," they invoked the memory of Tiananmen Square and stated that the Chinese authorities' denial of adequate facilities to NGOs stemmed from the government's fear of the trouble activists like themselves might cause. They explained to the press that it was imperative that groups who were "close to the women" in their countries attend the conference to ensure that women's "real needs" were expressed in the document that would become a "blueprint for women" in the generation to come. Finally, the speakers produced a petition to the secretary-general—a genre outside the usual scope of documents—and placed great emphasis on their individual signatures and the commitment these signified.

The plea was so passionate that the young members of the press sent to cover the event, who knew little about the organizations represented there, misinterpreted the event. Putting aside the question of what the secretary-general might do about improving conference site facilities, they focused instead on the activism: "Are you women hoping to risk your lives?" one reporter asked. "It could be very dangerous!" Others followed with similar questions—what would the Fiji government do, for example, to protect its activist citizens if the Chinese government resorted to violence to silence them? A nervous laughter fell upon the room. There had been a profound misunderstanding. The very attempt to enact the Real had only made visible the gap between networks and activism once again.

This activist register of bureaucratic activity was by no means unique to Fiji. In the second week of the PrepCom, for example, several states took the floor to speak about a Filipino migrant worker engaged as a maid in Singapore who had been mistakenly accused of a crime and was scheduled to be executed the following day. The delegates spoke passionately about the unwillingness of the government of Singapore to consider the testimony of new witnesses in the case and urged "you, madame chairperson, to do something." The issue took hold of the body, as one speaker after another spoke of the obligations of "this body to act." After much discussion, which included impassioned rejections of the procedural arguments of the delegate from Singapore that the matter already was being handled through bilateral consultations, the body decided that the chair should go personally to the secretary-general and ask him to intervene. "If you would do so right away, I know we would all be very grateful to you," said one delegate, "because a life, the life of a woman, is at stake." The chair hurried off to the secretary-general's office and reported back that although the latter was in a meeting of the Security Council his deputy had interrupted him to convey the message. The chair was confident that he would act on the matter, although of course there were certain practical problems such as the time change between New York and Singapore. The moment then passed, and the conference moved on to other business.

When people performed "Action," they did so with another subject in mind, a character whom they believed they encountered from time to time but ultimately understood to be distant from their daily lives. This character was the "activist." As one participant in the Beijing preparatory process told me in conversation:

> You should see some of the activists. . . . They move like nobody's business because basic human rights is a matter of life and death for them. For us, it's not, I mean, we come and talk about human rights, and women's rights, and then we go home and do our own thing, you know? Cook, have a nice time, go to the movies. But for them, it's a matter of life and death. . . . Here we are just waffling along, just writing whatever we want in the papers. To them, to write something is also a matter of life and death. . . . They are killed, they are hounded down and everything.

The "activist" was a source of considerable fascination. Others competed for her attention, invited her to speak on panels, rushed to assure her of their political commitment, and sought her endorsement of their own activities. Focal points often described themselves as facilitators of activists, disseminating information about "the struggle" on a more global scale by securing funding for activists or putting them in contact with international journalists in a position to publicize their causes.

Funding: A Desire for the Material

Among the standard and ubiquitous subjects of conversation among donors, government workers, and NGOs were accusations and counteraccusations of improprieties surrounding the accounting for and use of funds. Accusations usually centered around the fact that a particular person or institution had failed to follow the rules; it pointed to the gap between the way things were and the way they should be. The following passing comment from a local member of the clerical staff to a colleague at one donor institution was typical:

> M. rang. Wants money in cash. The check is made out to SPC. She says, "we're UNIFEM, how are we supposed to get the money?" I said, "you bank it and then you clear it! Tough luck, the grant is to SPC, not UNIFEM."

Funds were real, in this analysis, and had real consequences. Yet, like other manifestations of the Real, funds were also continually disappearing: Again and again, the parties commented about one another, as did one donor to me, that "in many cases you fund something in the Pacific and the money just disappears; there's no accountability." This donor complained bitterly that other funding agencies were just "dishing out funds" to the major organizations and therefore provided no incentive for reform.

The activities of donees aside, donors also experienced the lack of grounding of their activities in what in the "real world" were the hard facts of balancing the books and limited resources. The "gap" between the salaries and expenses of WID participants and the standards of the local economy was noted in chapter 2. One morning I arrived at the Asia Foundation to find the local project officer with calculator in hand scribbling across a series of charts and computer printouts. I asked what he was doing. "Cutting $150,000 from the budget—headquarters' orders," he smiled. I wondered aloud how on earth he could possibly achieve the task. He laughed and assured me that it would make no difference to the programs at all.

Like the levels of negotiated text that appeared within the brackets (chap. 3), therefore, the language of negotiation, the linkages of the networks, and the accounting procedures of international aid agencies created a grid through which participants regularly peered into the gaps to apprehend the "Real." What participants encountered in their excursions into the Real, in other words, was the gaps, what each form lacked or what proved elusive—meaning, activism, the fixity of the material.[5] The case of funding and the relationship between donors and donees will serve as a basis for a more general consideration of the absence of the Real in the pages that follow.

WID Funding in Suva: Distances within a Singular Form

The articulations of a desire for the Real emphasized the distance between institutional roles—between donors and donees, women and negotiators, or activists and bureaucrats. Translation of the Beijing document, for example, involved breaking the text down into units that corresponded to particular sectors or groups of actors, each with their "parts to play." This was particularly marked in relations between donors and donees. In the formal terms of employment contracts, funding agreements, correspondence, or conference participation, the distance between donors and donees was highly marked and acknowledged by all. While in a given institutional context an individual might represent both an NGO and a media organization, an international organization and an NGO, or even a government body and an NGO, the same individual could not represent both a donor and a governmental, nongovernmental, or media organization.

In practice, however, this distance between donor and donee was elusive. One popular view of the divide that portrayed donors as expatriate outsiders and donees as local insiders, for example, was difficult to substantiate when many donor representatives were Fiji citizens, while the representatives of donees included recent immigrants to Fiji, long-standing expatriates, and Fiji citizens who had spent the better part of the last ten years overseas. Most donors forwarded projects involving women to a special desk, a particular officer, or even a special office overseas for consideration. The staff of these desks by and large saw themselves as committed progressive women, and they viewed gender equity as a fundamental priority of their bureaucratic work. They also viewed their work as political in the sense that they favored some interests in Fijian society over others, although they often felt the need to shield this politics from direct and public view. One particular example of this covert activism on the part of donor staff will suffice: when I first approached AusAID on behalf of the Omomo Melen Pacific network, the network of women for the Pacific colonies, concerning the possibility of funding for focal points' attendance at the Beijing Conference, I was told that there would be a diplomatic problem with providing direct funding to a network that explicitly opposed the presence of the French government in the Pacific. However, AusAID eventually did provide major support to the network by funding one of its members from Kanaky, in her individual capacity, to attend the conference.

Another view of the distance between donors and donees emphasized the different political orientations of activists and international development experts. Yet this view also belied a situation in which both WID donors and donees imagined donors as feminist activists who, for better or worse, used their influence to inculcate into government and NGO activities the newest feminist vocabulary and values such as "gender equality" and "mainstreaming." This covert yet firm activist orientation on the part of aid agency staff members was reflected in the projects donors tended to fund. Only the most openly self-acknowledged "feminist" NGOs—Fiji Women in Politics, the Fiji Women's Crisis Centre, and the Fiji Women's Rights Movement, for example—received ongoing institutional support rather than piecemeal project-based aid. Likewise, the call in academic critiques of WID policies for a shift from "women" to "gender" and from "productivity" to "empowerment" (e.g., Escobar 1995: 187) was echoed far more forcefully among donors in Fiji than among NGOs.[6] In order to appeal to the activist in the aid agency staff member, NGO representatives often sought to demonstrate their progressive credentials in funding proposals and conversations with donor representatives.

What differentiated donors and donees, instead, was their relative position vis-à-vis the funding application and the distribution of funds. Funding for the most part was based on individual "projects" and thus was easily quantifiable or "accountable."[7] In chapter 2 I described the circle of donors and donees as a small and tight one, such that virtually every applicant for funding was personally known to donor staff. Yet, just as networks were personal relationships made technical, the disbursement of funds proceeded as if participants were anonymous applicants and evaluators whose relationship consisted only of the dossier of correspondence they produced.

The preparation of funding proposals demanded hours of painstaking effort for governmental organizations and NGOs in Suva, and their authors circulated them with pride. Some of the more successful NGO applicants were skilled at producing flawlessly word-processed proposals written in the technical English of international institutions, complete with a carefully designed layout and the latest terminology of the gender and development debates, while other applications conformed less successfully to the donors' ideal. In reviewing one another's proposals, people commented on the aesthetic qualities of a "good proposal" independent of the substance of the proposed project,[8] and in endeavoring to succeed in the application process they copied one another's conventions and innovations of form.

Funding proposals therefore conformed to a tight, standardized form. For example, the AusAID guidelines for projects related to funding for the Beijing Conference required applicants to submit a series of documents designed to provide information about the applicant's organization—audited financial statements, copies of annual reports, and constitutions. Proposals were documents of approximately fifteen pages written in narrative form but adhering precisely to an outline dictated by the funding agency. Necessary elements included objectives "in measurable terms, where possible" and lists that "quantified" the expected benefits of the project. The guidelines also asserted that a proposal must include "indicators (ways of measuring) to be used to monitor the proposed activity against its objectives" and asked applicants to prepare a time-line graph labeled "activity monitoring chart" filled in with x and o marks for proposed tasks and tasks actually completed (AIDAB 1994).

For donors,[9] the proposal format evidenced a desire to know something real and concrete about the applicants and their proposed projects, to instill a sense of fixity to the funding process through the form of the proposal itself. It also gave shape to a certain anxiety about donors' distance, as outsiders, from the "real action" among NGOs. Donors were always seeking "information" from me, as a fellow expatriate and observer of network activities, about what "really happened" at a particular conference or in a particular personal conflict among individuals or institutions. Their questions belied a sense of forever being one step removed from the "action." In the proposal, accessing the Real consisted of eliciting a series of units of information from the form filler. The desire was for a sense of proportionality or correlation among the units, as between objectives and outputs or units of time and units of projects. This desire for the Real facts took a particular form—the form of a rigid list that required a fine appreciation of a document genre to satisfy.

Yet, as with the demonstrations of activism, translation, and efficiency described earlier, this very facticity, the experience of capturing units of the Real, often made evident its own absence or lack: it exposed again a space for the Real. Consider, for example, one successful funding application by the Pacific NGO Coordinating Group for a meeting of NGO representatives to discuss the *Draft Platform for Action* and prepare for the PrepCom. The proposal included a highly detailed matrix listing areas of expenditure on one axis and a careful enumeration of estimated expenditures in each category on another. The text accompanying the table promised a complete accounting of expenses after the conference and a full report on conference proceedings. Even the use of U.S. dollar amounts for easy correlation with international donors' own accounting procedures evidenced shared approaches and expectations of "transparency." Yet the amounts that filled the spaces on the grids were so out of proportion with any common sense expectation of the cost of the budget items at issue that they subverted from within the effect of accountability in individualized components, the aesthetic of the measurability of units.[10]

At the Pacific area office of the Asia Foundation, an enormous chart hung on the wall behind the desks of the "local staff." The chart consisted of a grid-like table listing three "issue areas" on the vertical axis and next to each, a numerical value for the amount of funds the agency wished to allocate to projects in each area. On the horizontal axis, numbers (001, 002, 003) stood for "objectives" correlated to each issue and the projects approved and amounts already distributed during the year under each category.[11] In their daily work, the staff consulted the chart frequently and referred to its categories in conversation. For example, when the agency received a project proposal, staff members assessed it by considering the degree of "fit" with these categories, preferring projects that fit under several headings at once.

In its uses, TAF's matrix replicated in the internal evaluation processes the aesthetic of fixity that the same grid imposed on donees through the application process. Staff members often appealed to it precisely when they sought to demonstrate that funds were not simply fluid numbers on the books, out of proportion with real life and without any fixity of their own. For example, on one occasion representatives of a regional institution came to the office to sign a contract for funding for a short conference. After reviewing the program, from the agenda to the lunch menu, the representatives asked "if it would be pushing it" to ask the project officer to sponsor a cocktail party at the close of the event as well. The foundation staff member launched into a detailed explanation of the matrix and its system of allocating funds as a way of reaching the conclusion that "yes, it would be pushing it."

The Matrix, therefore, was a form shared among donors and donees that also internally marked the distance between the two. In each case, donees and projects filled in the blanks in the grids that donors generated. Both groups dedicated large amounts of energy to this form and pinned on it their desires. If donors and donees each viewed the other as outsiders to their own operations, as in the case of the Network, the distance between inside and outside was internal to the form.

The Matrix Form

As a design, therefore, the Matrix rivaled the Network in its ubiquity. At the Pacific office of the International Labour Organization, an oversized matrix listing each of the ILO conventions and their Pacific Island signatories covered the wall. At the SPC's Pacific Women's Resource Bureau, as at most international and regional agencies, staff produced and circulated extensive and detailed matrices listing their proposed "work programmes" for the year divided according to objectives, time frames, responsible staff members, and performance indicators (e.g., fig. 25). Even where documents included no formal matrix design the text often took an outline form, replete with bullets and headings, such that it was more a collection of points to be evaluated through a process of comparison, point by point, with other similar sections than a "text" to be read from start to finish. When negotiators evaluated a UN document, they engaged in a matrixlike comparison of "issues" incorporated into each successive draft. Comparison was one of the great analytical tasks of those working in institutions, and the Matrix brought the task into view. For example, the Fiji delegation's practical task in taking positions at the Beijing negotiations was simply to match the proposed language of other delegations with the language of Fiji's "national paper," thus comparing lists of suggested text. In its form, the Matrix suggested the comparability of all elements; it placed the elements in a singular plane and made of them entities of a singular scale.

Like network designs, matrices such as the TAF funding chart consisted of a collection of self-contained units connected only by a simple, systemic form. One of the general features of the matrix form was that the shape of the rectangular boxes allowed for a potentially endless number of units to be stacked one on top of the other without altering the form or the issues and paragraphs it contained. Even more rigid in form than the network diagram, the matrix made no allowances, for example, for the representation of differing distances between entities or the depiction of more than two relationships (horizontal and vertical) between elements in the figure. The matrix grid was a given entity not open to critical evaluation or interpretation, as was network design: It was never suggested that the issues to be discussed at Beijing should have a bearing on the form of the negotiations. If the Matrix provided the pattern, however, it did not provide context; each of the boxes and its contents took its form but not its interpretive meaning from the predetermined shape and dimensions of the grid.[12]

Consider for example "Turn the Words into Action!" (fig. 21), a matrix produced after the Beijing Conference and circulated to NGOs worldwide by WEDO, the prominent network that coordinated much NGO lobbying at the conference. The matrix decomposes the global *Platform for Action* into a series of "issues" and corresponding "key paragraphs." As it indicates, it is an "advocacy tool," that is, a form of translation and a way to "kick-start" the document, to show "concrete outcomes." In this sense, it was a device analogous to the commitments made by governments at the close of the conference.[13] As its title indicates, the objective of the matrix was to generate Action. In this sense, Fiji users of matrices considered them to be technical forms of the same genre as the Network. The Matrix enabled people to do something; it was an instrument, a tool, a means to another end—Action.

As in this example and the TAF matrix discussed above, matrices always included a left-hand column of "given" elements, usually known as "issues."[14] The definition of issue areas in the *Platform for Action*, for example, occurred long before the involvement of Pacific Islanders in the negotiation process, through the work of "experts" rather than through the politics of negotiation. In contrast to the academic conception of issues as that which is the subject of contention—that which divides women, for example—issues were entities around which there was consensus at the start, and they were almost always the same issues. "They have three issues," I was told when I first asked an insider about the Pacific NGO Coordinating Group, "everybody has three issues—let's see,

HUMAN RIGHTS

ISSUE & PARA REFERENCES	KEY PARAGRAPHS IN THE PLATFORM FOR ACTION (PFA)
Violence Against Women *See also:* PFA: paras 12, 113(a) - (c), 114, 117, 118, 119, 121, 124(a) - (s), 125(a) - (j), 131, 135, 136, 147(n), 224, 232(g), 283(a) - (d)	**124. By Governments:** (c) Enact and/or reinforce penal, civil, labour and administrative sanctions in domestic legislation to punish and redress the wrongs done to women and girls who are subjected to any form of violence, whether in the home, the workplace, the community or society; (i) Enact and enforce legislation against the perpetrators of practices and acts of violence against women, such as female genital mutilation, prenatal sex selection, infanticide and dowry-related violence and give vigorous support to the efforts of non-governmental and community organizations to eliminate such practices;
Trafficking *See also:* PFA: para 130(a) - (e)	130. By Governments of countries of origin, transit and destination, regional and international organizations, as appropriate: (b) Take appropriate measures to address the root factors, including external factors, that encourage trafficking in women and girls for prostitution and other forms of commercialized sex, forced marriages and forced labour in order to eliminate trafficking in women, including by strengthening existing legislation with a view to providing better protection of the rights of women and girls and to punishing the perpetrators, through both criminal and civil measures;
Internally Displaced *See also:* PFA: paras E.5, 133, 136, 147(a), (c), (d), (j) & (k), 226	147. By Governments, intergovernmental and non-governmental organizations and other institutions involved in providing protection, assistance and training to refugee women, other displaced women in need of international protection and internally displaced women, including the Office of the United Nations High Commissioner for Refugees and the World Food Programme, as appropriate: (b) Offer adequate protection and assistance to women and children displaced within their country and find solutions to the root causes of their displacement with a view to preventing it and, when appropriate, facilitate their return or resettlement;
Rape *See also:* PFA: paras 113(a), 117, 118, 129(c), 142(c), 144(b)	145. By Governments and international and regional organizations: (c) Urge the identification and condemnation of the systematic practice of rape and other forms of inhuman and degrading treatment of women as a deliberate instrument of war and ethnic cleansing and take steps to ensure that full assistance is provided to the victims of such abuse for their physical and mental rehabilitation; (d) Reaffirm that rape in the conduct of armed conflict constitutes a war crime and under certain circumstances it constitutes a crime against humanity and an act of genocide as defined in the Convention on the Prevention and Punishment of the Crimes of Genocide; take all measures required for the protection of women and children from such acts and strengthen mechanisms to investigate and punish all those responsible and bring the perpetrators to justice;
Religion and Culture	24. Religion, spirituality and belief play a central role in the lives of millions of women and men, in the way they live and in the aspirations they have for the future. The right to freedom of thought, conscience and religion is inalienable and must be universally enjoyed. This right includes the freedom to have or to adopt the religion or belief of their choice either individually or in community with others, in public or in private, and to manifest their religion or belief in worship, observance, practice and teaching. In order to realize equality, development and peace, there is a need to fully respect these rights and freedoms. Religion, thought, conscience and belief may, and can, contribute to fulfilling women's and men's moral, ethical and spiritual needs and to realizing their full potential in society. However, it is acknowledged that any form of extremism may have a negative impact on women and can lead to violence and discrimination.

Fig. 21. Sample page from *Turn the Words into action! Highlights from the Beijing Declaration and Platform for Action.* (From WEDO 1995: 6. Reproduced courtesy of the Women's Environment and Development Organization.)

what are their three? Decolonization, demilitarization, nuclear free Pacific, indigenous people . . . well, in any case, it's three out of those four."

The remainder of the form consisted of a collection of empty slots, geometrically arranged. It was this logic of slots that most often enabled the participation of Fiji delegates in international events. One delegate attended the Beijing Conference, for example, because the international donor agency responsible for funding her project wished to organize a panel at the NGO Forum, and it was imperative from the donor's point of view that there be "one from the Pacific" on the panel. Another participant in the NGO Forum was invited by WEDO to fill the need for someone to speak about the effects of U.S. militarism overseas after a member of the WEDO staff heard her make a presentation on that subject at another UN conference. NGO and government staff in Fiji were accustomed to filling slots at international conferences, like the words filled the boxes of the matrices described above. The form thus engendered a musical chairs-like politics among NGOs competing against one another to fill the same set of gaps in donors' plans. Knowledge about allotments of funds was in high demand, and the most skilled focal points steadfastly refused to reveal their funding sources while gathering information on the funding allotments of others.

This system of slots had a representative, even democratic aura about it. It was necessary that there be one young woman and at least two NGOs on each government delegation, for example, and the failure to include an Indo-Fijian representative in the delegation to the PrepCom exposed government and NGOs alike to critique (Momoivalu 1995). The Matrix also served as a solution to the gaps between projects and the Real in funding procedures. After dissatisfaction over the perceived nonrepresentative way in which the Pacific NGO Coordinating Group received funds to represent the entire Pacific at the PrepCom and then shared those funds only among Suva-based NGOs, AusAID implemented a highly structured application process for NGO funding to attend the Beijing Conference. The government aid agency placed advertisements in each national newspaper inviting all NGOs to submit applications and funded only one NGO from each country based on predetermined "criteria."

As a collection of rigidly aligned slots, then, the Matrix is a form that is apprehended incomplete. Its principal aesthetic feature is the way it demands further guided work on the part of the viewer to fill in the gaps left by the designer within the form.[15] It evidences desire in graphic terms. It is little surprise, then, that when Matrix designers spoke of the incompleteness of their form they often noted their desire that the Matrix would prompt its viewers to action. For example, as part of its role as "lead donor" for the Pacific for the Beijing Conference, AusAID each month produced a "coordination matrix" of project proposals relating to Beijing and their eventual sources of funding. The objective was the mutual energization of donors; by pointing to its own gaps, the Matrix spurred donors to become actively involved in funding Beijing-related activities as much as it coordinated their activities. As its administrator told me, "hopefully, this will encourage donors to look and see, hey, we're not doing much in this area, maybe we had better do more."

As an example of this task of stimulating Action, consider "Empowerment," the matrix produced by the staff of the DWC for a national consultation of government and NGOs held in Suva in January 1994 on the *Platform for Action* and its relationship to the Cairo Conference document (fig. 22). During the conference, participants broke into small groups to "discuss" and "fill in" the matrix. Each group then reproduced their matrix in poster form and presented it to the conference as a whole. As with "Turn the Words into Action!" the "issues" were given at the outset in the left-hand column, as was the systemic structure that divided the analytical problem into different kinds of possible institutional solutions, "political," "social," "eco," "health," and "legal." Although the session organizers suggested that these issues should not be considered exclusive, the typed placement of the text in the left-hand column, in vertical form, produced the effect of what was given (Kress and van Leeuwen 1996) and focused attention, rather, on the empty boxes that followed.

This, indeed, is what happened in the group in which I participated. In the short time available to discuss all the issues, participants did not attempt to reframe or expand them. Where in the final category ("legal") no issues were predetermined, participants simply abandoned the task of filling in the boxes rather than formulating issues of their own. Likewise, participants showed no interest in challenging the formal systemic division of the problem into institutional sections. As with the boxes of the Network diagram, these sections deflected attention away from themselves—in this case, onto the gaps.

The left-hand list of issues also provided the model for how the remaining boxes were to be completed. One unstated assumption among the members of our group was that all boxes should share in a singular genre. It seemed inappropriate to put sentences or paragraphs in some boxes and titular words in others, for example. When a member of the group formulated a statement or idea, therefore, others concentrated momentarily on how to phrase it so that it conformed to this titular style.

As the group worked through that matrix, participants demonstrated a collective desire to complete the work by filling in all the gaps. For most of those in attendance, the notion of issues, strategies, and roles was a new one, and they found it difficult to imagine exactly what they were expected to decide. Yet the gaps in the form seemed to generate their own impetus for completion, as participants rushed to finish the task within the allotted time frame.[16] Like the Network newsletter, the Matrix activated the participants; it drew them into its systemic logic and engaged their attention as it guided and channeled their thoughts about the (predetermined) issues at hand.[17]

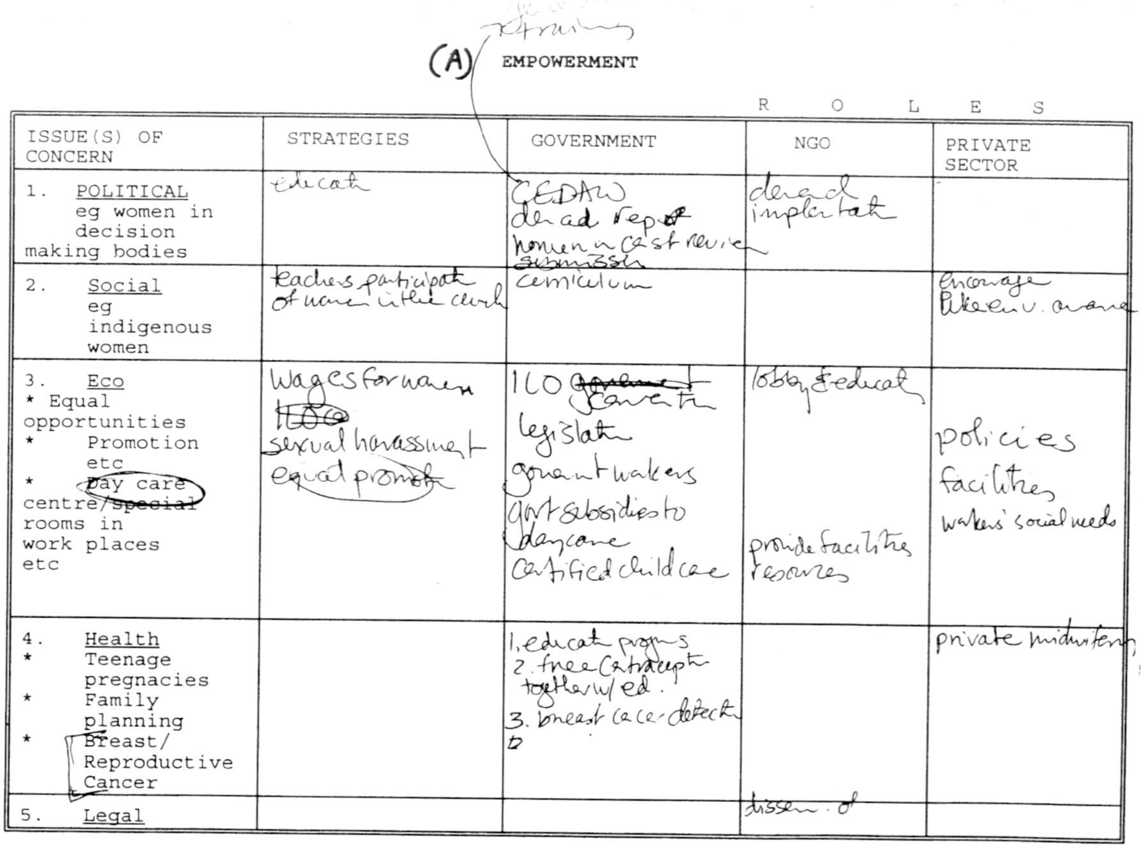

(A) Empowerment [strategies]

ISSUE(S) OF CONCERN	STRATEGIES	GOVERNMENT	NGO	PRIVATE SECTOR
1. POLITICAL eg women in decision making bodies	educat	CEDAW do ad rept women Cast revu curricula	clerical implemhat	Encourage & keen aware
2. Social eg indigenous women	Teaches participat of women whel cluh			
3. Eco * Equal opportunities * Promotion etc * Day care centre/special rooms in work places etc	Wages for women ILO sexual harassment equal promot	ILO convent legislat govt workers UN subsidies to daycare Cert Ffl childcare	lobby federal Provide facilities resource	policies facilities wohens social needs
4. Health * Teenage pregnancies * Family planning * Breast/Reproductive Cancer		1. educat progs 2. free contracept to the married 3. breast cancer chck		private midwifery
5. Legal			Assoc of	

Fig. 22. "Empowerment" matrix distributed at the Seminar on Beijing and the ICPD, a national preparatory conference of NGOs for the Fourth World Conference on Women, held at the headquarters of Soqosoqo Vakamarama in Suva, 18–19 January 1995. The writing on the figure is mine, as I participated in the matrix-filling activity described in the text.

In spurring its viewers to Action, then, the Matrix could be an activist tool. One young participant in our group emerged as the leader in this discussion and virtually dictated proposed contents of the matrix to the others. Although in other contexts such motivated intervention by a young Part-European woman at a meeting sponsored by this Fijian women's organization might have been resented by some, in this session everyone seemed grateful to her for providing something to write in each box. For her part, the young woman experienced her intervention as a dramatic coup, a successful incident of activism. The mood in the car trip home from the conference with this woman and her coworker had the spirit of a victory party after one of Fiji's rugby matches, as they whooped and screamed with joy at their accomplishment in convincing the members of conservative women's groups to include their items in the matrices and the final document produced from them.

In this case, Action was harnessed for the preparation of one of thousands of preparatory documents for the Beijing Conference; the Matrix turned Action into a document. Yet, as we saw, the WEDO matrix served to break the document down. The recurring uses of the Matrix thus evoked a temporal cycle in the negotiators' work that was absent from the Network's static designs. Where, as we saw in chapter 5, the Network made conceptual use of three-dimensional spatial distance in designing its own effectiveness into the two-dimensional figure, the Matrix made a parallel usage of distances of time.[18] The most common usage of the Matrix form in Suva was the calendar, and people showed a keen interest in making matrixlike time lines. Like simultaneous translation, and unlike the perusal of newsletter and network diagrams, viewers experienced their completion of the Matrix as taking place in real time. The Matrix seemed to encourage two simultaneous perspectives on time—the time of a project seen as a whole and the movement through time necessary for the analytical process of completing the chart from left to right (cf. Pickering 1997).

The Matrix, as form, energized participants, then. As with the moments of activism described in the early pages of this chapter, it spurred their commitment, at least for the moment of form filling. I now turn to the implications of this form for content and in particular for the notion of the Real.

The Matrix Inside Out

As we saw, the Matrix invites the viewer to think in terms of correspondences of facts to predetermined "issues," to fill in the details. The quantities with which matrix users filled in the gaps—amounts of funds, text, or strategies, for example—were self-contained, thinglike entities. For example, "Common Grounds" is a matrix produced for a 1995 DWC newsletter by the leader of Fiji's delegation to the PrepCom (fig. 23). The chart endeavors to illustrate that Fiji's "issues" had been incorporated into successive drafts of the *Platform for Ac-*

NATIONAL — COMMON — REGIONAL

CRITICAL CONCERNS	FIJI	PIC (Pacific Island Countries)
9. HEALTH	High incidence of STDs among younger females	Poor health situation of women is attributed to high fertility rates, high infant mortality rates, low immunisation rates, short birth intervals, early child-bearing, maternal mortality and lack of knowledge on hygiene, infectious disease and proper nutrition.
10. AGRICULTURE & FISHING		Lack of recognition of women's contribution in the primary industries and their lack of access to information and resources.
11. LEGAL AND HUMAN RIGHTS	Lack of awareness and commitment on internationally recognised legal instruments (e.g. CED) that recognise women's rights and improving appropriate national legislation that affect the rights of women.	Pacific women are unaware of their legal rights, social values often prevent women from gaining full protection from the legal system or exercising their rights, conflict between customary and religious laws on one hand and government and civil law on the other adversely affect women.
12. VIOLENCE	Increasing violence against women.	Incest, sexual harassment, rape and pornography
13. SHARED DECISION MAKING	Inequality of participation by women at all levels of decision-making	Women are under-represented in government and community decision-making bodies.
14. ECONOMIC EMPOWERMENT	Increase in the number of economically active women in the manufacturing and service sectors where they dominate in the lower wage bracket.	Women are over-represented in the lower wage earning brackets, they tend to concentrate in traditional occupations (nursing, teaching) and are under-represented at higher levels within an enterprise, need for more support for women's participation and contribution in the informal sector.
15. EDUCATION & TRAINING	Enrolment of women in non-traditional areas (e.g. engineering, agriculture) remain low.	Few women enter the school system, illiteracy is high among women, lack of women's participation at higher educational levels.

GROUNDS

INTERNATIONAL

ESCAP (Asia and Pacific Region)	C.S.W. (Draft Platform for Action)
Need for more health programmes on nutrition, basic health and reproductive health.	Inequality in access to health and related services and means of maximising the use of women's capacities.
Women's rights as human rights and elimination of discrimination against women, sexual exploitation and gender-based violence.	Lack of awareness of, and commitment to internationally and nationally recognised women's human rights.
Violence in the family, society, and in conflict situations and the implementation of CED	Violence against women.
	Inequality between women and men in the sharing of power and decision-making at all levels.
	Inequality in women's access to and participation in the definition of economic structures and policies and the productive process itself.
Empowering women through formal, non-formal and in-formal education.	Inequality in the access to education and related services and means of maximising the use of women's capacities.

Fig. 23. "Common Grounds." (From DWC 1995: 8–9. Reproduced courtesy of the Fiji Department of Women and Culture.)

tion at national, subregional, regional, and international levels of negotiation. It lists a series of issues on the vertical axis and each of the major "levels" of negotiations and drafts on the horizontal axis. Its designer then filled in the boxes with the issues under each category as included in each document. The factlike content of each box tells the viewer little about the issues in the left-hand column or the negotiated text listed in the right-hand columns. It simply expresses—as much in its graphic presentation as in the words—that the issue has been covered and included in the document, as in the matrix.

The extent to which all the boxes are filled in aims graphically to illustrate the "common ground" among the documents as a means, also, of demonstrating the effectiveness of Fiji's negotiating team. However, as it turned out, only one of the issues in Fiji's document (the issue of poverty) appeared in subsequent drafts of the *Platform for Action*. The facts did not generate the desired form of a completed chart: over half of the boxes could not be filled in. The designer therefore compensated by filling in the boxes with symbols and graphics photocopied from other newsletters and books of reproducible graphic symbols donated by IWTC. Once arranged in the boxes, these images have the same aesthetic effectiveness as the words; they fill in the spaces in the form.

In form, at least, therefore, persons, facts, language, and projects were substitutable kernels of Action, and, as in the case of "Common Grounds," the substitution was a potential source of effectiveness. What the contents of the Matrix spaces shared was precisely their substance, their authenticity, the Real within the spaces. To show the *Platform for Action* in matrix form (as did WEDO in "Turn the Words into Action!") (fig. 21) was to show the document as a set of real "commitments," not just analysis but the building blocks of Action.[19] As in "Common Grounds," the Matrix evidenced Action (in this case the action of NGO lobbyists at the conference) by evoking specificity, purpose, knowledge that did not conflate means and end.

The prototypical contents of the Matrix slot was an entity known as the "grass roots." Just as the designers of newsletters imagined their audience as "grassroots" women and organizations, in many cases, the designers of matrices imagined who and what filled in the Matrix in similar terms. The entire purpose of the exercise, in the case of the "Empowerment" matrix, for example, was to listen to the grass roots, to gather real information about their views and values and fundamental knowledge about what women wanted. At Beijing, also, the "grass roots" filled in a space—the "grassroots women's tent." As described to me and in public statements by the Fiji representative of the GROOTS network, who attended the Beijing Conference as a "representative of the grass roots in the Pacific," this new space for grassroots women was a great achievement of the Beijing Conference vis-à-vis previous women's conferences. As she explained it, the GROOTS network had emerged at the 1985 UN women's conference in Nairobi, where the absence of grassroots women meant that the conference was "out of touch." Grassroots women were precisely those who had been excluded, therefore, and in practice they could be identified with no more specificity than that. Her organization, the Fiji Catholic Women's League, had been chosen as the Pacific focal point of GROOTS because its membership was "90 percent grass roots," she said. An equally important factor in the choice, although one not explicitly acknowledged by the organization, was that she already participated in a number of existing networks. As she noted, the Catholic Women's League had been appointed Pacific focal point at the recommendation of the executive director of IWTC, whose previous work in Fiji was discussed in chapter 5. The impetus for the executive director's intervention, however, was the need to fill the gap. "Grass roots," then, was a factlike entity, a depoliticized, decontextualized term carved out precisely from the gaps in the networks at Nairobi.[20]

The grass roots was what was inherently, archtypically "outside," what one was *not*. Indeed, in stating that her organization's membership was 90 percent grass roots, the GROOTS Pacific focal point probably meant that most members *other than herself* were grassroots women. She herself worked as a secretary in an office in Suva and had attended the Nairobi Conference, at which, she said, grassroots women were not in attendance. "Grass roots" was a category that inherently applied to others. There was a productivity, an inherent sense of Action, to this "outside." Just as it was an "accomplishment" to include grassroots women in the Network, participants often referred to the persons or institutions that they considered "outside" with an admiring comment on their productivity. Thus, participants often noted how members of the Fiji press—the prototypical outside observers of institutional activity—"started early," worked hard, "were prepared," and "sang for their supper" at the Beijing Conference. Likewise, Fijian and Part-European delegates to the Beijing Conference often referred admiringly to delegates from India—the country they perceived of as home to the "other" portion of Fiji's population—as the most "impressive." They spoke with great respect of their organizing skills and of their ability to "agitate," to "push their issue" and get what they wanted. No wonder, then, that the secretary-general of the Beijing Conference and so many others referred to Action as the true mission of Beijing and the opposite of analysis. If analysis inhered in the forms, Action lay outside the form.

Yet in the Matrix, the outside presented something of a paradox: the outside—the grass roots, the Real information, and the material funds—were by definition entities with a place within the form. Indeed, the defining characteristic of the Matrix form lay in the way it literally contained its own outside within the gaps in the figure. Returning to the vocabulary of the previous chapter, we might say that the Real was the Matrix inside out.

Drawing upon the discussion in chapter 5 of how the Network, turned inside out, effectuated its own outside, we now also can understand the Real, as encountered within the gaps of the figure, as internally generated by the figure. Like the performances of the Real for the press alluded to in the earlier discussion of activism, the Real was snapshot-like units of authenticity made possible by the encompassing presence of the press (fig. 24). The funds distributed by international aid agencies were fundamental, material quantities precisely because of the way they filled the gaps in donors' matrices and donees' work schedules. The figure, like the Beijing document as described by the Fiji delegation leader at the opening of this chapter, dictated the way in which "everyone has a part to play." Funds were no more or less real than the facts, persons, symbols, or issues that also filled the gaps in the matrix, and, indeed, it was precisely the interchangeability of these that made the Matrix work, that turned funds into documents or documents into Action, thus internally solving the inherent problem of incompleteness in the form.

Yet, as in the case of the Network's systemic models of social relations, the evocation of matrix content as the form of truth, agreement, or conclusion did not necessarily require that matrix designers or users actually take the matrix contents as true, agreed upon, or conclusive.[21] Like the schematic representation of focal points in network diagrams, the words within the Matrix said very little about themselves. Their very conclusiveness, we might say, lay rather in the way they closed off the gap and directed attention, rather, to the next empty box within the figure. In the weeks following the national consultation described above at which we filled in the matrices, for example, another national meeting to discuss Fiji's ratification of the Convention on the Elimination of All Forms of Discrimination against Women (CEDAW) was held, and it became clear that in filling out the matrices at the previous conference the assembled organizations had not "agreed" on concepts behind the words in the matrices at all, as some delegates present at that first meeting simply repudiated the outcomes of the matrix-filling activity that had given the young activist such joy.

The Network Seen Twice

On this basis, we now can consider the relationship between the Matrix and the Network. Consider again the Fiji WIP diagram "Communication Line" and an extract from a matrix that accompanied it in Fiji WIP mission statements and funding proposals "Expected Outputs and Outcomes of Activities" reproduced in figure 25. At the outset, the two gridlike figures share an important similarity of form. Both involve a simple graphic interplay of lines and boxes aimed at ordering the information they provide. However, the Network design reveals the system that inheres in the pattern of Network action taken as a whole. In contrast, the bottom portion of figure 25 lists a series of concrete tasks: "secure office," "dialogue with political parties," "media watch" and so on. What it

Fig. 24. Participants in the Seminar on Beijing and the ICPD display the document they have drafted for a press photographer. The conference was held at the headquarters of Soqosoqo Vakamarama in Suva, 18–19 January 1995, and was funded by UNFPA. Above are Urmila Arya and Kuini Naqasima. Below are Senator Paula Sotutu and Ro Lady Lala Mara. (Reproduced courtesy of the *Fiji Times*.)

COMMUNICATION LINE

EXPECTED OUTPUTS AND OUTCOMES OF ACTIVITIES

ACTIVITY	TIME FRAME	PERSONNEL	TASKS	PERFORMANCE INDICATORS
I. Organisation of Office and Recruitment	August 1994 - February 1995	NCWF Volunteer, Project Manager and Clerk/Typist	1. Secure Office 2. Establish Office Procedures & Purchases 3. Convene Board 4. Establish contracts	1. Centre Established 2. Increase in workload due to women's awareness of Centre for FIJIWIP 3. Board tasks and procedures drawn up.
II. Targeting and Recruitment	May 1995 - July 1999	Project Manager, Project Assistant, Materials Developer, Statistician and Consultant	1. Opinion & Needs Survey 2. Materials production 3. Research Studies 4. Media Watch 5. Identify strengths for potential candidates 6. Dialogue with Political Parties	1. Women role models identified 2. Training Modules 3. Cadre of Researchers 4. Increased use of Media 5. WID Section in Party Manifestos
III. Leadership, Political Training & Research	June 1995 - January 1999	Project Assistant, Materials Developer, and Consultant	1. Workshops to build capacity for women in the political pipeline 2. Training for NGOs 3. Campaign Management 4. Voter Education etc. 5. Research Studies	1. Increase in Women's awareness 2. Increase in demand and supply of information 3. Cadre of trainers and potential women candidates

Fig. 25. "Communication Line," a schematic depiction of the Fiji WIP network; and "Expected outputs and outcomes of activities." (From Fiji WIP project proposal, August 1994, 10 and 18. Reproduced courtesy of the National Council of Women, Fiji.)

demonstrates, instead, is the order and type of these. Where the analytical power and aesthetic appeal of the Network lies in the way it crosses the spaces imagined to separate focal points—spaces that, as we saw, were generated by the optical effect of the design—in the Matrix the lines of the grid are given, and it is the spaces that demanded aesthetic and analytical attention.

If the discussion in this chapter has focused on the activating uses of the incompleteness of the matrix form, we now can recognize that the Network, also, evidenced an incompleteness of a kind. A careful scrutiny of "Communication Line," for example, might prompt a number of questions: What kind of "communication" is signified by the lines in this case? Do these acts of communication take place all at once or over time? Who exactly communicates with whom, why, how, and from where? The incompleteness of the Network as analysis inheres in the nature of formalism, and it engenders a desire for specifics internal to the device. The Network is a figure that points to its own gaps.[22]

Moreover, these literally are the same spaces depicted graphically in the Network diagram, for, as we saw, the spaces or distances crossed by the Network were not "real" geographical spaces but rather spaces generated by the way the Network made personal relationships technical. These are also precisely the spaces filled by the words in the Matrix in figure 25. The Matrix provides a wealth of specifics; it "historicizes" the Network's self-sociology, we might say, and even makes room for practice. It adds people and particular projects and their outcomes. Yet a careful perusal of this particular list generates questions of its own: what does the collection of persons and actions add up to in this case? If we do all the things listed on the Matrix, what do we have? The answer is "Communication Line." Viewed twice from the same point of view, the figure turns itself inside out so that the Network makes evident the outside form while in the Matrix it is the inside and content that come most easily into view.[23]

Action, then, consists of the movement from one form to the other, of the way the figure is viewed twice. If the Network and the Matrix are forms of analysis, then, as the comments of the Beijing Conference secretary-general indicated, Action is simply what analysis is not. An empty term, like "Network," and like the emptiness of the Network form, it is also a powerful concept that captures the very power of form itself. The periodic search for meaning, performances of activism, or appeals to fixity described as the articulation of desire earlier in this chapter, then, all can be understood as devices for moving back and forth between views, as is the alternative frustration and excitement people feel as they go about the work of networking, planning, drafting, or analyzing their documents—hence the periodic and temporary quality of the encounter with the Real.

We also now can understand better the character of "issues"—what was given in the Matrix and what provided the basis for filling it in. Issues also provide the organizational principle for Networks, as when people described a Network as having "three issues." As much as analytical outcomes, the new "issues" of the Beijing document, for example, were collections of women—displaced women, the girl child, older women, indigenous women, and so on. One member of the Pacific NGO Coordinating Group told me of her dissatisfaction with the Pacific issues (decolonization, denuclearization, and indigenous rights) because they seemed marginal to many "women's experience" (the

Real) in Fiji. When she raised this issue with other members of the group, however, they insisted that the Pacific needed these issues to "stand out" since every region had violence, gender discrimination, or poverty. What these focal points understood was that issues actually create the possibility of new networks; they are designs for a Network form, we might say. No wonder, then, that the issues were given in both the Matrix and the Network, that these alone remained fixed as the figure pivoted back and forth between views.

My point is that in the Matrix information, politics, issues, and all the other emblems of Action are purely and simply a design for a Network. What is important to understand, however, is that all of these are encountered in the register of analytical *failure*, as a lack or an absence—as if something is missing from the analysis. We can rephrase this as a matter of my own analysis: the possibilities and failures encountered in the previous chapters inhere in the character of the design. At once literally present and eternally elusive, the essence of substance and utterly vacuous, the Real is an apt subject for such a design. The following chapter considers some of the implications of the reach of the form.

CHAPTER 7

Network!

What was clear by the time of the Nairobi conference was that researchers and academic institutions, governments, the media, women's organizations, and interested individuals all needed information that was hard to obtain. Also, it was clear that a history and evolution of ideas translated into action and into official UN publications had to be documented. (Fraser 1987: x)

A further perceptual change needs, however to be added as the catalyst to action: that was the appearance of what has been rather inelegantly labeled the "can-do" mentality. This was the perception that complex social and economic problems were manageable, and did not need to be met with passive resignation. There was a procedural confidence, based upon a conviction that the underlying causes of difficulties were understood, which sustained a belief in the efficacy of action: in some areas, the mix of attitudes which led to the holding of the global conferences was extraordinary, and could not have arisen before the late twentieth century. (Taylor 1993: 122)

The necessary actions will not be taken for [women] based on some theoretical principle of equality. Women have researched and they have been the subjects of research. The statistics are much too gloomy in a number of key areas such as poverty, education and illiteracy, health, violence against women, governance and politics, and human rights. With the statistics and facts now well documented, there is no denying that women fare badly relative to men. . . . When the facts and statistics are disaggregated, the undeniable fact is that action is required to change the status quo. Action is the only way forward. There is no substitute. (Mongella 1995d: 10–11)

As I was completing this conclusion, the news came across the radio that President Clinton had ordered the bombing of sites in Afghanistan and the Sudan on the grounds that the sites were part of a "network of terrorists." In the *New York Times* account the following day, the statement did not appear in quotations—the term had become a *fact:* there existed a network of terrorists (Risen 1998: A1). What the president had done was to avail himself of the devices I have described—the Network in the broader sense: the absence of an analytical link between the targets of the American attack and the recent bombings of U.S. embassies in Kenya and Tanzania, or for that matter between the targets in the Sudan and those in Afghanistan, the absence of a link between cause and effect or means and end, could be overcome with an invocation of Network.

We have here a simple illustration of the central insight of this book: that the effectiveness of the Network is generated by the Network's self-description. As we have seen, the naming of a Network is the existence of a Network, and the existence of a Network is synonymous with Action on its behalf. The Network *is* analysis (the missing "link"), and it supersedes reality; in other words, one need not show a link once one pronounces the existence of a network. The "network of terrorists" also illustrates a second principal observation concerning the Network, and that is its inherent recursivity, the Network's endless reflection on itself. In the endless conferences and panel discussions that animated networkers' lives, as we saw, one was "doing" something for and on behalf of the Network by talking about the Network and the way others talked about it. I have aimed to suggest that the anxieties that globalization causes anthropologists might be better channeled into understanding the effectiveness of the forms of the global such as the Network—that is, the effectiveness of form in generating the effect of effectiveness.

Networks and networklike forms of analysis have captured the collective imagination across a span of contemporary disciplines and purposes. In international law and international relations theory, for example, networks as observable institutional organizations of governments and NGOs are widely viewed as more flexible, more progressive, more sophisticated forms of international action, which hold out the hope of success where the state system has failed (e.g., Jönsson 1986; Brysk 1993).[1] Liberal institutions such as the Ford Foundation have invested heavily both in research into the study of networks and in the establishment of networks of human rights activists, women's rights advocates, and environmentalists (Sikkink 1993: 420). One such foundation-supported network, Asia-Pacific Women in Politics, which, in January 1994, was launched and funded by the Asia Foundation, an international aid agency closely tied to the U.S. government, is the producer of the ingenious diagrams discussed in chapter 5. As described to me by its Fiji "focal point," however, the Network might raise questions for the democratic principles it is thought to implement:

> I think maybe for us we just decided to call it a network, because it is just limited to that, it's a loose, not so formal organization, sort of thing . . . [in] an organization, then you have to be accountable to an executive or to a

council or to a board or something like, which we are not. Each of us is just accountable to our Asia Foundation, which is funding in our country.

Nevertheless, networks, in the liberal international relations view, can serve as conduits for the flow not only of information but of enlightenment. Sikkink, for example, notes that they serve "as carriers of human rights ideas" (1993: 437). Documents and documentation processes play a key role in this process: Sikkink offers as an example of an international network success story the "documentation" of abuses by human rights networks, which pass their documents on to the U.S. State Department for inclusion in yet another document genre, the U.S. annual human rights report (422).

If the vision of political change presented here seems askance, the process-oriented aspect of the vision, with its emphasis on the implicit political and cultural impact of daily social practices, is highly reminiscent of sociological analysis: "Every report, conference, or letter from the network underscores an alternative understanding: the basic rights of individuals are not the exclusive domain of the state but are a legitimate concern of the international community" (Sikkink 1993: 441). Drawing upon the sociologist Nicholas Luhmann's systemic theory of social organization as autopoesis (e.g., 1985), the legal scholar Günther Teubner has embraced the Network as a corporate organizational form. The Network, Teubner argues, is "not *between*, but *beyond* contract and organization" (1993: 42) because of its self-organizing quality. It possesses the capability of internally distinguishing and calibrating opposing elements and demands such as variety against redundancy, hierarchy against egalitarian ad hoc arrangements, or collectivity against individual autonomy so that each network transaction leaves the system transformed (48–49): "self-referential circles loop together in such a way as to form new elements which constitute a new system" autonomous from the previous one (43). The international law and international relations theorist Anne-Marie Slaughter appeals to these same networked powers when she argues that in the "real new world order"

> [t]he state is not disappearing, it is disaggregating into its separate, functionally distinct parts. These parts—courts, regulatory agencies, executives, and even legislatures—are networking with their counterparts abroad, creating a dense web of relations that constitutes a new, transgovernmental order. (1997: 184)

Networks, in other words, are systems that create themselves.

The Network's claim to spontaneous, collective, and internally generated expansion and its ability to create systems that preserve the heterogeneous quality of their elements imbues its extension and enhancement with a certain normativity. Its existence is a good in itself. No one, it would seem, could possibly be "against" networks (whether or not they achieve other ends), for the Network is simply a technical device for doing what one is already doing, only in a more efficient, principled, and sophisticated way. When states or organizations can reach consensus about nothing else, they always can agree to "strengthen information networks." In this sense, the Network form is the opposite of political motive, strategy, or content. The seemingly universal appeal of networks, furthermore, is enhanced by the fact that networks are imagined as fragile entities: they are easily interrupted or destroyed by the cessation of funding, the waning of commitment, the creation of an alternative network, the ineffectiveness of the "links," or the inappropriate actions of the focal points. Networks must be created, sustained, and made to expand, and this need enlists collective interest and commitment to Action.

In its parody of social scientific analysis, moreover, the Network plays on academic sentimentality about finally having found a "people" who speak our language, who answer our questions on our own terms. It appeals to our collective fantasy about linking up with our subjects and finding in the "data" exactly what we set out to find. The idea of the Network, as the term is used here and by the subjects of this study as a form that supersedes analysis and reality, might also be imagined to borrow from the reflexive turn in the social sciences—from the notion that there is no longer such a thing as dependent and independent variables, that causes and effects are all mutually constituted in an endless feedback loop.

Social scientists' captivation with the Network in all its dimensions belies a rapprochement between institutional politics and social scientific analysis and perhaps even a collective responsibility for the borrowing of social scientific models to new globalizing effects. We academics are all inside the Network in one way or another[2]—we are skilled in the ways of funding applications described in chapter 5; we are members of "networks" of various kinds; and often we even participate in the policy arena of the kind described in this book. The Network also opens up opportunities for continuing existing projects in different guise. In their review of social movements scholarship, Simons, Mechling, and Shreier conclude that "whatever the political consequences of the protests of the 1960s and early 1970s, they surely yielded scholarly progress" (1984: 840). The dominant mode of analysis, I argued in chapter 4, has shifted from critique to networking.

Before we pronounce the Network as the new panacea, however, it may be worth considering what it leaves out.[3] Although in Beijing there was perhaps more agreement than ever before, this may have been because there was more that could not be said and did not even need to be excluded or argued over in the sound bite atmosphere engendered precisely by the aura of inclusiveness, the effort to give every voice its thirty seconds of airing.[4] One example will illustrate the nature of the exclusion.

The Consequences of Network Failure

In December 1994, a conference of women activists from the Pacific colonies and occupied territories launched a new network. Named the Omomo Melen Pacific (Women Lifeblood of the Pacific), the network brought together activists from Aotearoa (New Zealand), Australia, Bougainville, East Timor, Kanaky (New Caledonia), Tahiti, and West Papua (Irian Jaya). As one participant wrote in her report to the aid organization that funded her attendance at the meeting:

> It was agreed that we had to set up a clear agenda for the last day in order to activate our own network. Everyone felt very strong about this network being the first and most important goal of our meeting. As a network we can enter Beijing in a unified manner. It was also mentioned that not just Beijing is important but also the network in itself to help our respective struggles. . . . The most important aim was to work on forming a network. (Jouwe 1994)

The network was convened by Susanna Ounei, a veteran of the Kanak Liberation Movement then working as assistant director for decolonization at the Pacific Concerns Resource Centre (PCRC).[5] Mindful of the importance of "political analysis," Susanna had carefully chosen participants in whose politics she had personal confidence. The network's short-term goal was to participate in a visible way in the Beijing Conference: participants hoped to use their new organizational form to bring attention to liberation struggles in each country.

There was no discussion, at this meeting or subsequently, about why a "network" might prove the most appropriate or effective organizational form, what exactly a network might entail, or what limitations or constraints it might impose. Susanna showed little interest in the network form as such and never suggested any particular challenge to the concept of network or networking. To her and the other network members, it seemed like an a priori contentless entity—unlike "feminism," for example, which they saw as fraught with liberal First World values. Networks were inconsequential givens; what mattered was the particular character of *this* network.

From the beginning, however, despite ardent commitment to a common "struggle" and the network, they encountered organizational difficulties. Several participants could not attend the first meeting due to what many interpreted as political sabotage (in one case a plane ticket failed to reach a delegate from Kanaky; in another an activist from Bougainville fell ill just before her departure). Language differences compounded what participants described as the danger of "lack of follow-up." The network also struggled to procure funding from donors who feared that supporting it might constitute political involvement in the affairs of another state. After acquiring small amounts of money from activist groups and private aid agencies, Susanna ultimately turned to private donations and personal loans to keep the network afloat.

The network ideal of constant communication likewise seemed ambushed by hundreds of practical distractions and difficulties. Some of the Bougainvillian and West Papuan "members" of the network lived in remote villages and border camps a dangerous day's journey from a radio telephone, and relaying messages proved extremely difficult. For Susanna, the incongruity between the expectations of donors and the weakness of the communications links was a source of continual frustration. For example, in order to receive funding for a Kanak member of the network to attend the Beijing conference it was necessary to procure a one-page personal statement in English along with a set of passport photos and a completed form from a participant who lived in a remote village without a radio phone, spoke only Kanak and French, and had no photographic equipment at her disposal. Susanna's office, unlike those of other focal points, contained few newsletters or reports, and consisted only of several scattered piles of documents spread out on the floor beside a small desk.

Susanna also encountered numerous difficulties in soliciting responses to her faxes and getting network members to produce the written materials that constituted prototypical network outputs. Like all other networks, this one was to produce a "document" that it would "take to Beijing." When Susanna and I first discussed producing the document, I suggested that we follow standard network procedures and simply ask each focal point to contribute a certain amount of text, which we then could collate into a single document. Susanna laughed out loud at the suggestion; we would never receive the text if we requested it. Given the activist politics of this particular network, there was a political problem (in addition to the usual administrative difficulty) with writing accounts of others' liberation struggles. We solved the problem by resorting to another standard network tactic. Using my tape recordings of the initial network meeting, we transcribed each member's oral statement into textual form, thus transforming the meeting into a document. In the end, Susanna completed the preparations for the conference not through the formal linkages of the network but through one or two close personal connections who had little to do with the network per se. This preparation fell considerably short of the grand plan outlined at the network's first meeting.

If much of the expansive rhetoric of networks implicates a drive to develop linkages between networks, likewise, the Omomo Melen Pacific network seemed chronically out of step with the network ethos. Susanna was utterly, purposely unaware of connections of any kind other than her personal connections to other activists. Unlike other networkers in Suva, she showed little interest in how she came to be chosen to deliver a plenary speech at the Beijing Conference, for example, explaining offhandedly only that "some lady called. Can't remember her name." Invariably, she ignored both last names and institutional affiliations of the persons in the wider networks in which she interacted, referring to them only as Sue, Maria, or Makareta. The thought of working with other networks or focal points in Suva was impossible, likewise, since she distrusted them as "apolitical" or worse. The regional focal points had purposely given her the wrong information concerning the registration deadline for the PrepCom to keep the true Pacific activists from attending so that they could claim that status, she insisted. Other networkers in Suva admired Susanna as a prototype of "the activist," that is, what they claimed to be, and they even sought her endorsement for their own activism in many situations. But they also regarded her as a kind of terrorist, someone who would do as she pleased without regard for the unstated rules of proper conduct. For her part, it seemed that she sometimes wreaked havoc at conferences by publicly challenging speakers or denouncing host governments or aid agencies out of sheer boredom with the banality of Network politics. "I hate this place—it's killing me," she once said. "There are no good causes, arguing with these idiotic women. Even the scenery is dull here."

Likewise, in stark contrast to other networks in Suva, the principal analytical tool of Omomo Melen Pacific was critique (cf. chap. 4). For example, one of Susanna's great triumphs, from her own point of view, was a speech made at the UN PrepCom. The day before the speech, she had questioned the French delegate about the sincerity of her commitment to women in the context of French nuclear testing and colonization in Tahiti and Kanaky. The delegate had responded that such issues were "too specific for this forum"—a technically accurate response given the inadmissibility of concrete facts in the negotiation (see chap. 3). In her speech, however, Susanna seized on this notion of specificity. She listed a series of what she called "specifics"—women dying from the poisoning of radiation, women killed by French soldiers, women raped while imprisoned on trumped up charges—and in her speech she emphasized, sarcastically, that such matters apparently were "too specific" for the French delegation.

The Beijing Conference proved to be a disappointment for the Omomo Melen Pacific network. Several focal points from the French colonies never arrived, as their passports had mysteriously disappeared in the courier shipment from the Chinese Embassy after the issuing of their visas in Suva. One Bougainvillian could not travel due to the severity of the conflict there. The "document" that Susanna had labored so hard to produce likewise was held at customs without cause by the Chinese authorities for the duration of the conference, and she spent many precious hours attempting to reach the responsible customs agents by letter, telephone, and facsimile. In the sea of humanity, banners, fliers, and noise at the rain- and mud-drenched conference site, those members of the network who attended seemed to spend most of their time searching for one another. Even the simplest tasks, such as locating materials to make banners, proved inconceivably difficult—something the more experienced focal points had anticipated. In desperation, network members finally tore up their hotel bedsheets for makeshift national flags and banners.

Most of all, it seemed painfully difficult to attract attention to Pacific decolonization struggles in the face of thousands of other groups, each seeking to highlight its own causes and injustices in the few seconds of attention a journalist or participant might give it. The Asia and Pacific NGO Coordinating Group scheduled a press conference and invited Susanna and other members of the network to speak. Yet, when network members arrived for the press conference, they found a small outdoor space several meters square, just steps from other groups performing dances, holding demonstrations, and giving speeches and press conferences of their own. The only "press" that attended were one or two personal acquaintances of the speakers with media contacts in the Pacific and one or two young freelance writers without any clear prospects for publication. The network members did their best to present their case. Yet as each spoke of the human suffering in their own countries, the details were sacrificed for sake of brevity and comprehensibility to an (imaginary) outside audience. It would have been difficult to convey the importance of their message to an audience that had heard nothing but heart-wrenching accounts and important messages over the last week of the conference in any case. How could they compete, for example, against the eloquence and tears of the American actress Sally Field, who that morning had presented the story of her recent visit to a refugee camp to a cheering and suitably moved audience? How could the details of a massacre of twenty persons in New Caledonia, told in halting English, capture attention in the face of passing motorcades and the swirling colors of banners and costumes? The background noise of clashing cymbals and demonstration slogans seemed aptly to capture the impossibility of being heard.[6]

Fact Finding and the Form of Global Politics

International lawyers have long understood that to assert the existence of an international system is to bring it into existence (Kennedy 1987). However, in "information" and its networks there is a "new"[7] and even more effective tool than the rhetoric and doctrine that academics once used with these assertions. A small example will illustrate the device: in 1995, the UNDP issued a document entitled *Human Development Report* (UNDP 1995) containing statistical indicators that ranked UN member states according to the relative "status of women" in each. Fiji's relatively low ranking according to this "gender-related development index" caused considerable debate in the local press and was often cited by NGOs and government officials in speeches and documents. The competitive possibilities engendered by the simplicity of numerical ranking caught the attention of institutional participants in a way that admonitions or appeals to violations of international law had not.[8] In its emphasis on Action through information gathering, then, the Beijing Conference was emblematic of a growing trend.

International law is increasingly governance by *fact,* as fact-finding becomes one of the principal competencies of the UN and other intergovernmental institutions. The efficacy of the secretary-general over the last decade is often credited largely to the frequent and effective use of the office's fact-finding powers, for example. Since 1987, the office includes an Office for Research and the Collection of Information, which creates data banks, monitors potential emergencies, and produces weekly information bulletins. Christiane Bourloyannis, of the Codification Division of the UN Office of Legal Affairs, brushes aside member states' concerns about the infringement of such policies on national sovereignty, noting that in the end efficient information gathering is in the interest of all member states "[i]n the contemporary era of communication, in which information often is the determinant of power" (Bourloyannis 1990: 669). The UN's fact-finding activities likewise have become the contemporary site of cooperation and conflict between international organizations and NGOs (Steiner 1991: 66). The International Monetary Fund's governance of the developing world is accomplished through its fact-finding missions and reports as much as through the leverage of its purse strings (Harper 1998). A considerable literature in international politics analyzes the institutions of the European Union as a network—a "flexible and dynamic" entity that "receives a much higher level of commitment from its members" and is thus more sophisticated than an international organization (Keohane and Hoffman 1991: 10; cf. Borzel 1997). The European Union Council Regulation establishing the European Environmental Agency in 1990 likewise specifies that its tasks are

> To provide the member states and the Community with information; to collect, record and assess data on the state of the environment; to encourage harmonization of the methods of measurement; to promote the incorporation of European environmental information into international monitoring programmes; to ensure data dissemination; to co-operate with other Community bodies and international institutions. (Majone 1997: 263)

Under such conditions, "the environment," "women," or "culture" exist to be documented, exist *because* they are documented.

The standardization of informational processes is increasingly tantamount to the Rule of Law. The International Organization for Standardization, an organization of governments and international institutions based in Geneva and in consultative status with all the major UN bodies, is only one example. Since its founding in 1947, it has been devoted to producing international standards for information exchange. The organization has published ten thousand different kinds of communication standards; among the most influential is an official set of public information symbols, artifacts of graphic design empirically tested to demonstrate their intelligibility to people of different cultures. Old debates about the legal basis of international institutions, of their authority to act in the absence of the express consent of states, which have plagued international law since its inception (Hall 1880; Wheaton 1866; Franck 1988; Falk 1970), find themselves swept aside by the benign objective of information sharing and by the expediency of the call to Action.

Policy studies scholars now routinely argue that "indirect, information-based modes of regulation" that depend on powers of "persuasion" rather than compulsion are "actually more in tune with current economic, technological and political conditions" (Majone 1997: 264). The emphasis is on providing information about market and other forms of risk to private parties in cases of environmental problems, for example, rather than on banning a certain kind of high-risk activity outright, and this privatization of government is understood as a more compassionate form of governmentality—"persuasion" rather than "compulsion" (266–67). Majone adds that in order for this strategy to succeed, however, international agencies must enter into "networks" that will ensure that, like individuals in a team, the agencies have an incentive to uphold their commitments and professional standards (272).

The rationale for global governance by fact is a familiar one from the discussion of Action in chapter 6: the possibilities for measurement, comparison, or gridlike equivalency that inhere in the informational form—however metaphorical its relationship to the Real—prompt member states to action and engender *commitment* in a way that the doctrinal and political bases of international law have consistently failed to do. UN Secretary-General Boutros Boutros-Ghali appealed to these possibilities on the occasion of International Women's Day 1994:

> To examine the situation of women . . . is to provide both a yardstick, and a measure, of progress. We can see from the situation of women in a society whether power and entitlements are distributed fairly. We can see from women's health statistics, or from information about women's educational attainments, how developed a society really is. (INSTRAW and UNIFEM 1995)

To an anthropological mind, this ranking of societies according to a parallel ranking of the "situation of women" is perhaps disturbing. Yet, if we are to understand such comments ethnographically, we must read them as classic enlistments of the *form* of information, an effort to prompt the member states to action and commitment through an appeal to the yardstick, the measurement, the competitive possibilities of fact.

Unlike the designs of an early era of modernist activism, which aimed to transcend "real" distances and differences of culture, therefore, in the Network the question of transcultural efficacy is internal to the form. As we have seen, these forms displace the global/local with something far more mundane and in so doing foreclose the question of "cultural difference," at least for the moment of their apprehension. This effect of design is by no means simply a bureaucrat's trick. The reappearance of battle shields among the Wahgi of the Western Highlands of Papua New Guinea, after years of disuse following European pacification, has seen the addition to the shield designs of words, numbers, and graphic images from advertisements that are "significant *by virtue* of being graphical marks" (O'Hanlon 1995: 481). These graphics literally precede social groups in the imagined battles for which the shields are made. Graphics, for the Wahgi, then, are what is intelligible even to one's enemies; they are a face to the outside, a universal language.

By now, it will be no surprise that this turn to the facts in international law accompanies a turn away from midcentury realism "back to formalism, general rules and judicial processes, a formalism which, however, had always been latent in realism itself" (Koskenniemi 1995: 11). Whether in negotiation or fact-finding, therefore, design now precedes agreement, an earlier era's way of transcending so-called cultural difference. Indeed, a system of international law grounded in consent now seems almost quaintly outmoded in comparison with the designs that elicit commitment and desire even as they internally generate the very cultural difference they transcend.[9] Again, to critique such forms for the worldview latent in the facts would miss the point, for the character of the device is something much more powerful: the manufacture of desire through mundane "technicalities," the activating power of unnoticed forms.

Such patterns, which seemingly extend everywhere, might raise new questions about the place of academic analysis and critique. At the close of "The work of art in the age of mechanical reproduction," Benjamin considers the mass appeal and political uses of film. Noting that "reproduction [of film technology] is aided especially by the reproduction of masses" in patterns of parades and demonstrations that provided an image for such films ([1955] 1973: 243, n. 21), Benjamin concludes that through endlessly reproducible aesthetic devices such as film "Fascism sees its salvation in giving these masses not their right, but instead a chance to express themselves.... The logical result of Fascism is the introduction of aesthetics into political life" (234). The politics of early-twentieth-century propaganda films lay precisely in the opportunities generated by the form and the way in which the form enlisted *commitment*, demanded participation. The designs of the UN world conferences, with their endless cycles of inputs, might serve as a perfect example of a form in which everyone gets a chance, and nothing more than a chance, at self-expression (cf. Balkin 1992).[10]

Benjamin's solution lay in "politicizing art"—the Marxist call to political critique alluded to in chapter 4 and the Bauhaus call to high modernist activism through design alluded to in chapter 5. Yet the conferences described here pose a dual challenge to this call. On the one hand, in the ultimate victory of this modernist project of universal design, the UN conferences subvert critique of the aesthetics of politics by rendering it impossible to imagine a political life without "aesthetics." Conversely, in the world conferences and the designs described in this book we find design already "politicized" and even generating political commitment from within.

Of course, it is easy to see nonliberal politics as all about matters of form. As Benjamin and others have noted, fascism made of aesthetics an explicit question since the problem for critics was always how to explain the collective and irrational behavior that fascism engendered (Falasca-Zamponi 1997).[11] The forms of liberal rationalism, and its accompanying humanism (Malkki 1996), are more difficult to bring into view. Martin Jay describes a second tradition of critique, associated with Paul de Man and Terry Eagleton, which understands the "aesthetic ideology" of fascism as the *completion* of the politics of liberal reason rather than its opposite (1993: 75–76). In this view, "aesthetics is attacked not because it is formally cold and antihumane, but rather because it is human-all-too-human" (77).

To put the point in terms of the argument of this book, the forms of liberal rationalism are impervious to critique because they point not to themselves but to the gaps within the form, and beyond, to the Real: the point in President Clinton's justification is the terrorist, not the Network, and the same could be said of the place of "Women" in the networks I have described. Moreover, the forms considered in this book cleverly exploit our collective expectations that matters of rational agreement are not matters of form and vice versa and in so doing shade the forms that supersede and displace agreement itself.

International law and politics in the mode of information, then, represent not so much a revolution of norms as a perfection of form. What is interesting is the way form generates consensus where content and doctrine could never do so. One of the features most commented upon by delegates to the Beijing Conference and NGO Forum from Fiji and elsewhere who had attended previous women's conferences was the comparatively high degree of "consensus" on the "issues." Where delegates at previous meetings had been acrimoniously divided over whether structural adjustment or the Palestinian liberation were in fact "women's issues" (Fraser 1987: 2; Jacquette 1995), at this meeting Fiji's participants in the academic women's networks from "the South" who had led the fight for the expansion of what counted as women's issues at previous conferences found, to their own surprise, that most of the European and North American attendees at their sessions were in fact converts to their position (cf. Anand 1996). How and why this "consensus" might have arisen—the agreed bases of institutional knowledge—is the ultimate subject of this book.

If critical analysis is to have something more than a "place" in the figure, however, it now will be necessary to develop an alternative point of access. I have imagined the previous chapters as a series of experiments in working the form ethnographically against itself. By way of conclusion, I wish to address one further point of access, namely, the question of why the "global" of global conferences or the "international" of international law should be conceived as a scaled entity in the first place.

This book has focused on numerous instances of what I have called a figure seen twice. In each case, the trick of the device inhered in the way that a two-dimensional design generated an optical effect of dimension and depth. For example, a network diagram, seen twice, could be viewed as crossing great distances and incorporating persons, machines, or institutions. Likewise, as described in chapter 6, the matrix and network forms seen twice became inside and outside to one another. The appeal of the internally generated global form that ensued from the double vision inhered in the way that a simple, mundane, and ubiquitous organizational tool such as a matrix, drawn on a sheet of paper or printed from a computer, might frame and contain an entity of global proportions such as the Network and vice versa.

For the subjects of this study as for anthropological observers, the discovery of the design's internal possibilities for generating scale was aesthetically effective only because at times it was shielded from view. We have seen numerous examples of momentary and fleeting apprehensions of depth or scale proceeded and ultimately replaced by a design contained within a singular plane. In chapter 3, for example, the surface weave of the negotiated text gave way, at points, to infinite gaps within the brackets, just as there were moments in the course of negotiations in which delegates turned away from their focus on the technical details and were overcome with the sheer number of hours of work, people, conferences, and drafts that had preceded them in the production of the *Platform for Action*. Likewise, the optical effect generated by the Matrix as Network seen twice depended initially on the existence of a simple grid that placed entities of all kinds in a singular plane.

All of the forms considered here share another feature. As abstract graphic designs, they can be large or small while keeping the same form, and they provide no clues as to their scale, no internal means of evaluating their "size" or their "significance." The extension of the Network or the replication of the pattern of the *Platform for Action* structure into a newsletter in Fiji did not alter the pattern, for example. The same is true of percentages, indicators, and all the other forms of statistical data that brought "women" into view. The patterned relationship among members keeps its form whatever their size, that is, whatever their (external) reference points may be.

Ironically, it was the figures' internal failures that enabled this optical effect of variation in scale. The gaps within the Matrix, for example, engendered a desire for the figure's completion, and it was this apprehension of the figure's internal lack that generated the desire to fill in the gaps that in turn brought the Network diagram to the foreground. The uses of statistics as a "yardstick," in the UN secretary-general's term, for the status of women made of women (and UN governance) a coherent category by shielding the limitations of the numbers from view. To critique the statistics for what was left out, then, as anthropologists might feel compelled to do, ultimately would miss the point, for the "lack" is already well appreciated by the statistics' users. Yet this interest in size, and the apprehension of gaps in what was known among urban Whippys, for example, departed from the knowledge of land among the Whippys in Kasavu, where in informational terms, people lacked nothing. For them it was the land itself, not the tools of analysis, that generated possibilities of scale. At first view, a survey map was an entity of a different scale than the land, since it could be held by clan leaders, as an item in a collection of documents, as land could not. Yet where the sole analytical relationship between map and territory consisted in the fixed equation of quantity, one that a two-dimensional drawing could reproduce to perfection, then the map and the territory could also be viewed again as entities of identical scale. Strathern has noted the information loss that accompanies academics' shifts from analysis at one level of scale to another (1991: 95). The point is that such failure is internal to the form and is also the engine of its ultimate effectiveness, the means of turning inside out and thus stimulating the momentary apprehension of depth.

We now can understand better what the forms that generate the global share. Such forms leave room for infinite flexibility in their relationship to whatever might lie beyond and ultimately only signify the Real, as the outside, within the parameters of the design. Both perfectly complete and utterly vacuous, forms such as facts and matrices, brackets full of text, or numbers and networks enable viewers to share everything and nothing, as does, for example, "knowing the facts." As such, the celebration of humanity as commonality and difference enacted at the UN Fourth World Conference on Women is the ideal design for a new global politics.

"It was living inside *Time* Magazine!" one friend repeatedly said of the experience of serving as a Fiji government delegate to the Beijing Conference. She proceeded to describe the diversity of events and cultures all around her there, and the experience of becoming the subject of global news, as an example of being at the center of things. The experience of encompassment within a magazine's patterns of words and graphics no doubt is a common encounter with the forms that define "the global." Where the forms exploit their own internal spaces to produce the effect of being all around us, it is no wonder that much of the exhaustion that pervades our understanding of the literature on transnationalism and globalization derives from a sense that analysis has no further room to expand.

Notes

Preface

1. Research was conducted primarily in English in Suva and overseas and in both English and Fijian in Vanua Levu. Public events such as conferences and panel discussions were tape recorded and transcribed where feasible.

Chapter 1

1. In their study of anthropological context, Goodwin and Duranti write, "A relationship between two orders of phenomena that mutually inform each other to comprise a larger whole is absolutely central to the notion of context" (1992: 4).
2. I have also been inspired by Roy Wagner's parallel image of the "holographic or self-scaling form which differs from a 'social organization' or a cultural ideology in that it is not imposed so as to order and organize, explain or interpret, a set of disparate elements. It is an instantiation of the elements themselves" (1991: 166).
3. Sherry Ortner comments that "public culture is both the subject and object vis-à-vis the ethnographer" (1998: 414). She adds that the cause of the shift is the abandonment of the "anthropological trick" of distance and exoticism (433).
4. In referring to the aesthetics of information, I borrow Bateson's interest in information as an attention to "the pattern which connects" (1980: 8) and Strathern's definition of aesthetics as "the persuasiveness of form, the elicitation of a sense of appropriateness" (1991: 10). This understanding differs in important respects from more Kantian notions of aesthetics prevalent in the anthropology of art on the one hand and more Foucauldian approaches to the character of information and knowledge on the other, but it also finds parallels in the careful attention linguistic anthropologists have brought to matters of form and formality in communication (e.g., Brenneis 1996; Irvine 1996).

Bateson's definition of aesthetics, the outcome of his interest in information networks, sought to highlight the extent to which the viewer, producer, and artifact were integrated into the networks each described. Meaning, for Bateson, was synonymous with pattern, and communication worked through the redundancy or predictability of the pattern (1987b: 130). An art object's effectiveness, for example, stemmed from the extent to which it beckoned the viewer to appreciate it as both internally patterned and as part of larger patterns of various kinds (1987c: 130). Bateson's analysis effectively rids the study of art and aesthetics of any penchant for romanticism and demonstrates that to look at something (such as a document) as an aesthetic object need not entail rendering it exotic or strange. Rather, aesthetics, in this definition, stresses identification with both the heterogeneity of actants and their systemic integration.

In a recent essay on the history of mutual influence between anthropology and art, Marcus and Myers (1995: 12–13) cite the notion of "pattern" as influenced by Kroeber in the works of Sapir, Benedict, Mead, Levi-Strauss, and Geertz as a principal influence of early modernist art criticism on the development of anthropology. Bateson's use of the term no doubt borrows from Benedict, whose *Patterns of Culture* he credited for many of his insights in *Naven* and beyond. If Marcus and Myers are correct in their genealogy, one might imagine my redeployment of this term as a return on the debt.

5. In a commentary on the anthropological treatment of events and history, Marilyn Strathern has called for the extension of the conception of the artifact to include events and performances—something "that cannot be domesticated in quite the same way as texts," something prone to display that "draws attention to form" and, as in the case of the museum object, something that resists straightforward contexualization (1990: 40). Most importantly, however, to treat events as artifacts is "to talk about people using an event the way they use a knife, or creating an occasion the way they create a mask." To treat information as artifact, as I do in this book, is to confront the opposite problem, for here is an entity that Euro-Americans straightforwardly assimilate to the knives and masks of others as instruments, technologies, means to other ends. One challenge of this study, therefore, is to see the way in which, in the bureaucratic contexts at the very heart of the Euro-American conception of technology and instrumentality, information might also be event, that is, to make use of the decontextualizing element of the museum term, to anthropological ears, to hear the possibilities that inhere in the familiar without resorting to making it strange.

6. Amitav Ghosh, for example, describes the ethnography of international peace-keeping missions as "a yet uninvented discipline" (1994: 413), while an anthropologist present at the UN Earth Summit has noted that "[s]uch events also open up an entire new field of ethnographic analysis" (Little 1995: 265). Linda Basch, Nina Schiller, and Cristina Blanc, likewise, write of transnationalism as an "idea whose time has come" (1994: 7).

7. For anthropology, the opportunity lies in the willingness of so many scholars and practitioners outside of the discipline to associate the problem of globalization with that old province of anthropology, culture. The sociologist Roland Robertson asserts that "all of international politics is cultural," and he even terms the present "a period of globewide *cultural* politics" (1992: 5, emphasis in the original; cf. Hannerz 1992a). Arjun Appadurai (1991) has noted the appropriation of the anthropological notion of culture in the global domain by literary and cultural studies, and John Borneman has commented on the same appropriation in policy and business studies (Borneman 1998: 6–7). A cultural perspective has found adherents among international lawyers eager to exploit the techniques of ethnography to refute critiques of international law by demonstrating that international law is a "culture" of its own, and thus a viable enterprise, whatever its "legal" premises (e.g., Kennedy 1993). Ironically, then, the global provides both new terrain and a new audience for familiar methods and projects.

8. Keck and Sikkink (1998), for example, argue that "transnational advocacy net-

works" share the following characteristics: "the centrality of values or principled ideas, the belief that individuals can make a difference, the creative use of information, and the employment by nongovernmental actors of sophisticated political strategies in targeting their campaigns" (1998: 2). As this definition suggests, they begin with the assumption that such networks exist to fulfill instrumental ends and thrive in so doing. Conclusions are based on a limited number of interviews with NGO leaders (mostly in the United States and northern Europe) about the purposes and achievements of their networks, not on observation of what "networks" actually "are" and "do."

9. For their part, anthropological writings on international institutions also have tended to take the "expert" knowledge practices of institutional actors as familiar and to concentrate attention on the encounter between such practices and non-Western cultures (e.g., Hobart 1994). The trend belies more than a simple matter of interest, in my view; it points to a problem in accessing institutions in anthropological terms.

10. Michael Herzfeld has made a similar point concerning the strategic invocations of essentialism in everyday life (1997).

11. One example of the replicative rather than transformative character of analyses of the global concerns the lack of critical analytical perspective in this literature on the enhancing, enabling character of information technology. The existence and revolutionary effects of "new communications technologies" are most often assumed, rather than ethnographically explored. Often, the technology that is most enhanced by such an assumption is the theorist himself or herself. For example, a central point of Edwards's discussion (1994) of his ethnography of Afghan culture in the context of military conflict is the innovation of his own displacement—the fact that rather than conducting fieldwork in an Afghan village he finds himself monitoring electronic mail conversations, spending time in a border camp, and meeting with refugees in Washington. Like the information imagined to flow through NGO networks, the anthropologist's knowledge is presented as expanding beyond the horizons of what he or she can physically apprehend. Arthur Stinchcombe (pers. comm.) notes that historical documents have served a similar purpose for sociologists and anthropologists.

In contrast, Richard Harper notes in the context of uses of information technology by British police that empirical studies have shown the actual benefits of these to be very few, although they do alter the character of bureaucratic activity (1991).

12. The governmental portion of the conference was held in Beijing on 4–16 September 1995. The NGO Forum was held in Huairou, China (approximately one hour from Beijing by bus), from 30 August to 8 September.

13. These were: the United Nations International Women's Year Conference held in Mexico City in 1975; the Mid-decade Conference on Women held in Copenhagen in 1980; and the End of the Decade Conference on Women held in Nairobi in 1985.

14. From the point of view of the subjects of this book, the most notable were the Earth Summit (UN Conference on Environment and Development) held in Rio de Janeiro in June 1992, the World Conference on Human Rights held in Vienna in June 1993, the UN Global Conference on the Sustainable Development of Small Island Developing States held in Barbados in April–May 1994, the International Conference on Population and Development (ICPD) held in Cairo in September 1994, and the World Summit for Social Development held in Copenhagen in March 1995.

15. See the interpretive statement by the United States, at the close of the Beijing Conference, that "the Platform, Declaration and commitments made by the States . . . are not legally binding, and they consist of recommendations" (UNFWCW 1995c: 173).

16. Official NGO participation in UN global conferences takes place through NGOs' "consultative status" with the Economic and Social Council (ECOSOC). The criteria for consultative status appear in Article 71 of the United Nations Charter and in ECOSOC Resolution 1296 (XLIV). The most important of these is that the organization must be "international in its structure" (para. 7) and must "represent a substantial proportion, and express the views of major sections, of the population or of the organized persons within the particular field of its competence, covering, where possible, a substantial number of countries in different regions of the world" (para. 4). The sixty-five members of the committee of NGOs (CONGO) who have such status are established, predominantly European and North American NGOs. The only member organizations of CONGO with any contact in the Pacific were the Young Women's Christian Association (YWCA), the Girl Guides, and the International Council of Women. Of the thirty-two NGOs given consultative status with ECOSOC at the founding of the UN, ten were women's organizations (Connors 1996: 151).

One of the changes of procedure at global conferences, beginning with the Rio Conference, was the expansion of the list of consultative NGOs to include a so-called B list of NGOs given consultative status on a one-time basis for that particular conference, based on their competency in the subject matter of the conference, thus enabling groups that might never have had a reason to seek general consultative status to attend a particular conference. In order to gain access to the conference, organizations were required to prove that their "purpose" bore a significant relationship to the meeting and that they were not "purely local" in character (United Nations General Assembly 1993). There was considerable controversy among delegates at the PrepCom and FWCW and in the press surrounding the secretariat's decision, subsequently affirmed by ECOSOC in a number of cases, to deny accreditation to some groups from Tibet and Taiwan, to some lesbian groups, and to several other "controversial" groups (see APWG 1995a).

The second significant change in the negotiation procedure at UN global conferences was the broadening of access to the negotiated text and even to actual negotiation sessions for these NGOs (cf. Willetts 1996). The UN's fostering of parallel NGO Forums at each of the world conferences has further broadened participation beyond accredited organizations and their official delegates (Harris 1985).

17. As Paul Taylor writes of the Rio Conference on the Environment,

> The mixture of technical facilities, together with confidence about the rightness and effectiveness of chosen courses of action, which lay behind efforts in the area of population control, for instance, could only have arisen in recent decades. . . . On the one hand there was a realization of global problems and they demanded the application of a wide range of skills: they demanded a holistic approach. On the other hand was a feeling that learning and research was becoming increasingly compartmentalized and detached from the real world. . . . One consequence of this was that there emerged a new concern to try to link together various branches of knowledge, which showed a tendency to go their separate ways, and to apply them to the

solution of particular problems. There was the need to rearrange the universe of knowledge in order to make it applicable to the real world. (Taylor 1993: 122–24)

18. For its part, the NGO Forum was designed as a formal counterweight to the governmental meeting; it was precisely what that meeting was not. From structural adjustment to yoga, the program of activities advertised a choice of 350 workshop topics each day. As one NGO newsletter emphasized:

> The Forum is not designed to take formal positions; it has no fixed "agenda," and does not adopt resolutions as a body. . . . It is a means of creating and exchanging ideas, and not an end in itself . . . its success lies in the follow-up activities at national level. (APDC 1994: 5)

The parallel NGO Forum has been a standard element of UN world conferences since the 1972 Stockholm Conference on the Environment (Fraser 1987).

19. The twelve critical areas of concern were:

(1) The persistent and increasing burden of poverty on women;
(2) Inequalities and inadequacies in and unequal access to education and training;
(3) Inequalities and inadequacies in and unequal access to health care and related services;
(4) Violence against women;
(5) The effects of armed or other kinds of conflict on women, including those living under foreign occupation;
(6) Inequality in economic structures and policies, in all forms of productive activities and in access to resources;
(7) Inequality between men and women in the sharing of power and decision-making at all levels;
(8) Insufficient mechanisms at all levels to promote the advancement of women;
(9) Lack of respect for and inadequate promotion and protection of the human rights of women;
(10) Stereotyping of women and inequality in women's access to and participation in all communication systems, especially in the media;
(11) Gender inequalities in the management of natural resources and in the safeguarding of the environment;
(12) Persistent discrimination against and violation of the rights of the girl child. (UNFWCW 1995: chap. 3)

20. Fiji government preparations for the Beijing conference included the preparation of "country reports" on the status of women in Fiji and progress reports concerning Fiji's efforts to implement the previous UN world conference document (the "Nairobi Forward Looking Strategies"); the drafting and ministerial endorsement of a *Pacific Platform for Action* together with other Pacific governments; the negotiation and ministerial endorsement of an Asia-Pacific Platform for Action; the formulation of "sub-regional objectives" (for the "Melanesian subregion"); and the formulation of a negotiating position concerning the *Platform for Action*.

21. Officially, the PrepCom was known as the thirty-ninth annual meeting of the Commission on the Status of Women (CSW), an organization of member states established in 1946 to highlight problems concerning women's equality and to formulate development plans aimed at women. Member states are elected on a rotating basis to two-year terms from the wider membership of ECOSOC, the major UN organ of which the CSW is a part. All UN member states and official observers were invited to send delegations to the PrepCom and the FWCW.

22. Throughout this book, the terms *Pacific, South Pacific, Pacific Islands,* and *Pacific Island states* are used not as analytical terms but in the sense in which they are used by the subjects of this book, that is, to signify the member states of the regional intergovernmental institutions—the South Pacific Forum and the South Pacific Commission (now known as the Secretariat of the Pacific Community). The member states of the South Pacific Commission are American Samoa, the Cook Islands, the Federated States of Micronesia, Fiji, French Polynesia, Guam, Kiribati, the Marshall Islands, Nauru, New Caledonia, Niue, the Northern Mariana Islands, Palau, Papua New Guinea, Pitcairn, the Solomon Islands, Tokelau, Tonga, Tuvalu, Vanuatu, Wallis and Futuna, and Western Samoa. In addition, Australia and New Zealand are members of the South Pacific Forum only and are often, although not always, included in this definition.

23. Prior to the Rio Conference, few NGOs from the developing world had the consultative status that would allow them to attend UN conferences, and none of the Pacific NGOs had the funds, knowledge, connections, or international stature to do so.

24. Cris Shore encounters a similar problem in his anthropological study of European Community bureaucrats who seek to create a European identity by deploying symbols and fostering informational exchange among community citizens. As he notes in his contribution to a volume on the anthropology of consciousness, for his informants consciousness is an indigenous category theoretically informed by the same debates as his own (1995: 232).

25. In his comments on Yolngu aesthetics, Weiner writes:

> The inside and outside of Yolngu knowledge refers not to the way such social political conditions differentiate types of knowledge—rather, the facts of social and political differentiation are themselves contingent upon how such knowledge is brought forth in particular ways, through the displaying of painting or the reciting of myths, for example. Inside and outside are descriptions of the contrasting limits within the Yolngu's form-producing procedures, and what such limits make it possible to create as socially enacted perceptual contrasts. The iconicity of Yolngu designs are not the true shape of their world, but a visual rendering of the kinds of forces that make connectivity a vital constituting force of that world. (1995: 44)

26. "As entities in themselves, sets of information proliferate as much from the possibility of magnifying the detail of individual parts as from increasing the whole number of entities being considered" (Strathern 1991: xiv).

27. The "fractal" of chaos theory Strathern borrows as an organizing device is defined by the way in which the same form repeats itself to infinity at every level of scale. The structure of Strathern's account then repeats itself again and again, demonstrating, in ef-

fect, how the problems of collecting and analyzing data repeat themselves in precisely the same pattern at every "level."

28. In *The Meeting*, a study of the institutional culture of a mental health facility, Helen Schwartzman tackles materials similar to those considered here. Her approach "invites the reader to walk into a social system backwards in order to see it and the forms that produce it, in a new way" (1989: 4).

29. The discursive critiques of anthropological writing of the last fifteen years have been built upon the assertion that given the process of selection and ordering that this infinity of information demands, all ethnographic writing is a fiction of sorts. Against this interest in anthropology's truth claims, what I am proposing is not so much a new epistemology as a new aesthetic. One consequence of borrowing one's method from the ethnographic material at hand, however, is that method becomes far more contingent. In other words, contrary to an ethnographic imagination of methods as universal and data as particular, I understand the "method" to be no more general or particular than the "data" to which it is applied. To state the point another way, the contribution of this work is its challenge to the distance between data and method in the ethnographic imagination of information.

30. One design theorist defines the craft according to the following criteria:

> (1) the possibility of a separation of the maker from someone who is responsible for the "blueprint" of the artifact;
> (2) the location of decisions about what is to be produced in the hands of the person who commissions the artifact, usually on the basis of a brief;
> (3) the possibility of multiple "runs" of the object for which the designer constructs a model;
> (4) a tight relationship between this modeling and the economic function of the object in question. (Palmer 1996: 4)

Compare this definition with that of institutional policy that "design is the creation of an actionable form to promote valued outcomes in particular context" (Goodin 1997: 31). Goodin himself expressly disclaims any connection between institutional and graphic design.

31. Of course, the task of making choices from a seemingly infinite body of information is a hallmark of all late modern analysis (Geertz 1973: 10) and one to which chapters 3 and 4 aim to offer something of a counterpoint.

Chapter 2

1. Judith Irvine has described Wolof exchanges of payments for praise songs, a parallel example of "a case where linguistic objects and performances are exchanged for cash and goods" (1996: 259). In drawing attention to the way in which "[t]he verbal sign . . . relates to a political economy in many ways: by denoting it; by indexing parts of it; by depicting it . . . and by taking part in it as an object of exchange" (278), she challenges social scientists' dichotomization of the sign and the material that would render events such as the collapse of PAWORNET a puzzle in the first place.

2. For a survey-based typology of "voluntary organisations" in Suva and their relative importance among different cultural and economic groups during this period, see Mamak 1974.

3. The delegate was a young woman whose family now lived overseas and who was returning from university studies in the United States. Although PPSEAWA had not planned to send a representative, at the woman's mother's request the organization's president agreed to sponsor her as their representative.

4. During the term of my fieldwork, the group sponsored only one meeting, a workshop on the protection of turtles.

5. As she stated in a newspaper interview at the time of her studies, "My interests remain in effective communication techniques for non-formal adult education programmes. . . . The ways in which people communicate with each other and with the rest of the community, the community itself have always been of particular interest to me" (*Fiji Times*, 27 September 1975).

6. In 1976, that conflict came to a head. The Board of Directors fired the director and several other top administrators, and the remainder of the staff staged a strike. The activist contingent responded by calling a meeting of the membership to oust the board. They rewrote the constitution, elected new board members, and ultimately reinstated the director ("Two mole Y staff expelled" 1976; "Suva Y votes" 1976; Reid 1976). Nevertheless, the director resigned the following year (YWCA 1977).

7. However, during the course of my fieldwork one such person took up a major position in a regional WID organization and participated actively in the Beijing Conference in that capacity. Likewise, the former director of the Fiji YWCA returned to Suva from many years' work at YWCA headquarters in Geneva and was hired by UNIFEM.

8. In 1987, a military coup overthrew the democratically elected Labour and National Federation parties government. The postcoup political leadership justified the coup in terms of the necessity of safeguarding indigenous Fijian interests and of upholding the status of Christianity in Fiji given the presence of Fiji Indians in the elected government.

9. Although Fiji's Methodist Church follows the Wesleyan teachings associated with other Methodist churches worldwide, it is entirely independent.

10. The SPC-sponsored Seminar of South Pacific Women, which recommended the establishment of the PWRB, was the first intergovernmental conference focusing on women of this genre. This conference enlisted expert consultants, engaged in document drafting, and was funded by large quantities of overseas aid (SPC 1981; Pryor 1981). The comments of delegates recorded in the press foreshadow the practices described in this book. As one delegate said: "We're fed up with meetings where people ask us to identify our needs. . . . We want action" (Goodwillie 1981).

11. Pacific Islanders were not alone in this perception. For example, Line Robillard Heyniger, of the U.S. National Commission for UNESCO, says of the Copenhagen women's conference that

> When women met five years ago in Mexico City, the conference was called a global "consciousness raising." When they met in Copenhagen, the buzzword was "networking." . . . Women from all continents came to Copenhagen for two basic reasons: to get information on how to mobilize other women in their own countries

and to establish links across cultures, classes, and ideologies from a common cause. (Kneerim and Shur 1982: 4)

12. The earliest examples of documents drafted in the form discussed in chapter 3 that I was able to locate in Fiji are a "Fiji country paper" prepared for a Pacific women's meeting sponsored by ESCAP in 1980 and a "Plan of Action" prepared by the Fiji National Council of Women (FNCW) in 1981.

13. The South Pacific Commission was established by Australia and New Zealand in 1944. Now known as the Secretariat of the Pacific Community, it administers regional development programs in the areas of education, fisheries, agriculture, and media in addition to the women in development programs of the Pacific Women's Resource Bureau discussed in the chapters that follow. SPC has a staff of approximately 130 based in Suva and Nouméa, New Caledonia. The bulk of its budget is funded by contributions from Australia, the United States, New Zealand, France, and (until 1995) Britain (Hoadley 1992: 57–60).

14. The South Pacific Forum is a political and economic alliance of independent Pacific Island states modeled on the European Economic Community and devoted to political and legal harmonization of law and policy in areas such as trade, maritime, environmental, defense, and foreign policy. Founded in 1971, the forum serves as an umbrella organization for a variety of more specialized regional associations such as the Forum Fisheries Agency, the Regional Committee on Trade, and the South Pacific Regional Environment Programme. It has observer status at the United Nations. SPF is funded primarily by contributions from the member states, prorated according to GNP, and from large grants from the European Union, Japan, and the United Nations (Hoadley 1992: 60–70). The forum has no specialized women's desk and played only a minor role in the Beijing Conference and its preparatory activities.

15. According to UNDP and SPC, there are approximately 1,012 NGOs (including church-based and "community" groups) in the Pacific, of which over half are women's organizations (UNDP 1994).

16. According to a 1985 comparative study of development projects of UN agencies, only 5 percent of all such projects were "designed exclusively with women in mind," 12 percent were "designed to include women," 56 percent affected women "but with no provision for women's participation," and 27 percent were "of no interest to women" whatsoever (UN Secretary-General 1994: 9). In contrast, in 1996, the New Zealand Official Development Assistance Programme (NZODA), for example, aimed to ensure that 50 percent of its projects would be "WID integrated" by 1997. It required all projects to include "gender desegregated data" in their terms of reference and treated the support of NGOs working in WID-related processes as a major target area in the Pacific (NZODA 1992). By 1994, all of the major donors with a presence in Fiji listed WID as one of their top five priority areas.

17. The SPC's Pacific Women's Resource Bureau convened a monthly meeting of government focal points via PEACESAT, and the Pacific NGO Coordinating Group for the Beijing Conference convened a parallel monthly PEACESAT meeting of NGOs.

18. Interviews with donor staff working outside the WID area indicated that this focus on information dissemination, coordination, training, and conference attendance was not limited to WID funding. This usually was justified in terms of a desire not to in-

terfere in the domestic affairs of a sovereign state, on the one hand, and a desire not to foster dependence on outside sources for exhaustible material resources on the other. For example, I once interviewed a senior official of the World Health Organization (WHO) in Suva about its projects in Fiji. At the close of an interview in which the official detailed the organization's many educational and training projects aimed at curbing the rapid spread of sexually transmitted diseases in Fiji, I asked him whether WHO had considered providing disposable epidermic needles to Fiji's hospitals since the reuse of needles then posed a fair risk of contracting illness while in the hospital. This comparatively inexpensive project would be against organization policy, he explained, as it would foster dependence on outside donations.

19. The first mention of networking among women's organizations in conference documents appears in a regional conference of Pacific women's organizations sponsored by the South Pacific Commission in 1985. Delegates at that meeting arrived at the following joint statement:

"Networking" involves information exchange with other people. This involves:

(a) recognition of a personal and general need to obtain and exchange information for particular purposes;
(b) identification, approach and use of sources (e.g., people, government departments, statistics offices, libraries, book shops, radio and television services, publishers, IGOs and NGOs);
(c) acquisition and organization of resource materials for future use;
(d) extracting and organizing data for a particular purpose;
(e) organization and production of information in forms appropriate to the intended users (audio-visual, interview, speech, letter, newsletter, article, report, project document);
(f) getting feedback from the users and building on this to provide further information;
(g) keeping appropriate records of exchange activities (free and exchange mailing lists, subscription lists, useful address and expertise lists, correspondence files).

(SPC 1985: 38)

20. As Helen Schwartzman has noted in the context of institutional culture in an alternative mental health facility:

[It is] important to understand how meetings reproduce themselves, and this requires making a break with cultural assumptions about the purpose of meetings. Instead of accepting task-focused assumptions that suggest that decisions, crises, conflicts, and the like are what meetings are about, the opposite is proposed here, that is, *that meetings are what decisions, problems, and crises are about.* (1989: 9; emphasis in the original)

21. From the point of view of the comparative study of institutions, it is interesting to note how the purpose of the organization comes to be reflected in the form of its bureaucratic activity. Although Network participants would declare themselves to be conforming purely to an ideal type of action devoid of "cultural characteristics," there were

qualities to these meetings that one would not find elsewhere. Compare, for example, the practice of treating meetings as collective "therapy" among bureaucrats at an alternative mental health facility (Schwartzman 1989: 244) or the uses of prose and syntax in the politics of internal memoranda writing among editors at the Book of the Month Club (Radway 1997: 98).

22. Carol Heimer and Arthur Stinchcombe have noted that "[a]lthough many organizational routines purport to be about 'opening up the decision process,' one could argue that they are in fact about legitimate ways of keeping it closed. 'Opening a decision process' often means producing routines for access" (1999: 8). As they point out, some such limits are imagined by the actors involved as intentional, while others, like limitations on one's time, are not. In her ethnography of editors at the Book-of-the-Month Club, Janice Radway offers a number of powerful illustrations of the more subtle and nonintentional dimensions of such practices, as when an editor proclaims that the average reader, on whose behalf the editorial work is done, is "a generalist like me" (1997: 93).

23. And of course in my case they were correct.

24. For example, at one post-Beijing community meeting, the president of the Fiji YWCA, an owner of a local clothing store chain, asked one member of the Pacific NGO Coordinating Group why her colleague, the Asia-Pacific NGO focal point and former regional focal point of PAWORNET, had appeared so often in the CNN coverage of the Beijing Conference. Although the response emphasized her colleague's communications skills, it also located agency squarely beyond the colleague herself:

> We were members of the facilitating committee, which was like the secretariat for the whole conference. None of the facilitating committee could face up to the media. They would always push [the colleague] to go speak on their behalf.... [CNN] picked [her] because she was articulate, where others didn't. They wanted fire and I suppose they got fire.

25. When I asked NGO focal points why they had failed to enroll, most offhandedly mentioned the high costs involved. Yet this explanation seems unsatisfactory when the same NGOs routinely spent the cost of a yearly subscription on a single lavish conference lunch. Unlike the hosting of a lunch, it would seem, sending e-mail was not an effective genre for performing their connections.

26. According to internal registration records of the Association for Progressive Communications (APC), an organization dedicated to developing computer networks and putting them to use for political action, which maintained a sign-in sheet for computer use at the Beijing Conference and the NGO Forum, a full 57 percent of the users of free computer facilities at the Beijing Conference were U.S. nationals. Canadian nationals constituted the second largest category with 5 percent of total users. Only two Fiji nationals used these facilities. One was an academic, and the other was a former employee of a Fiji-based NGO living in Japan. I am grateful to APC for providing these statistics.

27. This is not to say that these people were absorbed into a Suva expatriate community. In fact, they came into contact with expatriates only for brief exchanges in the context of conferences or meetings between donors and donees.

28. Fiji Indians are the descendants of Indians who came to Fiji in the nineteenth century (cf. Kelly 1991) as indentured laborers and today make up almost 48 percent of the population (Fiji Government 1996).

29. Gender was rarely discussed outside the formal networks. The absence of men from these organizations and projects in essence made the difference between men and women a nonissue. As discussed further in chapter 6, "Woman" was a formal analytical category that referred to what was outside the network (as in "the women asked for this policy").

30. Fred Myers has described his own difficulty in understanding why Pintupi meetings "rarely resulted in decisions or plans for concerted action" (1996: 242). He concludes that what is created at such meetings is the polity itself: "the meeting does not stand for but is the polity" (245).

31. Kinship did not serve as an organizational or divisive form, however, as there were only one or two cases of relations reckoned in kinship terms.

32. Stacy Zabusky (1995) comments on her exhaustion at incessant conversation among European Space Agency scientists concerning stereotypical differences between nationalities. She notes that this conversation was experienced as dreary by her informants as well, although without it, there seemed to be nothing to say.

33. Myers has made a similar observation concerning the turn taking rules of meetings. He comments that "[t]he organization of discourse has the effect of creating a sense of a meeting as a set of discrete bits from which speakers' egotism, will, and responsibility are detached. It is as if the outcome—the consensus no one opposes—is 'found' rather than created, and the group reflexively derives from it" (1996: 244).

34. In one of these cases, the selection of a male middle-level administrator in the SPC bureaucracy as director for the SPC's Community Education Training Centre, a facility intended primarily for Pacific women, sparked a major controversy, as women's groups denounced the appointment in the press and in letters to the government. Although the focus of these protests concerned the gender of the applicant and the lack of transparency in the selection process, many of the protesters acknowledged that they acted as much out of shock and disappointment that a veteran of their institutions was not selected.

35. For social network analysts, a network was "always personal" (Epstein 1969). The concept of "action sets," for example, aimed to describe the set of network actors that an actor might personally mobilize in fulfilling a goal such as inducing a political opponent to agree to a compromise (Wheeldon 1969). Although it was implicitly assumed that actors were individualistic, rational choice–oriented human actors, little else was clear about the personal character of the network actors on which so much depended. Barth, for example, proposed that "[p]ersons in Western society are characterized by large personal repertoires" (1978: 180) of connections and that these explained the person's capacity for forming complex networks around the self. Tautological explanations of this kind led to the internal criticism that, while the entire objective of network analysis had been to escape the dichotomy of individual and society, social network analysis had unwittingly replicated this dichotomy in the most direct way (e.g., Blok 1973).

36. Adam Reed (n.d.) has described how, for prisoners in Papua New Guinea, personal friendship is a means of purposely refusing relationality. For networkers in Suva, in contrast, relationality did not even need to be refused.

37. For a useful summary of the American tradition of social network analysis from the 1930s onward, see John Scott 1991. Equally interesting from an ethnographic point of view is Scott's own networked understanding of the network analysis tradition, reproduced in the following figure. He argues that

> There are numerous very diverse strands in the development of present-day social network analysis. These strands have intersected and fused with one another at various times, only to diverge once more on their separate paths. Nevertheless, a clear lineage for the mainstream of social network analysis can be constructed from this complex history. (7)

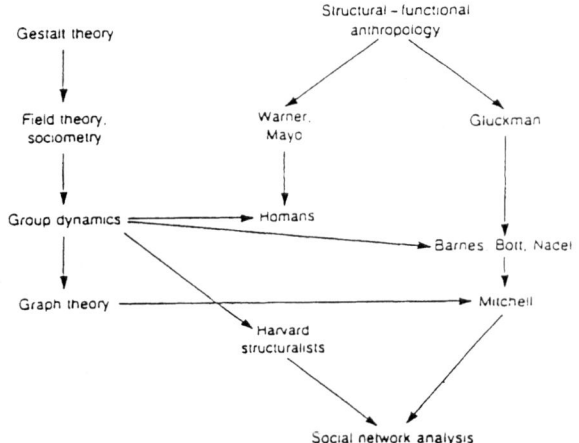

"The lineage of social network analysis." (Reproduced from J. Scott, *Social Network Analysis* [London: Sage Publications, 1991], 7. Reprinted by permission of Sage Publications Ltd.)

Barnes, the author of the first network analysis study, recounts that he borrowed the term from Fortes's *Web of Kinship* and Radcliffe-Brown's characterization of social structure as a "network of actually existing relations." Barnes surmises that the latter may have picked the term up from popular English usage, as in "the old boy network" (1968: 108–11), although it is likely that both were also influenced by the already extensive tradition of network analysis in the United States at the time.

38. Mitchell identified three principal types of linkage "content" that moved through social networks—communication content (information), exchange content, and normative content (1973: 23–26).

39. Hannerz oscillates between the view that networks actually exist in a global ecumene and the view that the Network is an analytical tool for describing transnational culture (1992b: 47). At times, he asserts that culture itself is a network; at others, that it is something that "flows" through a network; and at others that it is a product of the net-

work (51). This slippage is a classic example of the recursive quality of network analysis I aim to describe.

40. As Jean Baudrillard wrote in a critique of McLuhan's notion of the global village, "cybernetics presents itself as neo-humanism" ([1972] 1981: 199).

41. "My imploded story insists on the inextricable weave of the organic, technical, textual, mythic, economic, and political threads that make up the flesh of the world" (Haraway 1995: xii).

42. I borrow the metaphor from the world of UN conferences, in which the imagination of the world as a collection of networked focal points is premised on the existence of an earlier imagination of the world as a system of "regions." It has become commonplace among international actors to critique the usefulness of thinking of the world as a set of regions. Yet this does not mean that regions have fallen from view. Rather, where they used to be imagined as analytical devices—as useful organizing principles, like networks—they now are imagined as the Real (chap. 5), as prior to analysis (chap. 4), and as demanding a further tool, the Network, to apprehend.

43. In the United States during this period, this interest in mathematics was taken to even further extremes, with attempts to develop algebraic equations that could model kinship and other social relations (Scott 1991: 33).

44. Frederick Barth's study (1978), although not a particularly sophisticated example of the method, was emblematic: even taking himself as sole informant, self-observed for a period of only fourteen days, he could not account for the totality of his linkages nor draw significant conclusions about them.

45. "[T]he principle of symmetry suggests that there is no privilege—that everything can be analysed, and that it can (or should) be analysed in the same terms. So it erodes distinctions that are said to be given in the nature of things, and instead asks how it is that they got to be that way" (Law 1994: 12).

46. In fact, one could read the 1960s and 1970s literature in the rhetoric of social movements as another version of the Network: an exercise in rendering a phenomenon (social movements) real by analyzing it.

47. When, for example, the director of the Department of Women and Culture wrote to the local AusAID Beijing coordinator—a person much her junior who in other situations would be expected to show her considerable deference—seeking funds for the department to attend the Beijing Conference, she received in response a courteous but brisk admonition to pursue the matter through proper channels.

48. That this liberal project is deeply implicated in the modernist aesthetics described in this chapter is illustrated by the fact that no funding agency in Suva would have proposed that women get together to make mats instead of documents (see chap. 3).

49. I am grateful to Art Stinchcombe for bringing this essay to my attention.

50. As a PAWORNET newsletter explained:

> Networking means literally to "work a net," a net which links and binds us together, a net which underpins and supports our activities, a net which weaves a collective strength out of our individual and small-group efforts. Women are natural "networkers"—weaving and linking people together within their extended families, among church groups, in their communities. What we need to do more of is net-

working on a broader scale—from one community to another, across our islands, nationally, even internationally. (PAWORNET 1990: 4)

Chapter 3

1. The Pacific Ministerial Conference on Women and Sustainable Development was convened by SPC in Nouméa from 2 to 6 May 1994 as preparatory negotiations for the Beijing Conference at the subregional level.

2. This subtitle, and especially the phrase "sustainable development," was adopted largely at the urging of the UNDP, which played a major role in the funding and organization of this meeting. At the conference, well-known politicians were enlisted to give lectures on different aspects of the concept. The presence of this term at the center of the image might be taken as graphic evidence of the powerful role international agencies play in the production of even the "local," "natural," and "grassroots" documents at issue in this chapter.

3. In addition to the actual intergovernmental agreements, many other kinds of "documents" are produced in the course of this process, including shadow documents drafted by NGOs, newspaper articles, newsletters, films, and demonstrations. In this chapter I limit the discussion to the analysis of the official negotiated document. Throughout, therefore, "the document" is the *Draft Global Platform for Action* unless otherwise specified.

4. Following local convention I use "Fiji NGOs" or "Fiji delegates" to refer to NGOs and delegates from Fiji rather than to ethnic Fijians.

5. When delegates at the Nouméa Conference sought to eliminate several sections of the *Draft Pacific Platform for Action* prepared by SPC staff and to adopt an alternative format, they were informed by UN authorities that they could not do so, as they were "required" to conform to "UN style" for the sake of the uniformity of documents.

6. Such uses of text may be more pervasive than is often acknowledged. Brenda Danet (1997) has described a similar processing of knowledge with respect to electronic hypertext:

> The advent of hypertext is changing the rhythms with which we read, and undermining the authority of the author and the fixity of the text. Texts written in modular chunks and having an associative, rather than a linear structure may be read in different sequences by different readers, and even by the same reader on different occasions. Links between portions of texts and between different texts may be instantly activated. (6)

Similarly, studies in cognitive psychology have demonstrated that the use of documents such as timetables should be understood as "analogical reasoning" rather than reading since they require entirely different skills focused on the comparison of elements in the document and the location of specific facts rather than the acquisition of knowledge (Guthrie 1988: 181, 197).

7. I borrow the term *digital* from Gregory Bateson's commentary on the difference between "digital" and "iconic" patterns (Bateson 1987b). Bateson's argument concerns the way in which pattern that is digital at one "level" can be iconic at another.

8. This regional ministerial meeting was convened by the UN Economic and Social Council for Asia and the Pacific (ESCAP) from 7 to 14 June 1994.

9. Feminist scholars Sallie Baden and Anne Marie Goetz capture the nature of the divide between academic and activist uses of documents:

> As feminist researchers we felt it important in the build-up to Beijing to forge alliances with activists and campaigners within NGOs and women's organizations who are attempting to change the policies of public institutions. This proved challenging in a number of ways. Specifically, it highlighted our distance from the language used in the lobbying process, in both its conceptual underpinnings and style: our proclivity for academic rigour, complexity and critique seemed at times to be in direct opposition to the demands of consensus building, political utility and direct campaigning messages. (Baden and Goetz 1997: 8)

10. In speaking of an academic point of view, I do not mean to imply that actual "academics" never encounter the kind of knowledge practices described here. The presence of some academic feminists at the Beijing Conference and the anxious discussions within academic feminist networks such as DAWN over whether to participate in document drafting or take an entirely critical stance toward the conferences are evidence of important interconnections.

11. In Wagner's study of the fundamental "constitutive and organizing power" of meaning in human cultural life (1986: ix), for example, we learn that it is in the elicitation of meaning that knowledge expands (31), crosses from one scale to another, and grows from one "order" to the next (126).

12. Brinkley Messick (1993) similarly describes the past treatment of legal documents by judges in Yemen, for whom "an oral core is complemented by a written surround" (209). The resemblance to UN documents is not complete, however, because Messick tells us that, like the ethnographer, the Yemeni scribe aims to describe the social world in the text of his document (224).

13. Michael Herzfeld has made a similar point concerning the tensions between officials' insistence on the transparency of bureaucratic language and their own uses of the inherent opacity of language (1992: 115). The interesting aspect, Herzfeld points out, is the way in which bureaucrats continue to insist on the clarity of literal words even as they are "well aware of the inconsistencies that abound in the legal system they are supposed to uphold" (118). As he illustrates, such claims on behalf of language can in turn be substantiated only by the "tautologous" practices of producing yet more documents at further stages or levels of activity (121). It is through the bureaucrat's movement between an apprehension of the transparency and opacity of language, in other words, that documents beget further documents and further "levels."

14. This is not to say, however, that delegates were naively unaware that language was not in fact "firm," as academics engaged in "critique" of the Platform for Action at the conferences and in outside writings sometimes assumed. Indeed, the entire game of the negotiation consisted in lulling oneself and others into an apprehension of the concrete-

ness of language even as one knew that meanings must fail to hold. For example, after initially opposing a paragraph affirming women's equal right to own land, the Fiji delegation later dropped its objection on the grounds that the text could be read as asking for nothing beyond the communal "land rights" Fijian women nominally "had" in their native clans. If the strategy lay in the interpretive possibilities of terms such as *land rights*, the strategy was at least a double one. For at least some members of the delegation, it also was a way of supporting a call for land reform in Fiji that as individuals they believed to be imperative but that, as government officials, they could not ratify. If words could be decomposed, so could institutional identities and allegiances.

15. Margaret Jolly (1996) has described a similar conference of Vanuatu NGO representatives sponsored by overseas aid agencies on the topic of violence against women. Jolly's argument that the *allure* of human rights language (182) among the educated urban ni-Vanuatu women who attend such conferences is neither "familiar" nor "unfamiliar" (185)—an artifact neither of local culture nor of international institutions—is well illustrated in the ease with which a brochure for that conference gathered together Christian allusions, quotations from a speech by a well-known American feminist activist given at a UN conference, a title from a book authored by the owner of the Body Shop, calls for "educating" and "empowering" women in language evocative of UN documents, and an account of the local history of the Vanuatu Women's Center (179–180).

Chapter 4

1. The principal feature of this new global society, for Castells, is a conflict between segmented identities (selves) and informational "flows" (networks) (31). Although Castells shows a certain sympathy for "tribes" against "flows" (31), it is not difficult to predict which of these wins out in the end. As Kay Warren has noted, the same can be said of anthropological studies of social movements: "It is not uncommon for scholars of new social movements to treat their goals and organizations as self-evident and thus, to focus on the formal ideologies and established collectivities that people embrace" (Warren 1998: 209–10). In a response to Castells, Emily Martin aptly flags the romance of system (1996: 50) that gives sociological appeal. "The intriguing problem," she notes, "is how we can describe the emergence of flexible flows without at the same time becoming caught up in them" (51).

2. Al Gore, for example, aligns the U.S. government's current information policy to its old agricultural policy, "which left grain rotting in thousands of storage silos while people were starving. We have warehouses of unused information 'rotting,' while critical questions are left unanswered and critical problems are left unsolved" (1991: 110).

3. The only demographic study to include Part-Europeans as a separate category, conducted in 1966, found that over 50 percent married other Part-Europeans, while over 20 percent married "Europeans" and 25 percent married Fijians (Kelly 1966: 5). Many Part-Europeans also trace their ancestry to newcomer Europeans, Tongans, Samoans, and other Polynesians.

4. Over 83 percent of the land in Fiji is held in "native trust"—allocated to specific Fijian clans, inalienable, and administered by the government. This is the result of a colonial policy, discussed extensively elsewhere (e.g., France 1969), to limit the alienation of Fijian land. As part of this policy, a Land Claims Commission was established

immediately after cession to investigate the validity of every "European title." On the commission's recommendation, the governor in council issued Crown Grants to Europeans in only a minority of cases. For example, of the ten claims submitted to the Land Claims Commission by the heirs of David Whippy, only five ultimately were endorsed by the colonial administration. Except for a short period during the administration of Governor Im Thurn (1905–8), the sale of Fijian land has been prohibited by law since then and continues to be prohibited today.

5. During the colonial period, Part-Europeans living in the urban areas formed a kind of artisan class specializing in carpentry, boat building, and the manufacture and repair of machinery for the sugar refining industry (cf. Kelly 1966). For example, until recently members of the Whippy clan owned a shipyard in Suva where they built high-quality small and medium-sized vessels. The postcolonial period has seen the demise of the markets for these trades, and few Part-Europeans alive at the time of my research still knew the skills of boat building, although those living in the cities worked in large numbers as mechanics, telephone or gas utilities employees (in the case of men), and clerks and secretaries (in the case of women).

6. A person born into a Part-European clan is considered a member of his or her father's clan. Women join their husbands' clans at marriage, and residence is virilocal. However, a person also may choose to live with his or her mother's kin and to participate fully in kin affairs (albeit while retaining the father's surname in the cases familiar to me). Some do this formally by presenting food and valuables to their mother's kin; more commonly, a person simply takes up residence on his or her mother's land or is willed land by his or her mother and moves to that land to cut copra.

7. Almost everyone in Kasavu had visited the cities on occasion, and about half of the men had worked in the shipyards or in other manual labor positions for a period lasting from several weeks to several years.

8. Kasavu was the name of a Fijian village located on the land before Tui Cakau, the high chief of Cakaudrove, gave the land to David Whippy and moved the villagers further north. Modern-day Kasavu is not a village in official terms because there is no common land. The entirety of the land is subdivided into separately owned tracts of freehold land.

9. In many respects, the clan's common orientation toward the life and image of David Whippy and his partner William Simpson conforms to observations in the anthropological record concerning Fijians' notion of *vu* (ancestral spirit), a "heroic ancestral leader of a major immigration party" (Sahlins 1962: 228) and perceived genitor of a clan, whose exploits and human attributes are taken to be emblematic of the character of the clan as a whole (Hocart 1952: 45). David Whippy's photograph hangs prominently in the Whippy church in Kasavu, side by side with and facing an image of the Crucifixion of the same size. The same photograph also hangs in a place of honor in most houses in Kasavu. David Whippy's reportedly tricky and somewhat mischievous character often is imputed to the clan as a whole, as are his supposed intelligence and bravery. Yet the Whippys do not actually refer to David Whippy as a *vu*. That relationship is traced through their ancestral links with the Tui Levuka clan so that the *tauvu* relationship (special relationship between clans that share a common *vu*) serves as an important basis of affinity with Fijian clans.

10. The Whippys said that David Whippy held the special title of *Matakibau* (facing

Bau) or representative of the settler population to the chief of Bau, and they often referred to their ancestor simply as Matakibau while William Simpson was known as *Matakivunivesi* (facing Vunivesi). According to the archival record, Whippy and Simpson acquired their considerable holdings in land from various Fijian chiefs in exchange for boat building, for transporting them or carrying ships full of exchange goods to other chieftainships on ceremonial occasions, and for serving as semipermanent "counsellors" in matters of administration and war. They owned two cutters built by Simpson, which in the boom days of settlement ferried people and goods from Levuka to the outer islands and back again. They served as guides for early British and American expeditions to Fiji and also cleared and planted the estates now owned by their respective clans (Brown 1886; Bulu 1871; Eagleston n.d.; Young 1984).

11. In this respect, the Whippys and Simpsons are typical of many of the original Part-European clans of Fiji. The Simpson clan is subdivided in a manner similar to the Whippy clan. Each clan is undifferentiated from the point of view of the other. Members of both clans were only vaguely aware of the existence of the other's subclans and could not identify them with any particularity.

12. As Hocart observed, the term *tavale*, often translated as "cross-cousin," actually refers more to a category of marriageable persons, persons in ego's generation from the opposing moiety, than to genealogical cross-cousins. Hocart (1952) insisted that this was not simply a case of the "extension" of kin terms but rather a form of reckoning different from the European genealogical one. In practice, only a small number of marriages among Whippys and Simpsons, relative to the data reported for Fijians (e.g., Sahlins 1962: 161), involve actual or classificatory cross-cousins if these are reckoned in genealogical terms (cf. Quain 1948).

13. The practice of marrying *tavale* had broken down among urban Whippys by the time of my fieldwork, although a preference for marrying *tavale* was expressed by urban and rural clan members alike.

14. Unlike Fijians (e.g., Toren 1990), Part-Europeans do not use Dravidian kinship terminology unless in conversation with Fijians or making a particular point regarding their Fijian ties. However, like Fijians, their terms of address accentuate the differences between generations. All males and females of the first ascending generation, on both the mother's and father's sides, other than one's father and mother are referred to as "uncle" and "auntie," respectively, while males and females of the second ascending generation on both sides who are brothers and sisters (i.e., MoMoSi, or FaFaSi) are referred to in English as "pa" and "ma" or "bubu," respectively. These are terms of respect, and to fail to use them, even when there is no difference in age among persons of different generations, is an affront that is bound to initiate a cycle of bad feelings. However, it is interesting that males and females of the second ascending generation who are more distantly related to ego (i.e., one's mother's mother's *tavale*) are referred to as "uncle" or "auntie," thus collapsing the distinction between first and second ascending generations.

15. I.e., ego marries a classificatory Mo.

16. The ineffectuality of clan membership as a divisive principle was made particularly apparent to me when it was necessary to divide the population of Kasavu for the purposes of competitive fund-raising for the settlement primary school. The usual spatial divisions would not do since not all school alumni were associated with particular parcels

of land. Rather than resort to clan membership, Kasavu leaders arbitrarily invented four "houses" of different colors and invited people to choose at random which house to join.

17. This pattern of division accords with practices with respect to lands owned by other portions of the Whippy clan elsewhere in Fiji as well as with practices among other Part-European clans.

18. For example, the plots shown in the plan in figure 15 reflect the subdivision of one small portion of land one generation ago. At the time of my fieldwork, each of these portions had been further subdivided informally into four or five shares by tracing the future line of division with a piece of string. Those living there hoped to register their division and obtain separate legal titles in the near future, as some persons sharing in these informally subdivided plots already wished to divide them again.

19. At the time of my fieldwork, the land was divided into plots of approximately twenty-five acres, yielding five to six tons of copra each year, which the Whippys sold for around F$350 (US$180) a ton. As each plot usually was owned in common by several brothers, they took turns harvesting the copra in alternate months, thus sharing the annual income of the land evenly. Some also grew small quantities of kava on their land for sale in the market at Savusavu. In addition to copra, the Whippys planted taro, cassava, and other root crops and fished for subsistence. A handful of people also drew some cash income from contributions from relatives overseas, government disability assistance, or wages from such activities as serving as the settlement's preschool teacher or working on a government ship.

20. Although many said that deference should be given to the eldest member of each generation, there was considerable debate about who was in fact the eldest.

21. Indeed, the church, too, had divided into separate congregations according to the major divisions of land, and in the absence of permanent ordained ministers the same clan leaders served as lay preachers. Holding onto the truth of one's claim in the face of parallel challenges, therefore, was as futile as attempting to hold onto resources in the face of others' demands.

22. This identity of land and documents has a genealogy for the Whippys and other Part-Europeans that traces back to their early ancestors' eagerness to obtain deeds and other documentary proof of conveyance from Fijians long before such deeds had any legal enforceability. Early settlers placed great emphasis on the significance of their deeds, registered these meticulously with American and British agents, and produced them for the captains of visiting warships to enforce. David Whippy's house in Levuka served as a repository for the deeds of American citizens in Fiji, and many were lost in a succession of fires that, according to the Kasavu Whippys, were purposely set by neighboring Fijians with the intention of destroying these documents.

23. Consider, for example, how the Whippy universe might differ if land were divided according to some other logic, thus generating plots of other geometrical forms that do not partake in this simple numerical correlation. Bertrand Russell credits Pythagoras with the discovery of the concept of "incommensurability" in the course of attempting to make numerical sense of the form of a triangle. The triangle had a side length of one but a hypotenuse of a length of the square root of two, "which appeared not to be a number at all" ([1919] 1993: 4).

24. Debbora Battaglia (1995) has described the productive uses of nostalgic con-

ceptions of "home" by low-ranking Trobrianders who have achieved a new standing in the urban areas. It is interesting here, in contrast, that the collective invention of the Whippy family does not draw on images of Kasuva nor of home. Place does not figure on the family tree; organizers held the last family reunion in Suva on the understanding that it might take place anywhere. The productive images, in this case, rather, are those of original ancestors and their exploits, as well as the patterned image of the family tree.

25. The organizer of the genealogy session at the family reunion, a senior member of the clan, was a bishop in the Church of Latter Day Saints, and his church's approach to the collection of genealogical data directed the form in which genealogical data was collected at that reunion. However, other Whippys in Suva, most of whom were Methodists, privately expressed distaste for his use of their family tree for his own religious purposes and insisted that their interest in family history was not influenced by his.

26. For example, absent in the Whippys' ancestral stories are the metaphors or actual experiences of traveling so often encountered among Fijians and other Austronesian peoples (e.g., Munn 1996).

27. For example, in the Fijian case the problem addressed by kinship terminology concerns how to bring a potentially infinite field of persons into the fold of immediate kin (Sahlins 1962: 154).

28. "What has happened is that the perceptual technology of written representation, with its contingent conceptions of the sign and the possibility of constructing an analytic language about language, has been upstaged by a perceptualist self-act, a scoping of the scope. A scholarship of 'constructionism' is reduced to finding segmental or semiotic equivalents, analytic 'redescriptions,' for images that do not need them, trading on the marginal advantage through which its anthropology has exploited so-called oral literatures and indigenous poetics. . . . A scopic prose makes all of this unnecessary, not by resuscitating oral tradition and turning the world, as Marshall McLuhan has suggested, into a global village, but by imitating insight in its own artifact, making its own presentation the need for a need, as advertising does" (Wagner 1995: 63–64).

29. I do not mean to imply that academic analysis has been reduced solely to networking, just as one cannot reduce a previous generation's analysis simply to critique.

Chapter 5

1. As Barnes wrote: "We construct analytical tools not because they look beautiful but because we have a job of work to do with them. In particular we take measurements not for the joy of counting . . . but in order to prove or disprove some hypothesis." (1968: 109)

2. These two aesthetic genres have parallels in many spheres of network activity. For example, the structure of UN global conferences always involves a highly regimented and "technical" meeting of governments, which is strictly limited to insiders through a system of accreditation procedures, while the free, festivallike NGO Forum held in tandem with the official meeting is imagined as a space in which all viewpoints, no matter how outlandish or unique, can find a place.

3. Most newsletters and other documents were designed primarily by one person and machine but were circulated among a group of several focal points for comment before distribution.

4. Kress and van Leeuwen quote Mondrian's allusion to the shapes of circles and squares of the kind that pervade every network diagram as "pure, quasi-scientific 'atoms' of the visible world, a 'pure manifestation of the elements,' the 'universal-as-the-mathematical'" (1996: 51).

5. The letter of invitation to the conference asked focal points to nominate two participants—one each from the governmental and nongovernmental sectors, both of whom were to be:

> (i) Technically competent to follow the program of the Workshop and implement its outcome
> (ii) Presently involved in women-related information work
> (iii) Familiar with the organizational features of the WINAP
> (iv) Fluent in English

The paper that each nominee was to produce had equally precise requirements:

> It must be 10–15 pages and entitled "recent developments in women's information in Fiji" or "recent developments in women's information in the NGO sector in Fiji." There is a set outline:
>
> (1) Organizational developments (structure, staff, policy)
> (2) Database developments (bibliographic databases, statistical databases, directories, thesaurus used)
> (3) Research activities (new issues, new methodologies, research needs)
> (4) Recent statistics (new issues, new methodologies, data needs)
> (5) Computerization (software, hardware, training)
> (6) Network developments (networking within the government organizations, national networks, inter-country networks, sub-regional networks, global networks)
> (7) Recent publications
> (8) Budget (funding sources)
> (9) Obstacles encountered
> (10) Training/advisory services
> (11) Future plans (project proposals, planned meetings, activities to prepare for Beijing)

(VanRoy 1992)

6. Bateson argued that the technical "skill" required to produce an aesthetically pleasing artifact inhered in the maker's ability to reflect and elaborate upon the layered patterns of the conscious and unconscious minds. For him, the mind was a networklike integration of multiple heterogeneous elements, both data and analyst:

It is not that art is the expression of the unconscious, but rather that it is concerned with the relation *between* the levels of mental process. . . . Artistic skill is the combining of many levels of mind—unconscious, conscious, and external—to make a statement of their combination. (1987c: 470)

The difference between conscious and unconscious thought, in his formulation, is the way in which meaning is apprehended in terms either of substance or relationship: While the conscious mind focuses on entities (e.g., persons or things) and at a secondary stage notes the multiple potential relationships between them, the unconscious apprehends the patterns of relationships as primary and plays with the possible substitutions of entities to be related (e.g., in the way "actual" relationships are represented as involving other persons or places in a dream) (1987b).

7. Kress and van Leeuwen note that it is possible that diagrams "have been affected by the structure of English, with its lexical distinction of verbs/processes and nouns/objects" (1996: 63).

8. Design theorists sometimes differentiate design from art precisely on the grounds of the strict limits on form imposed by the technological requirements of the creation (e.g., Pye 1978: 11).

9. For a discussion of the significance of the spatial arrangement of persons for social hierarchies in Fiji, see Christina Toren (1990).

10. This image is also a good example of how graphics circulate among NGOs. Originally created by IWTC, it was borrowed, free of whatever textual explanations accompanied it in the IWTC publication, and reproduced in this flier but was credited to IWTC.

11. One important difference between the focal point and the linkage as aesthetic devices was that linkages could be verbalized and critiqued. In this sense, linkages were repositories of information that might take other analytical forms, and they generated discussion. In contrast, one could not put the attraction of focal points into words.

12. Kinross even notes the influence of cybernetics on some designers in the Bauhaus school and the desire it generated that "human transactions might have the same order and essential simplicity as an electrical circuit" (1989: 140).

13. In Beijing, tension developed between the Pacific Islander participants and their Australian "facilitators" over the extent of participant control over the project. For many, this conflict found voice around questions of aesthetics. The entire product looked wrong, participants complained. Instead of a brightly colored, tentlike covering for their booth, there should have been a mat, a Micronesian representative insisted, and instead of documents there should have been people talking and making things. And there should have been men, she added.

14. In their study of British teenagers' responses to AIDS awareness campaigns, Briggs and Cobley quote a girl overcome by the attractiveness of a jeans advertisement. When asked whether she would buy the jeans, she balked, stating that she would like to buy the *ad,* not the jeans (1996: 186). If the image had succeeded on an aesthetic level, it had failed miserably in its intended transmission of the message.

15. Kress and van Leeuwen note that what they term the "analytical structure" of design can contain within it at another level a "transactional structure" that emphasizes movement, transformation, and narrative change (1996: 48–49).

16. One thinks of the old trick of 3-D movies in which differently tinted lenses placed over the left and right eyes enable the viewer to see the figure twice, thus engendering an effect of depth.

17. As Shore notes in his study of European Commission bureaucrats' efforts to create a European consciousness, data, for them, serve as an agent, just as persons might:

> Depending on how we define it, almost anyone or anything might constitute an "agency" of consciousness; the only qualifying criterion is that these are persons or objects through which power is exerted. . . . EC bureaucrats define themselves as "agents" of European consciousness, but they see information policy, symbols, statistics, history books, "communications experts" and the mass media as agencies through which European consciousness can be inculcated among European citizens. (1995: 232)

18. Latour and Woolgar demonstrated that in the laboratory they studied, scientific facts did not exist a priori but were created through political contest and that their separation from the specific context in which they were created was only the final stage in their creation (Latour and Woolgar [1979] 1986: 175).

19. Daston ([1991] 1994) has described how in the sixteenth and seventeenth centuries the prodigy moved from being understood as a *sign* of God's will to a natural *fact* that could not be explained. Daston's argument is that it is in the closure of signification and the possibilities of interpretation that the fact emerges as an entity distinct from interpretation.

20. Michael Barnett writes of his experience as a UN bureaucrat in Rwanda that "the knowledge that mattered most was not the particulars about Rwanda but rather the culture of the policy-making process in the U.S. government and the UN" (1997: 554). This knowledge was conceived of as a possession of "facts" about the bureaucracy: "who handled the issues, who had access to key decision makers, who my counterparts were in other missions to the UN and other departments in Washington, what had transpired in the Security Council, and what the precise language of past mandates was. Over time, I accumulated a stock of facts regarding the issues that I covered, and I became fluent in the acronyms of the UN and the policy process" (554–55).

21. For example, in debate in a negotiation session at the Beijing Conference over the inclusion of a reference to a recommendation from the office of the secretary-general that gender balance should be achieved in troops sent on peacekeeping missions, some states objected that each state should decide for itself what constituted gender balance. The chair responded, "Can we all agree on a reference to the Secretary-General's report, which, I think, is a factual report. It is we, the Member States, who asked him to make the report." At that statement, those objecting grudgingly rescinded. When the chair claimed that a certain formulation was "factual," this had the effect of closing the debate.

22. In this respect, the appeal of statistics is of the same kind as the appeal of focal points' language, replete with nominalizations and bureaucratic jargon. Both foreclosed interpretive possibilities and rendered the units more susceptible to arrangement into pattern. Mary Poovey (1998) has described how the invention of double-entry book keeping in sixteenth-century England rendered factual accuracy as an effect of the accounting firm:

Because double-entry book keeping's sign of virtue—the balance—depended on a sum that had no referent—the number added simply to produce the balance—the rectitude of the system as a whole was a matter of formal precision, not referential accuracy. (55)

23. This is not to say that feminist statisticians are unaware of the way in which statistics generate an internal coherence at the expense of a certain distance from the "realities" they quantify. For an excellent review of the problems associated with efforts to compile and evaluate gender data and some suggestions for its "critical use," see Danner, Fort, and Young 1999.

Chapter 6

1. Remarks delivered at the Seminar on Beijing and the ICPD held at the Soqosoqo Vakamarama headquarters, Suva, 19 January 1995 (transcript).
2. Fijian delegates were not certain what the fifth gender was supposed to be.
3. Catholic Women's League post-Beijing briefing, 28 September 1995 (transcript).
4. Present was the coordinator of the Pacific Media Desk, the vice president of the National Council of Women, the director of the Fiji Women's Crisis Centre, and other prominent focal points.
5. In her ethnography of the European Commission, Irene Bellier comments on the parallel way in which the staff of the commission imagine their project as "incomplete" and thus live with an eye to the future. This orientation toward the future, she notes, finds itself challenged to the core at intervals by wider skepticism about the European Community (1997:101). Like activists in Suva, commission staff experience their project as alternatively moving forward and utterly vanished.
6. In October 1994, at a high-level "Pacific WID donors conference" held in Suva, one representative from the home office of a major donor rose to present an extensive argument for the "need for a gender approach, not a women's approach." The presentation portrayed the "women's approach" as a conceptual dinosaur and the "gender approach" as both politically and technically correct. The presentation prompted other delegates to rush to assert that they too already had taken that point into account, having instituted "gender awareness guidelines," developed "gender checklists," and "mainstreamed gender concerns."
7. This emphasis on projects came in for extensive criticism at a regional workshop of Pacific women in 1987 (see the comments of Noeleen Heyzer and a general discussion in Griffen 1989: 77–87). Interestingly, however, this criticism of project-based development assistance never surfaced in any conference or workshop I attended during the period 1994–96, although one founding member of the Women and Fisheries Network recalled a discussion at the time of the founding of that network (1992) about the members' desire not to become involved in "projects."
8. In recalling for me the history of PAWORNET, for example, several people commented admiringly upon the new level of sophistication attained by its project funding proposal.
9. Local and expatriate staff of donor agencies evaluated these proposals and often solicited comments from other NGOs and government representatives in Fiji. Some

donors forwarded the most successful candidates to their home offices for a final decision, while others made the decision in Fiji.

10. The proposal requested U.S.$1,800 per participant for four nights of accommodation, despite the fact that the conference was to be held at a government guest house where participants would share rooms at minimal cost, and it included such additional expenditures as U.S.$1,000 for "opening ceremonies." The proposal ultimately was funded by UNDP.

11. The issue areas for 1995 were as follows:

(1) Strengthening the institutional capacity, role, and responsiveness of Pacific Island parliaments
(2) Increasing the legal rights and political participation of Pacific Island women
(3) Strengthening the capacity, efficiency, and responsiveness of Pacific Island legal systems
(4) Increasing the regional cooperation and participation of Pacific Island nations in regional and international affairs

The objectives listed under Issue 2 were:

(1) To advance the status, role, and participation of women in the political process ($75,000)
(2) To protect and promote women's legal and human rights ($42,600)

12. Jack Goody early on drew attention to the way a tabular list allows information to be sorted according to parallel criteria (1977: 89). He emphasized in particular the list's qualities as a tool for categorization:

> The list relies on discontinuity rather than continuity; it depends on physical placement, on location; it can be read in different directions, both sideways and downwards, up and down, as well as left and right; it has a clear-cut beginning and a precise end, that is, a boundary, an edge, like a piece of cloth. Most importantly it encourages the ordering of the items, by number, by initial sound, by category, etc. And the existence of boundaries, external and internal, brings greater visibility to categories, at the same time as making them more abstract. (81)

Yet a comparison and categorization are not always identical activities. Goody's formulation places more emphasis on the implications of the list form for "content" or "meaning" than is warranted in this case.

13. As WEDO wrote in its analysis of the GPFA that accompanied the matrix: "We consider both paragraphs [calling on governments to make concrete commitments and calling on governments to develop 'national action plans'] strategic tools for NGOs as organizing hooks in the post-Beijing implementation stage. The specific commitments announced by governments in Beijing were a tactical means of 'kick-starting' the larger and more difficult process of implementation" (1995b).

14. Escobar quotes Adele Mueller's conclusion in her study of WID policies that the

"topics" of WID discourse "are not entities in the real world, merely there to be discovered, but rather are already constructed in procedures of rule" (1995: 179).

15. The form of the matrix recalls Gluckman's (1965) view of the nature of legal concepts as *absorbent* in the way that they draw in facts and also are permeated with any set of (culturally specific) principles.

16. Sociological research on form-filling behavior finds that the defining characteristic of the stylized genre of interaction between the form filler and the form-originating body generated by the use of forms is that "the only acceptable response to a written question is an answer. The same restriction does not apply in natural conversation" (Frohlich 1986: 57).

17. The Matrix's effectuation of Action by pointing to its own gaps recalls Andrew Pickering's recent argument for the extension of the Science Studies interest in nonhuman agents to the agency of concepts (Pickering 1997). This "disciplinary agency," he argues, "leads disciplined practitioners through a series of manipulations within an established conceptual system" (41). His particular example is the application of mathematical models to new analytical problems, and he describes mathematical modeling as a temporally determined three-step process of "bridging" (applying the model to a new situation), "transcription—the copying of established moves from the old system into the new space fixed by the bridgehead," and "filling, completing the new system in the absence of any clear guidance from the base model" (42). Although bridging and filling are acts of human agency, he argues, transcription is the act of the model itself (61).

In making this claim, Pickering argues against efforts in the sociology of science to explain the appeal or success of particular models with reference to social relations of individuals or groups of scientists, that is, by referring to the social realities beyond the model: "I want to stress that on my analysis *nothing* substantive explains or controls the extension of scientific culture" (66). His description of his project in some respects mirrors the "inside out" analysis that has characterized this book: "Where [the sociology of science] necessarily looks outward from metaphysics (and technical culture in general) to quasi-emergent aspects of the social for explanations of change (and stability), I have looked inward, to technical practice itself. There is an emergent dynamics in that practice which goes unrecognized by [sociologists of science]" (74).

18. There is a considerable body of design theory on the question of how agency can be strongly or weakly signified in design terms. One of the most effective tricks represents categories as actors by projecting a chart, with its categories, onto a time line so that the categories appear to act in time (Kress and van Leeuwen 1996: 104–6).

19. In a textual analysis accompanying this chart, the organization made a strong argument that the Beijing Conference should be viewed as a success.

20. This conclusion recalls Chris Tennant's study of the treatment of indigenous people in the literature of international institutions in which he argues that the image of the indigenous person as an entity in harmony with nature but "threatened" and "on the brink of survival" due to development policies is internal to the modernist rhetoric of institutions. The slot created for the indigenous in the materials of the International Labour Organization and the UN that he describes will be familiar from the analysis above. He notes a "recurring idea that every issue demands an institution to take responsibility for it" (1994: 33) as well as the ideal of "participation" (49), which recalls the system of

slots in the Matrix. These forms culminate in "the single idea," "the call for *action*" (35), which most often takes the *form* of the "study" or "report" (36).

21. Recent discussions of data bases in social science and critical theory have tended to view these as instruments of social and political control that force the inherent complexity of the real world into simple categories, thereby subtly defining what can or cannot be expressed. Influenced by the Foucauldian critique of mechanisms of surveillance and also implicitly by popular ambivalence about the newness of the technology of which he writes, for example, Poster has emphasized the rigidity of the form in which information must be inserted into the data base and the sheer size of contemporary data bases as signs of their function in controlling knowledge (1990: 96). In a similar vein, Ferguson has critiqued the World Bank's analyses for "the way that extremely controversial and widely disputed claims are blandly asserted as simple, incontestable, scientific facts" (1993: 86). Yet, if categorization entails taking an inherently complex and messy set of elements and ordering them, the matrices described here cannot be said to involve categorization at all. There was no confusion or messiness in the constitution of what counted as "one Pacific Islander" on a panel or "one PPSEAWA member" as a representative of the organization in Beijing. All that mattered was that the panel organizer had found someone to fill the slot and the donor had found someone to fund. The matter then was closed and the work was done.

22. Christopher Pound notes of computer networks that

> the goal of computer networking is, first of all, to establish a grid to cross some space—in fact, to create that space in a telecommunicative sense. Then, at the same time, computer networks operate to erase or repress every inch of their own gridness, their spatiality. On the computer screen, there is to be no distance or difference between the user and the data. (1995: 536)

23. As Strathern has written in another context: "Gaps seem to give us somewhere to extend: space for our prosthetic devices" (1991: 115).

Chapter 7

1. They differ from "movements," for example, in the diverse kinds of actors they link (Sikkink 1993: 439). In contrast, other international relations scholars have applied institutional and status political theory to explore the symbolic quality of liberal institutional processes and the "epistemic communities" they create (Haas and Adler 1992), and hence to challenge the notion that transnational phenomena associated with liberal institutions serve instrumental purposes alone (e.g., Boyle and Preves 1998).

2. For example, Keck and Sikkink (1998) fail to consider how their own funding from the Ford Foundation to analyze the very networks funded by the Ford Foundation colors their description of the roles of funding and donor agencies. This at once legitimates the research, the networks, and the agency that funds them—by serving to convince the reader that there is a Real out there. This usage of social science to argue for the existence of a transnational phenomenon by describing and evaluating it has a lengthy history in United Nations institutions as well (e.g., Rittberger 1983).

3. Keck and Sikkink acknowledge that only certain kinds of issues seem to mobilize

NGO networks to "action." They point, for example, to global organization around violence against women (1998).

4. Laura Nader (1995) notes a similar normalization of political conflict in international negotiations. At the NGO Forum, participants sometimes puzzled over the ironies of this paradox. Panelists at a plenary session on the media, for example, described how the influx of women into journalism had changed very little. It was not necessary for the owners of newspapers to impose their views on their publications because journalists mysteriously assimilated themselves to an image of "what sells" without any explicit encouragement. DAWN's panelists likewise noted that, despite gains in certain areas such as violence against women, the very possibility of talking about the effects of the growth model of economic development now was foreclosed and women's groups seemed increasingly disinterested in critiquing "systemic inequalities" outside the parameters of a liberal paradigm.

5. The Pacific Concerns Resource Centre, the "secretariat" for the Nuclear Free and Independent Pacific Movement (NFIP), is an umbrella alliance of over 150 "grassroots organizations" throughout the region. Based in Suva and staffed by leaders of member organizations and veterans of major political struggles in the region, the PCRC organizes conferences, gathers information, translates materials between French and English, conducts press campaigns, produces newsletters, and handles similar tasks that are not easily coordinated by small groups with few resources. The PCRC therefore stands at a juncture between the institutional world of UN conferences and development policies and the demonstrators, liberation armies, trade unions, and tribal organizations gathered under the NFIP umbrella. As one activist explained in a speech at a recent NFIP conference, the PCRC joins "the struggle" to "the network":

> Our [the PCRC] job is to feed information from our struggles. Our movements initiate the campaigns, provide the background information and then the office sends that information out to all the networks and support groups throughout the world. (Halkyard-Harawira 1990: 5)

6. After Beijing, Susanna resolved to hold a follow-up meeting of the network in her native village on the island of Ouvéa. Some members were skeptical. Beijing had proven the network a failure, they said. They were tired; perhaps it would be best to concentrate scarce time and resources elsewhere. The meeting was postponed repeatedly due to a lack of funds, difficulties in arranging logistics on the remote island, and the death of a member of the network.

7. One intriguing aspect of the Network form, in contrast to "moments" or "organizations," for example, is the way its "newness" is intrinsic and hence timeless.

8. The competitive possibilities of ranking had a particular appeal in Fiji, where forms of all kinds are activated by competition. However, numerical ranking is by no means a purely Fijian fascination. In July 1996, the UNDP again issued its document entitled *Human Development Report*, which focused this time on the gap between rich and poor in each UN member state. Britain's ranking "behind" many of its former colonies on this scale was front page news in the British national newspapers (Lean and Bell 1996: 1).

9. The political implications of the Beijing Conference have been a subject of debate among feminist scholars of international law. Hilary Charlesworth offers a mutedly pos-

itive evaluation of the UN conference's generation of commitments. Nevertheless, she concludes that "[T]he documents help articulate women's rights but generally allow women access only to a male-defined world and so do not challenge the international political order" (Charlesworth 1996: 546). Diane Otto concludes that the dominance of an "equality" paradigm in the *Platform for Action* and the emaciation of issues of development and peace preclude the possibility that the document might serve as a catalyst for transformative change (Otto 1996: 28).

10. Matthias Finger has described how organizers of the UN Conference on Population and Development envisioned a space for NGOs as "providers of data and expertise" (1994: 186). This "input function," as he terms it, was mentioned again and again at the Beijing Conference and preparatory meetings in the remarks of UN officials, members of the Fiji delegation, and NGO representatives. Finger points out that at the Cairo Conference this formulation served the interests of NGOs identified as groupable into "sectors" such as science, women, and indigenous people, as well as NGOs from the north and representatives of business interests, much better than it did those that Finger terms "political environmental" NGOs, which complained "that they were only allowed to contribute information, but not to participate meaningfully in the decision-making" (201).

11. Martin Jay has described the critique of the aestheticization of fascist politics as a critique of aesthetics "self-referentially," that is, its indifference to other kinds of values and concerns (Jay 1993: 72–73), and of the treatment of the audience (i.e., "the masses") as a passive receiver rather than an active participant in the artistic process (74). Both of these critiques could be equally extended to the networks I have described.

References

Official Publications and Documents

Annan, Kofi. 1997. Preface. In *The world conference: Developing priorities for the 21st century*. New York: UN Department of Public Information.

Asia Pacific NGO Working Group (APWG). 1995a. *Reaching Out* 3 (1) (May 1995). Kuala Lumpur, Asia and Pacific Development Centre.

Asia Pacific NGO Working Group (APWG). 1995b. *Asia and Pacific NGOs: Asia-Pacific souvenir booklet*. Beijing: NGO Forum on Women.

Asian and Pacific Development Center (APDC). 1994. *NGO Forum on Women, Beijing '95, Issues in Gender and Development* 7 (August 1994). Kuala Lumpur, Asia and Pacific Development Centre.

Australian International Development Assistance Bureau (AIDAB). 1994. *UN Fourth World Conference on Women: Project proposal guidelines*. Canberra: Australian International Development Assistance Bureau.

Boutros-Ghali, Boutros. 1995. Secretary-general's statement at meeting of Advisory Group on Fourth World Conference on Women. UN Department of Public Information Press Release, 20 March, WOM/819.

Brown, Mary Cushman. 1886. Letter to Josiah and Julia. MS 166. National Archives of Fiji, Suva.

Department of Women and Culture (DWC). 1994. National report on women in Fiji—situation, analysis and strategies: In preparation for the Fourth World Conference on Women, action for equality development and peace. Suva, Fiji.

Development Alternatives with Women for a New Era (DAWN). 1995. *Markers on the way: The DAWN debates on alternative development—DAWN's platform for the Fourth World Conference on Women, Beijing, September 1995*. Barbados: Development Alternatives with Women for a New Era.

Fiji Department of Women and Culture (DWC). 1994. *News of Women* 2 (October 1994). Suva, Fiji DWC.

Fiji Department of Women and Culture (DWC). 1995. *News of Women* 3 (January 1995). Suva, Fiji DWC.

Fiji Government. 1996. 1996 Census of Fiji. Suva: Fiji Government Bureau of Statistics.

Fiji Land Claims Commission. 1880. Land Claims Commission Report no. 875, claim of Samuel and Peter Whippy to Lovonisikeci. On file at the National Archives of Fiji.

Fiji National Council of Women (FNCW). 1981. Fiji women's United Nations' mid-decade plan of action, 1981–1985. On file at the USP Library, Pacific Collection.

Fiji National Council of Women (FNCW). 1995. *Women's Information Network* (fourth quarter). Suva.
Fiji Women in Politics (FijiWIP). 1994. Project proposal. Suva.
Goodwillie, Diane. 1988. Posters. From Practical Skill Training Workshop.
Griffen, Vanessa. 1975. "Pacific women's chance." *Pacific Islands Monthly*, July.
Griffen, Vanessa. 1976. "Pacific women speak up." *Pacific Islands Monthly*, February.
Griffen, Vanessa, ed. 1989. *Women, development, and empowerment: A Pacific feminist perspective*. Kuala Lumpur: Asian and Pacific Development Center. Report of a Pacific women's workshop, Naboutini, Fiji, 23–26 March.
Halkyard-Harawira, Hilda. 1990. Opening speech. In *Sixth N.F.I.P. Conference, Aotearoa, 1990*. Auckland: Pacific Concerns Resource Centre for the Nuclear Free and Independent Pacific Movement. Conference report.
International Women's Development Agency (IWDA). 1995. *Beneath paradise: Concept paper for an exhibition being prepared by women from grassroots NGOs of the Pacific to be presented at the NGO Forum '95*. Victoria, Aust.: International Women's Development Agency.
International Women's Tribune Centre (IWTC). 1995a. *The Tribune: A Women and Development Quarterly* 54 (August 1995). New York, International Women's Tribune Centre.
International Women's Tribune Centre (IWTC). 1995b. *The Tribune: A Women and Development Quarterly* 53 (July 1995). New York, International Women's Tribune Centre.
Jouwe, Nancy. 1994. Report on the meeting for women of the Pacific colonies in preparation for Beijing, 1995. 13–16 December. Report submitted to Bread for the World, Nadi, Fiji.
Kneering, Jill, and Janet Shur. 1982. *The Exchange report: Women in the third world*. New York: The Exchange.
Mongella, Gertrude. 1995a. Beijing Conference must elicit commitments to action and of resources, Commission on the Status of Women is told. 39th session of the Commission on the Status of Women. UN Department of Public Information press release, 15 March, WOM/813.
Mongella, Gertrude. 1995b. Statement by the president of the conference on the commonly understood meaning of the term "gender," in *Report of the informal contact group on gender*. 7 July, 1995, A/CONF.177/20/Add.1. New York: UN Department for Policy and Sustainable Development.
Mongella, Gertrude. 1995c. Statement at the opening of the Fourth World Conference on Women. UN Department of Public Information press release, 4 September, WOM/BEI/12.
Mongella, Gertrude. 1995d. Opening address at the Fourth World Conference on Women. 4 September, A/CONF.177/20/Add.1, annex 2.
New Zealand Official Development Assistance Programme (NZODA). 1992. *Women in development policy statement*. Wellington: NZODA.
Pacific Women's Information/Communication Network (PAWORNET). 1990. *Tok Blong Ol Meri* 2 (June 1990). Suva, PAWORNET.
Pacific Women's Information/Communication Network (PAWORNET). 1992. Pacific

subregional workshop on the technical processing of information concerning women in development. Report, Suva, 4–15 May.
Pacific Women's Resource Bureau (PWRB). 1994a. *Pacific Women's Resource Bureau: Proposed work program, 1995–1997.* Suva: PWRB.
Pacific Women's Resource Bureau (PWRB). 1994b. Letter from PWRB to network focal points. 19 September.
Pacific Women's Resource Centre (PWRC). N.d. *Report on the Second Pacific Women's Conference, November 20–27, 1978.* Suva: PWRC.
Pan-Pacific and Southeast Asian Women's Association (PPSEAWA). 1978. *International Bulletin* (November 1978). Kuala Lumpur, Pan-Pacific and Southeast Asian Women's Association.
Planning Committee for the Pacific Regional Women's Conference. 1975. *Women speak out.* Suva.
Pryor, Pamela Takiora Ingram. 1981. Island women draft proposals. *New Pacific,* September-October.
South Pacific Commission (SPC). 1981. Seminar of South Pacific women, Papeete, Tahiti, French Polynesia, 20–24 July 1981. Conference report, Nouméa.
South Pacific Commission (SPC). 1985. *Regional meeting of Pacific islands women's non-governmental organisations. Rarotonga, Cook Islands, 19–23 March 1985.* Nouméa: South Pacific Commission Report.
South Pacific Commission (SPC). 1994a. *Pacific Platform for Action.* Nouméa: South Pacific Commission.
South Pacific Commission (SPC). 1994b. *Sixth regional conference of Pacific women, Nouméa, New Caledonia, 2–4 May 1994.* Nouméa: South Pacific Commission.
United Nations Branch for the Advancement of Women. 1988. *Women 2000.* New York: United Nations.
United Nations Department of Public Information. 1997. United Nations conferences: What have they accomplished? DPI/1825/Rev.4. http://www.un.org/News/facts/confrnes.htm.
United Nations Development Program (UNDP). 1992. United Nations in the South Pacific, Pacific subregional workshop on the technical processing of information concerning women and development, Suva, 4–15 May 1992. UNDP press release, 1 May.
United Nations Development Program (UNDP). 1994. *Pacific human development report.* Suva: UNDP.
United Nations Development Program (UNDP). 1995. *Human development report.* Washington, D.C.: United Nations.
United Nations Division for the Advancement of Women. 1995. Agents for change. *Women on the Move* 8. New York, United Nations.
United Nations Economic and Social Council (ECOSOC). 1995. Second review and appraisal of the implementation of the Nairobi forward looking strategies for the advancement of women. Report of the secretary-general to the Commission on the Status of Women, 10 January, E/CN.6/1995/3.
United Nations Fourth World Conference on Women (UNFWCW). 1995a. *Platform for Action.* In Report of the Fourth World Conference on Women. A/Conf. 177/20. New York: United Nations.

United Nations Fourth World Conference on Women (UNFWCW). 1995b. Draft Platform for Action. 15 May 1995 version, Future A/CONF. 177/L.1.

United Nations Fourth World Conference on Women (UNFWCW). 1995c. Report of the Fourth World Conference on Women. A/CONF.177/20. New York: United Nations.

United Nations General Assembly. 1993. Eighty-fifth plenary meeting: Implementation of the Nairobi forward-looking strategies for the advancement of women. 20 December, A/RES/48/108.

United Nations International Research and Training Institute for the Advancement of Women (INSTRAW) and United Nations Fund for Women (UNIFEM). 1995. *Women and the UN, 1945–1995.* New York: United Nations.

United Nations Secretary-General. 1994. Technical assistance and women: From mainstreaming towards institutional accountability. Report of the secretary-general to the Commission on the Status of Women, 19 December, ECN.6/1995/6.

VanRoy, Edward. 1992. Letter to Fiji Department of Women and Culture, Re: Pacific Subregional Workshop on the technical processing of information concerning women in development, Suva, 4–15 May, 1992. 17 March.

Women's Environment and Development Organization (WEDO). 1995a. *A brief analysis of the UN Fourth World Conference on Women Beijing Declaration and Platform for Action.* New York: Women's Environment and Development Organization.

Women's Environment and Development Organization (WEDO). 1995b. *Turn the words into action! Highlights from the Beijing Declaration and Platform for Action.* New York: Women's Environment and Development Organization.

World Association for Christian Communication—Pacific Region (WACC). 1995. *Pacific handbook for the United Nations Fourth World Conference on Women NGO Forum, 1995.* Suva: Pacific Women in Christian Communication.

Young Women's Christian Association (YWCA). 1962. List of members on the committee of the Young Women's Christian Association for 1962. On file at the archives of the YWCA, Suva.

Young Women's Christian Association (YWCA). 1977. *Arena* 3 (December) Suva, YWCA.

General Publications

Abbott, Kenneth W. 1993. "Trust but verify": The production of information in arms control treaties and other international agreements. *Cornell International Law Journal* 26:1–58.

Abel, Richard. 1973. Law books and books about law. *Stanford Law Review* 26:175–228.

Abu-Lughod, Lila. 1995. The objects of soap opera: Egyptian television and the cultural politics of modernity. In *Worlds apart: Modernity through the prism of the local,* ed. Daniel Miller. London and New York: Routledge.

Anand, Anita. 1996. Beijing: Exhausting, frustrating, exciting. *Indian Journal of Gender Studies* 3:127–32.

Anderson, Benedict. 1983. *Imagined communities.* London: Verso.

Appadurai, Arjun. 1991. Global ethnoscapes: Notes and queries for a transnational an-

thropology. In *Recapturing anthropology: Working in the present*, ed. Robin Fox. Santa Fe, N.M.: School of American Research Press.
Appadurai, Arjun. 1996. *Modernity at large: Cultural dimensions of globalization*. Minneapolis: University of Minnesota Press.
Augé, Marc. [1992] 1995. *Non-places: Introduction to an anthropology of supermodernity*. London: Verso.
Baden, Sally, and Anne Marie Goetz. 1997. Who needs [sex] when you can have [gender]? Conflicting discourses on gender at Beijing. *Feminist Review* 56:3–25.
Baker, James N. 1992. The presence of the name: Reading scripture in an Indonesian village. In *The ethnography of reading*, ed. Jonathan Boyarin. Berkeley: University of California Press.
Balkin, J. M. 1992. What is postmodern constitutionalism? *Michigan Law Review* 90 (7): 1966–90.
Barnes, J. A. 1968. Networks and political process. In *Local-level politics*, ed. Marc J. Swartz. London: University of London Press.
Barnett, Michael N. 1997. The UN Security Council, indifference, and genocide in Rwanda. *Cultural Anthropology* 12 (4): 551–78.
Barth, Frederick. 1978. Scale and network in urban Western society. In *Scale and social organization*, ed. F. Barth. Oslo: Universitetsforlaget.
Basch, Linda, Nina Glick Schiller, and Cristina Szanton Blanc. 1994. *Nations unbound: Transnational projects, postcolonial predicaments, and deterritorialized nation-states*. Langhorne, Pa.: Gordon and Breach Science Publishers.
Bateson, Gregory. 1980. *Mind and nature: A necessary unity*. London: Fontana.
Bateson, Gregory. 1987a. Cybernetic explanation. In *Steps to an ecology of mind*. Northvale, N.J.: Jason Aronson.
Bateson, Gregory. 1987b. Style, grace, and information in primitive art. In *Steps to an ecology of mind*. Northvale, N.J.: Jason Aronson.
Bateson, Gregory. 1987c. Form, substance, and difference. In *Steps to an ecology of mind*. Northvale, N.J.: Jason Aronson.
Battaglia, Debbora. 1994. Retaining reality: Some practical problems with objects as property. *Man* 29:1–15.
Battaglia, Debbora. 1995. On practical nostalgia: Self-prospecting among urban Trobrianders. In *Rhetorics of self-making*, ed. D. Battaglia. Berkeley: University of California Press.
Baudrillard, Jean. [1972] 1981. *For a critique of the political economy of the sign*, trans. Charles Levin. St. Louis: Telos.
Baudrillard, Jean. 1994. *Simulacra and simulation*, trans. Sheila Faria Glaser. Ann Arbor: University of Michigan Press.
Beidelman, Thomas O. 1986. *Moral imagination in Kaguru modes of thought*. Bloomington: Indiana University Press.
Bell, Daniel. 1973. *The coming of post-industrial society*. New York: Basic Books.
Bell, Daniel. 1979. *The cultural contradictions of capitalism*. London: Heinemann Educational.
Bellier, Irene. 1997. The commission as an actor: An anthropologist's view. In *Partici-*

pation and policy-making in the European Union, ed. Helen Wallace and Alasdair R. Young. Oxford: Clarendon.

Benjamin, Walter. [1955] 1973. The work of art in the age of mechanical reproduction. In *Illuminations*, trans. Harry Zohn. London: Fontana.

Blok, Anton. 1973. Coalitions in Sicilian peasant society. In *Network analysis: Studies in human interaction*, ed. Jeremy Boissevain and J. Clyde Mitchell. Paris: Mouton.

Born, Georgina. 1995. *Rationalizing culture: IRCAM, Boulez, and the institutionalization of the musical avant-garde*. Berkeley: University of California Press.

Borneman, John. 1998. *Subversions of international order: Studies in the political anthropology of culture*. Albany: State University of New York Press.

Börzel, Tanja A. 1997. What's so special about policy networks? An exploration of the concept and its usefulness in studying European governance. European Integration Online Papers 1, 16. http://eiop.or.at/eiop/texte/1997-016a.htm.

Bouquet, Mary. 1996. Family trees and their affinities: The visual imperative of the genealogical diagram. *Journal of the Royal Anthropological Institute* (n.s.) 2:43–66.

Bourloyannis, M.-Christiane. 1990. Fact-finding by the secretary-general of the United Nations. *New York University Journal of International Law and Politics* 22:641–69.

Boyle, Elizabeth H., and Sharon E. Preves. 1998. National legislating as an international process: The case of national anti-female-genital-cutting laws. Article under review.

Brenneis, Donald. 1994. Discourse and discipline at the National Research Council: A bureaucratic bildungsroman. *Cultural Anthropology* 9:23–36.

Brenneis, Donald. 1996. Grog and gossip in Bhatgaon: Style and substance in Fiji Indian conversation. In *The matrix of language: Contemporary linguistic anthropology*, ed. D. Brenneis and R. K. S. Macaulay. Boulder: Westview.

Brenneis, Donald. 1999. New lexicon, old language: Negotiating the "global" at the National Science Foundation. In *Cultural anthropology now: Unexpedited contexts, shifting constituencies, changing agendas*, ed. George E. Marcus. Santa Fe: School of American Research Press.

Briggs, Adam, and Paul Cobley. 1996. Designing HIV awareness strategies: An ethnographic approach. In *Design and aesthetics: A reader*, ed. Jerry Palmer and Mo Dodson. London and New York: Routledge.

Brysk, Alison. 1993. From above and below: Social movements, the international system, and human rights in Argentina. *Comparative Political Studies* 26 (3): 259–85.

Bulu, Joeli. 1871. *Joeli Bulu: The autobiography of a native minister in the South Seas translated by a missionary*. London: Wesleyan Mission House.

Burke, Kenneth. 1969. *A rhetoric of motives*. Berkeley: University of California Press.

Burke, Kenneth. 1984. *The philosophy of literary form*. Berkeley: University of California Press.

Callon, Michel. 1986. Some elements of a sociology of translation: Domestication of the scallops and the fishermen of St. Brieuc Bay. In *Power, action, and belief: A new sociology of knowledge?* ed. John Law. London: Routledge and Kegan Paul.

Callon, Michel. 1991. Techno-economic networks and irreversibility. In *A sociology of monsters: Essays on power, technology, and domination*, ed. John Law. London: Routledge.

Castells, Manuel. 1996. The net and the self. *Critique of Anthropology* 16:9–38.
Charlesworth, Hilary. 1996. Women as sherpas: Are global summits useful for women? *Feminist Studies* 22: 537–47.
Chayes, Abram, and Antonio Handler Chayes. 1995. *The new sovereignty: Compliance with international regulatory agreements.* Cambridge: Harvard University Press.
Chinkin, Christine. 1989. The challenge of soft law: Development and change in international law. *International and Comparative Law Quarterly* 38:850–66.
Clifford, James. 1988. *The predicament of culture: Twentieth-century ethnography, literature, and art.* Cambridge: Harvard University Press.
Clifford, James. 1994. Diasporas. *Cultural Anthropology* 9:302–38.
Comaroff, Jean, and John Comaroff. 1992. *Ethnography and the historical imagination.* Chicago: University of Chicago Press.
Comaroff, Jean, and John Comaroff. 1995. *Modernity and its malcontents: Ritual and power in postcolonial Africa.* Chicago: University of Chicago Press.
Connors, Jane. 1996. NGOs and the human rights of women at the United Nations. In *"The conscience of the world": The influence of non-governmental organisations in the UN system,* ed. P. Willetts. Washington, D.C.: Brookings Institution.
Coote, Jeremy, and Anthony Shelton, ed. 1992. *Anthropology, art, and aesthetics.* Oxford: Clarendon.
Crapanzano, Vincent. 1992. *Hermes' dilemma and Hamlet's desire: On the epistemology of interpretation.* Cambridge: Harvard University Press.
Crary, Jonathan, and Sanford Kwinter, ed. 1992. *Incorporations.* New York: Zone.
Crocombe, Ron G., and William F. E. Marsters. 1987. Land tenure in a test tube: The case of Palmerston Atoll. In *Land tenure in the atolls,* ed. Ron G. Crocombe. Suva: Institute of Pacific Studies of the University of the South Pacific.
Danet, Brenda. 1997. Books, letters, documents: The changing aesthetics of texts in late print culture. *Journal of Material Culture* 2:5–38.
Danner, Mona, Lucia Fort, and Gay Young. 1998. International data on women and gender. Resources, issues, critical use. *Women's Studies International Forum* 22 (2): 249–59.
Danziger, Eve. 1996. Parts and their counterparts: Spatial and social relationships in Mopan Maya. *Journal of the Royal Anthropological Institute* (n.s.) 2:67–82.
Das, Veena. 1995. On soap opera: What kind of anthropological object is it? In *Worlds apart: Modernity through the prism of the local,* ed. Daniel Miller. London and New York: Routledge.
Daston, Lorraine. [1991] 1994. Marvelous facts and miraculous evidence in early modern Europe. In *Questions of evidence: Proof, practice, and persuasion across the disciplines,* ed. James Chandler, Arnold I. Davidson, and Harry Harootunian. Chicago: University of Chicago Press.
De Sousa Santos, Boaventura. 1987. Law, a map of misreading: Towards a postmodern conception of law. *Journal of Law and Society* 14:279–302.
Dezalay, Yves, and Bryant G. Garth. 1996. *Dealing in virtue: International commercial arbitration and the construction of a transnational legal order.* Chicago: University of Chicago Press.
DiMaggio, Paul J., and Walter W. Powell. 1991. The iron cage revisited: Institutional

isomorphism and collective rationality in organizational fields. In *The new institutionalism in organizational analysis*, ed. W. W. Powell and P. J. DiMaggio. Chicago: University of Chicago Press.

Durkheim, Emile. [1915] 1957. *The elementary forms of the religious life*, trans. Joseph W. Swain. London: Allen and Unwin.

Eagleston, John. N.d. Ups and downs of Captain John Eagleston. Manuscript on file at the Salem Museum, Salem, Massachusetts.

Edwards, David B. 1994. Afghanistan, ethnography, and the new world order. *Cultural Anthropology* 9:345–60.

Epstein, Arnold L. 1969. The network and urban social organization. In *Social networks in urban situations*, ed. J. Clyde Mitchell. Manchester: Manchester University Press.

Escobar, Arturo. 1992. Culture, practice and politics: Anthropology and the study of social movements. *Critique of Anthropology* 12:395–432.

Escobar, Arturo. 1995. *Encountering development: The making and unmaking of the third world*. Princeton: Princeton University Press.

Ewins, R. 1982. *Mat-weaving in Gau, Fiji*. Fiji Museum Special Publications, no. 3. Suva: Fiji Museum.

Falasca-Zamponi, Simonetta. 1997. *Fascist spectacle: The aesthetics of power in Mussolini's Italy*. Berkeley: University of California Press.

Falk, Richard. 1970. *The status of law in international society*. Princeton: Princeton University Press.

Faubion, James D. 1988. Possible modernities. *Cultural Anthropology* 3:365–78.

Faubion, James D. 1993. *Modern Greek lessons: A primer in historical constructivism*. Princeton: Princeton University Press.

Feinberg, Richard. 1981. What is Polynesian kinship all about? *Ethnology* 20:115–31.

Ferguson, James. 1990. *The anti-politics machine: "Development," depoliticization, and bureaucratic power in Lesotho*. Cambridge: Cambridge University Press.

Ferguson, James. 1993. De-moralizing economics: African socialism, scientific capitalism, and the moral politics of "structural adjustment." In *Moralising states and the ethnography of the present*, ed. Sally Falk Moore. American Ethnological Society Monographs, no. 5. Arlington, Va.: American Anthropological Association.

Finger, Matthias. 1994a. Environmental NGOs in the UNCED process. In *Environmental NGOs in world politics*, ed. Thomas Princen and Matthias Finger. London: Routledge.

Finger, Matthias. 1994b. NGOs and transformation: Beyond social movement theory. In *Environmental NGOs in world politics: Linking the local and the global*, ed. Thomas Princen and Matthias Finger. London: Routledge.

Firth, Raymond. 1957. A note on descent groups in Polynesia. *Man* 57:4–8.

Fisher, Julie. 1993. *The road from Rio: Sustainable development and the nongovernmental movement in the Third World*. Westport: Praeger.

Fisher, William F. 1997. Doing good? The politics and antipolitics of NGO practices. *Annual Review of Anthropology* 26:439–64.

Foerster, H. von. 1951. *Cybernetics: Circular causal and feedback mechanisms in biological and social systems*. New York: Josiah Macy Jr. Foundation.

Foster, Robert J. 1995. Print advertisements and nation making in metropolitan Papua

New Guinea. In *Nation making: Emergent identities in postcolonial Melanesia*, ed. Robert J. Foster. Ann Arbor: University of Michigan Press.

Foucault, Michel. 1972. *The archaeology of knowledge and the discourse on knowledge.* New York: Pantheon.

Foucault, Michel. [1979] 1991. *Discipline and punish,* trans. Alan Sheridan. London: Penguin.

France, Peter. 1969. *The charter of the land: Custom and colonization in nineteenth century Fiji.* Melbourne: Oxford University Press.

Franck, Thomas M. 1988. Legitimacy in the international system. *American Journal of International Law* 82:705–59.

Franklin, Sarah. 1997. *Embodied progress: A cultural account of assisted conception.* London: Routledge.

Fraser, Arvonne S. 1987. *The U.N. Decade for Women: Documents and dialogue.* Boulder and London: Westview.

Frege, Gottlob. [1884] 1983. The concept of number, trans. Michael S. Mahoney. In *Philosophy of mathematics*, ed. Paul Benacerraf and Hilary Putnam. 2d ed. Cambridge: Cambridge University Press.

Frohlich, D. M. 1986. On the organisation of form-filling behaviour. *Information Design Journal* 5:43–59.

Fulmer, Mara Jevera. 1996. *Symbols and patterns of grassroots culture in the Fiji Islands.* Suva: University Media Centre, University of the South Pacific.

Galtung, Johan. 1986. On the anthropology of the United Nations system. In *The nature of United Nations bureaucracies*, ed. David Pitt and Thomas G. Weiss. Boulder: Westview.

Geertz, Clifford. 1973. *The interpretation of cultures.* New York: Basic Books.

Geertz, Clifford. 1988. *Works and lives: The anthropologist as author.* New York: Polity.

Gell, Alfred. 1985. How to read a map: Remarks on the practical logic of navigation. *Man* (n.s.) 20:271–86.

Gell, Alfred. 1992. The technology of enchantment and the enchantment of technology. In *Anthropology, art, and aesthetics*, ed. Jeremy Coote and Anthony Shelton. Oxford: Clarendon.

Ghils, Paul. 1992. International civil society: International non-governmental organizations in the international system. *International Social Science Journal* 44 (5): 417–31.

Ghosh, Amitav. 1994. The global reservation: Notes toward an ethnography of international peacekeeping. *Cultural Anthropology* 9:412–22.

Giddens, Anthony. 1990. *The consequences of modernity.* Cambridge: Polity.

Ginger, Ann Fagan, Anne Paxton Wagley, and Rob Markfield. 1996. Nonprofits have a new role in ensuring human rights in the United States. *University of South Florida Law Review* 30:427–76.

Ginsburg, Fay. 1994. Embedded aesthetics: Creating a discursive space for indigenous media. *Cultural Anthropology* 9:365–82.

Gluckman, Max. 1965. *Ideas in the Barotse jurisprudence.* New Haven: Yale University Press.

Goodin, Robert E., ed. 1997. *The theory of institutional design*. Cambridge: Cambridge University Press.
Goodwin, Charles, and Alessandro Duranti. 1992. Rethinking context: An introduction. In *Rethinking context: Language as an interactive phenomenon*, ed. Alessandro Duranti and Charles Goodwin. Cambridge: Cambridge University Press.
Goody, Jack. 1977. *The domestication of the savage mind*. Cambridge: Cambridge University Press.
Gore, Al. 1991. Infrastructure for the global village. *Scientific American* 265 (3): 108–11.
Gray, Chris Haldes, and Steven Mentor. 1995. The cyborg body politic: Version 1.2. In *The cyborg handbook*, ed. Chris Haldes Gray. New York and London: Routledge.
Gray, Chris Haldes, Steven Mentor, and Heidi J. Figueroa-Sarriera. 1995. Cyborgology: Constructing the knowledge of cybernetic organisms. In *The cyborg handbook*, ed. Chris Haldes Gray. New York and London: Routledge.
Griffen, Vanessa. 1971. The part European association: A report. Manuscript filed at the University of the South Pacific Library.
Griffen, Vanessa. 1994. Women, development, and population: A critique of the Port Villa Declaration. In *Sustainable development or malignant growth? Perspectives of Pacific island women*, ed. 'Atu Emberson-Bain. Suva: Marama.
Griffin, L. M. 1969. A dramatistic theory of the rhetoric of movements. In *Critical responses to Kenneth Burke*, ed. W. H. Rueckert. Minneapolis: University of Minnesota Press.
Groom, A. J. R. 1989. Reflections on a changing system. In *Global issues in the United Nations' framework*, ed. Paul Taylor. New York: St. Martins.
Guattari, Felix. 1992. Regimes, pathways, subjects. In *Incorporations*, ed. Jonathan Crary and Sanford Kwinter. New York: Zone.
Gunning, Isabelle R. 1991. Modernizing customary international law: The challenge of human rights. *Virginia Journal of International Law* 31:211–47.
Gupta, Akhil. 1992. The song of the nonaligned world: Transnational identities and the reinscription of space in late capitalism. *Cultural Anthropology* 7:63–79.
Guthrie, John T. 1988. Locating information in documents: Examination of a cognitive model. *Reading Research Quarterly* 23:178–99.
Haas, Peter M., and Emanuel Adler. 1992. Conclusion: Epistemic communities, world order, and the creation of a reflective research program. *International Organization* 46 (1): 367–90.
Habermas, Jürgen. 1984. *The theory of communicative action*, trans. Thomas McCarthy. Boston: Beacon.
Hall, William E. 1880. *International Law*. Oxford: Clarendon.
Hanks, William F. 1996. Language and communicative practices. Boulder: Westview.
Hannerz, Ulf. 1992a. The global ecumene as a network of networks. In *Conceptualizing society*, ed. Adam Kuper. London: Routledge.
Hannerz, Ulf. 1992b. *Cultural complexity: Studies in the social organization of meaning*. New York: Columbia University Press.
Haraway, Donna. 1990. A manifesto for cyborgs: Science, technology, and socialist feminism in the 1980s. In *Feminism/postmodernism*, ed. Linda J. Nicholson. New York: Routledge.

Haraway, Donna. [1989] 1992. *Primate visions: Gender, race, and nature in the world of modern science*. London: Verso.
Haraway, Donna. 1995. Cyborgs and symbionts: Living together in the new world order. In *The cyborg handbook*, ed. Chris Haldes Gray. New York and London: Routledge.
Harper, Richard H. R. 1991. The computer game: Detectives, suspects, and technology. *British Journal of Criminology* 31 (3): 292–307.
Harper, Richard H. R. 1998. *Inside the IMF: An ethnography of documents, technology, and organisational action*. San Diego: Academic.
Harris, Rosalind W. 1985. A note on parallel conferences. In *Forum '85: NGO Planning Committee, final report, Nairobi, Kenya*. New York: International Women's Tribune Center.
Harrison, Simon. 1989. Magical and material polities in Melanesia. *Man* (n.s.) 24:1–20.
Harvey, Penelope. 1996. *Hybrids of modernity: Anthropology, the nation state, and the universal exhibition*. London and New York: Routledge.
Heimer, Carol A., and Arthur L. Stinchcombe. 1999. Remodeling the garbage can: Implications of the origins of items in decision streams. In *Organizational and institutional factors in political life*, ed. Morten Egeberg and Per Loegreid. Oslo: Scandinavian University Press.
Herzfeld, Michael. 1992. *The social production of indifference: Exploring the symbolic roots of Western bureaucracy*. Chicago: University of Chicago Press.
Herzfeld, Michael. 1997. *Cultural intimacy: Social poetics in the nation-state*. New York: Routledge.
Hoadley, Steve. 1992. *The South Pacific foreign affairs handbook*. Sydney: Allen and Unwin.
Hobart, Mark. 1994. Introduction: The growth of ignorance? In *An anthropological critique of development*, ed. M. Hobart. London: Routledge.
Hobart, Mark. 1995. As I lay laughing: Encountering global knowledge in Bali. In *Counterworks: Managing the diversity of knowledge*, ed. Richard Fardon. London: Routledge.
Hocart, A. M. 1952. *The northern states of Fiji*. London: Royal Anthropological Institute.
Hofstede, Geert. 1989. Cultural predictors of national negotiation styles. In *Processes of international negotiations*, ed. Frances Mautner-Markhof. Boulder: Westview Press.
Hooper, Paul F. N.d. Feminism in the Pacific: The Pan-Pacific and Southeast Asia Women's Association. Paper on file at the University of the South Pacific Library, Pacific Collection.
Hulme, David, and Michael Edwards. 1997. *NGOs, states and donors: Too close for comfort?* New York: St. Martin's Press.
Humphrey, Caroline. 1995. Creating a culture of disillusionment: Consumption in Moscow, a chronicle of changing times. In *Worlds apart: Modernity through the prism of the local*, ed. D. Miller. London and New York: Routledge.
Irvine, Judith T. 1996. When talk isn't cheap: Language and political economy. In *The matrix of language: Contemporary linguistic anthropology*, ed. D. Brenneis and R. K. S. Macaulay. Boulder: Westview.

Jacquette, Jane S. 1995. Losing the battle/winning the war: International politics, women's issues, and the 1980 Mid-Decade Conference. In *Women, politics, and the United Nations,* ed. Anne Winslow. Westport, Conn.: Greenwood.

Jacquette, Jane, and Irene Tinker. 1987. UN Decade for Women? Its impact and legacy. *World Development* 15:419–27.

Jameson, Fredric. 1998. Notes on globalization as a philosophical issue. In *The cultures of globalization,* ed. Fredric Jameson and Masao Miyoshi. Durham: Duke University Press.

Jay, Martin. 1993. *Force fields: Between intellectual history and cultural critique.* New York: Routledge.

Jolly, Margaret. 1996. Woman ikat raet long human raet o no? Women's rights, human rights, and domestic violence in Vanuatu. *Feminist Review* 52:169–90.

Jönsson, Christer. 1986. Interorganization theory and international organization. *International Studies Quarterly* 30:39–57.

Kant, Immanuel. 1952. *The critique of judgement,* trans. J. Meredith. Oxford: Clarendon.

Keck, Margaret E., and Kathryn Sikkink. 1998. *Activists beyond borders: Advocacy networks in international politics.* Ithaca: Cornell University Press.

Kelly, D. L. 1966. The Part-Europeans of Fiji. M.S. thesis, Department of Geography, University of Wellington.

Kelly, John D. 1991. *A politics of virtue: Hinduism, sexuality, and countercolonial discourse in Fiji.* Chicago: University of Chicago Press.

Kennedy, David. 1987. *International legal structures.* Baden-Baden: Nomos Verlagsgesellschaft.

Kennedy, David. 1993. Autumn weekends: An essay on law and everyday life. In *Law in everyday life,* ed. Austin Sarat and T. R. Kearns. Ann Arbor: University of Michigan Press.

Keohane, Robert O., and Stanley Hoffmann. 1991. Institutional change in Europe in the 1980s. In *The new European Community: Decisionmaking and institutional change,* ed. Robert O. Keohane and Stanley Hoffmann. Boulder: Westview.

Kinross, Robin. 1989. The rhetoric of neutrality. In *Design discourse: History, theory, criticism,* ed. Victor Margolin. Chicago: University of Chicago Press.

Kirshenblatt-Gimblett, Barbara. 1995. Confusing pleasures. In *The traffic in culture: Refiguring art and anthropology,* ed. George E. Marcus and Fred R. Myers. Berkeley: University of California Press.

Koskenniemi, Martti. 1995. International law in a post-realist era. *Australian Year Book of International Law* 16:1–19.

Kress, Gunter, and Theo van Leeuwen. 1996. *Reading images: The grammar of visual design.* London: Routledge.

Laclau, Ernesto, and Chantal Mouffe. 1985. *Hegemony and socialist strategy: Towards a radical democratic politics,* trans. Winston Moore and Paul Commade. London: Verso.

Lash, Scott. 1994. Reflexivity and its doubles: Structure, aesthetics, community. In *Reflexive modernity: Politics, tradition, and aesthetics in the modern social order,* ed. Ulrich Beck, Anthony Giddens, and Scott Lash. Stanford: Stanford University Press.

Latour, Bruno. 1990. Drawing things together. In *Representation in scientific practice*, ed. M. Lynch and S. Woolgar. Cambridge: MIT Press.

Latour, Bruno. 1993. *We have never been modern*, trans. Catherine Porter. Cambridge: Harvard University Press.

Latour, Bruno, and Steve Woolgar. [1979] 1986. *Laboratory life: The construction of scientific facts*. Princeton: Princeton University Press.

Law, John. 1994. *Organising modernity*. Oxford: Blackwell.

Lean, Geoffrey, and Graham Bell. 1996. UK most unequal country in the West. *Independent on Sunday*, 21 July 1996, 1.

Lipnack, Jessica, and Jeffrey Stamps. 1984. Creating another America: The power and the joy of networking. In *People centered development: Contributions toward theory and planning frameworks*, ed. David Korten and Rudi Klaus. Hartford, CT.: Kumarian. Quoted in Julie Fisher, *The road from Rio: Sustainable development and the nongovernmental movement in the Third World* (Westport: Praeger, 1993).

Lipschutz, Ronnie D. 1992. Reconstructing world politics: The emergence of global civil society. *Millennium: Journal of International Studies* 21:389–420.

Little, Paul E. 1995. Ritual, power and ethnography at the Rio Earth Summit. *Critique of Anthropology* 15:265–88.

Luard, Evan. 1990. *The globalization of politics: The changed focus of political action in the modern world*. Basingstoke: Macmillan.

Lupton, Ellen. 1989. Reading isotype. In *Design discourse: History, theory, criticism*, ed. Victor Margolin. Chicago: University of Chicago Press.

Lyotard, Jean-François. 1984. *The postmodern condition: A report on knowledge*, trans. Geoff Bennington and Brian Massumi. Manchester: Manchester University Press.

Majone, G. 1997. The new European agencies: Regulation by information. *Journal of European Public Policy* 4 (2): 262–75.

Makarov, Igor' Mikhailovich. 1987. *Cybernetics of living matter: Nature, man, information*. Moscow: MIR.

Malkki, Liisa. 1992. National geographic: Rooting of peoples and the territorialization of national identity among scholars and refugees. *Cultural Anthropology* 7:24–44.

Malkki, Liisa. 1995. *Purity and exile: Violence, memory, and national cosmology among Hutu refugees in Tanzania*. Chicago: University of Chicago Press.

Malkki, Liisa H. 1996. Speechless emissaries: Refugees, humanitarianism, and dehistoricization. *Cultural Anthropology* 11 (3): 377–404.

Mamak, Alexander F. 1974. *Pluralism and social change in Suva City, Fiji*. Ph.D. diss., University of Hawaii. Ann Arbor: University Microfilms.

Marcus, George E. 1995. Ethnography in/of the world system: The emergence of multi-sited ethnography. *Annual Review of Anthropology* 24:95–117.

Marcus, George E. 1996. Introduction to the volume and reintroduction to the series. In *Connected: Engagements with media*, ed. George E. Marcus. Chicago: University of Chicago Press.

Marcus, George E., and Fred R. Myers. 1995. The traffic in art and culture: An introduction. In *The traffic in culture: Refiguring art and anthropology*, ed. George E. Marcus and Fred R. Myers. Berkeley: University of California Press.

Martin, Emily. 1994. *Flexible bodies: Tracking immunity in American culture from the days of polio to the age of AIDS*. Boston: Beacon.
Martin, Emily. 1996. The society of flows and the flows of culture. *Critique of Anthropology* 16:49–56.
Mathews, Jessica T. 1997. Power shift. *Foreign Affairs* 76:50–66.
Maurer, Bill. 1997. *Recharting the Caribbean: Land, law, and citizenship in the British Virgin Islands*. Ann Arbor: University of Michigan Press.
McCarthy, J. D., and M. N. Zald. 1973. *The trends of social movements in America: Professionalization and resource mobilization*. Morristown, N.J.: General Learning Press.
Messick, Brinkley. 1990. Literacy and the law: Documents and document specialists in Yemen. In *Law and Islam in the Middle East*, ed. Daisy Hilse Dwyer. New York: Bergin and Garvey.
Messick, Brinkley. 1993. *The calligraphic state: Textual domination and history in a Muslim society*. Berkeley: University of California Press.
Meyer, J. W., and B. Rowan. 1991. Institutionalized organizations: Formal structure as myth and ceremony. *The new institutionalism in organizational analysis*, ed. Walter W. Powell and Paul J. DiMaggio. Chicago: University of Chicago Press.
Mitchell, J. Clyde. 1973. Networks, norms, and institutions. In *Network analysis: Studies in human interaction*, ed. Jeremy Boissevain and J. Clyde Mitchell. Paris: Mouton.
Mitchell, J. Clyde. 1974. Social networks. *Annual Review of Anthropology* 3:279–99.
Miyazaki, Hirokazu. 1997. Artefacts of truth. Ph.D. thesis, Department of Anthropology, Research School of Pacific and Asian Studies, Australian National University.
Moisy, Claude. 1997. "Myths of the global information village." *Foreign Policy* Summer:78–87.
Mol, Annemarie, and John Law. 1994. Regions, networks, and fluids: Anaemia and social topology. *Social Studies of Science* 24:641–71.
Momoivalu, Mere. 1995. Concern over no Indian women representation, *Fiji Times*, 17 March 1995, 4.
Morgenstern, Felice. 1986. *Legal problems of international organizations*. Cambridge: Grotius.
Mueller, A. 1986. The bureaucratization of feminist knowledge: The case of women in development. *Resources for Feminist Research* 15:36–38.
Mueller, A. 1987. Power and naming in the development institution: The "discovery" of "women in Peru." Paper presented at the Fourteenth Annual Third World Conference, Chicago.
Munn, Nancy D. 1973. *Walbiri iconography: Graphic representation and cultural symbolism in a central Australian society*. Ithaca and London: Cornell University Press.
Munn, Nancy D. 1995. An essay on the symbolic construction of memory in the Kaluli Gisalo. In *Cosmos and society in Oceania*, ed. Daniel de Coppet and André Iteanu. Oxford: Berg.
Munn, Nancy D. 1996. Excluded spaces: The figure in the Australian Aboriginal landscape. *Critical Inquiry* 22:446–65.
Myers, Fred R. 1986. *Pintupi country, Pintupi self: Sentiment and politics among western desert Aborigines*. Washington, D.C.: Smithsonian Institution Press.
Myers, Fred R. 1996. Reflections on a meeting: Structure, language, and the polity in a

small-scale society. In *The matrix of language: Contemporary linguistic anthropology*, ed. D. Brenneis and R. K. S. Macaulay. Boulder: Westview.
Nadel, Laurel. 1975. *Meeting in Mexico: The story of the world conference of the International Women's Year.* New York: United Nations.
Nader, Laura. 1969. Up the anthropologist: Perspectives gained from studying up. In *Reinventing anthropology*, ed. Dell Hymes. New York: Pantheon.
Nader, Laura. 1995. Civilization and its negotiations. In *Understanding disputes: The politics of argument*, ed. Pat Caplan. Oxford Providence: Berg.
Nicholson, T. 1994. Institution building: Examining the fit between bureaucracies and indigenous systems. In *Anthropology of organizations*, ed. Susan Wright. London and New York: Routledge.
O'Hanlon, Michael. 1995. Modernity and the "graphicalization" of meaning: New Guinea highland shield design in historical perspective. *Journal of the Royal Anthropological Institute* (n.s.) 7 (1): 469–93.
Ong, Walter J. 1982. *Orality and literacy: The technologizing of the word.* London and New York: Routledge.
Ortner, Sherry B. 1998. Generation X: Anthropology in a media-saturated world. *Cultural Anthropology* 13 (3): 414–40.
Otto, Dianne. 1996. Holding up half the sky, but for whose benefit? A critical analysis of the Fourth World Conference on Women. *Australian Feminist Law Journal* 6:7–28.
Palmer, Jerry. 1996. Introduction to part 1. In *Design and aesthetics: A reader*, ed. Jerry Palmer and Mo Dodson. London: Routledge.
Parry, John T. 1989. Planters and plantations in Viti Levu, 1875: An historical geography. *Domodomo* 1–4: 1–23.
Pickering, Andrew. 1997. Concepts and the mangle of practice: Constructing quaternions. In *Mathematics, science, and postclassical theory*, ed. Barbara Hernstein Smith and Arkady Plotnitsky. Durham: Duke University Press.
Poovey, Mary. 1998. *A history of the modern fact: Problems of knowledge in the sciences of wealth and society.* Chicago: University of Chicago Press.
Poster, Mark. 1990. *The mode of information: Poststructuralism and social context.* Oxford: Polity.
Pound, Christopher. 1995. Imagining in-formation: The complex disconnections of computer networks. In *Technoscientific imaginations: Conversations, profiles, and memoirs*, ed. George E. Marcus. Chicago: University of Chicago Press.
Princen, Thomas. 1994. NGOs: Creating a niche in environmental diplomacy. In *Environmental NGOs in world politics: Linking the local and the global*, ed. Thomas Princen and Matthias Finger. London: Routledge.
Pye, David. 1978. *The nature and aesthetics of design: A design handbook.* London: Herbert.
Quain, Buell. 1948. *Fijian village.* Chicago: University of Chicago Press.
Rabinow, Paul. 1989. *French modern: Norms and forms of the social environment.* Cambridge: MIT Press.
Rabinow, Paul. 1996. *Essays on the anthropology of reason.* Princeton: Princeton University Press.
Radway, Janice. 1994. On the gender of the middlebrow consumer and the threat of the culturally fraudulent female. *South Atlantic Quarterly* 93 (4): 871–93.

Radway, Janice. 1997. *A feeling for books: The Book-of-the-Month Club, literary taste, and middle-class desire.* Chapel Hill: University of North Carolina Press.

Reed, Adam. N.d. Under constraint. Writing about loss and transformation in a Papua New Guinea Prison. Manuscript.

Reid, Keith. 1976. Teeth and talons bared at Suva Y. *Pacific Islands Monthly,* September.

Riles, Annelise. 1994. Representing in-between: Law, anthropology, and the rhetoric of interdisciplinarity. *University of Illinois Law Review* 1994:597–650.

Riles, Annelise. 1995. The view from the international plane: Perspective and scale in the architecture of colonial international law. *Law and Critique* 6:39–54.

Riles, Annelise. 1997. Part-Europeans and Fijians: Some problems in the conceptualization of a relationship. In *Fiji in transition,* ed. Brij V. Lal and Tomari R. Valcatora. Research Papers of the Constitution Review Commission, vol. 1. Suva: School of Social and Economic Development, University of the South Pacific.

Riles, Annelise. 1998a. Division within the boundaries. *Journal of the Royal Anthropological Institute* 4:409–24.

Riles, Annelise. 1998b. Infinity within the brackets. *American Ethnologist* 25 (3): 378–98.

Riles, Annelise. 1999. Models and documents: Artefacts of international legal knowledge. *International and Comparative Law Quarterly* 48:809–30.

Risen, James. 1998. U.S. says it has strong evidence of wide-ranging terror network. *New York Times,* 21 August, A1.

Rittberger, Volker. 1983. Global conference diplomacy and international policy-making: The case of UN-sponsored world conferences. *European Journal of Political Research* 11:167–82.

Robertson, Roland. 1992. *Globalization: Social theory and global culture.* London: Sage.

Rouse, Roger. 1995. Thinking through transnationalism: Notes on the cultural politics of class relations in the contemporary United States. *Public Culture* 7:353–402.

Russell, Bertrand. [1919] 1993. *Introduction to mathematical philosophy.* London and New York: Routledge.

Sahlins, Marshall. 1962. *Moala: Culture and nature on a Fijian island.* Ann Arbor: University of Michigan Press.

Salmond, Ann. 1982. Theoretical landscapes: On cross-cultural conceptions of knowledge. In *Semantic anthropology,* ed. David Parkin. London: Academic. Quoted in Mark Hobart, As I lay laughing: Encountering global knowledge in Bali, in *An anthropological critique of development,* ed. M. Hobart (London: Routledge, 1994).

Scarry, Elaine. [1985] 1987. *The body in pain: The making and unmaking of the world.* New York and London: Oxford University Press.

Scarry, Elaine. 1994. *Resisting representation.* Oxford: Oxford University Press.

Scelle, Georges. 1953. The evolution of international conferences. *UNESCO International Social Science Bulletin* 5:241–77.

Schneider, David M. 1984. *A critique of the study of kinship.* Ann Arbor: University of Michigan Press.

Schwartzman, Helen B. 1989. *The meeting: Gatherings in organizations and communities.* New York and London: Plenum.

Scott, John. 1991. *Social network analysis.* London: Sage.

Shore, Cris. 1995. Usurpers or pioneers? European Commission bureaucrats and the question of "European consciousness." In *Questions of consciousness*, ed. Anthony P. Cohen and Nigel Rapport. London and New York: Routledge.

Sikkink, Kathryn. 1993. Human rights, principled issue-networks, and sovereignty in Latin America. *International Organization* 47:411–41.

Silverstein, Michael, and Greg Urban. 1996. The natural history of discourse. In *Natural histories of discourse*, ed. Michael Silverstein and Greg Urban. Chicago: University of Chicago Press.

Simmel, Georg. [1955] 1964. *Conflict; the web of group-affiliations*, trans. Kurt H. Worlff and Richard Bendix. New York: Free Press.

Simons, Herbert W., Elizabeth W. Mechling, and Howard N. Schreier. 1984. The functions of human communication in mobilizing for action from the bottom up: The rhetoric of social movements. In *Handbook of rhetorical and communication theory*, ed. Carroll C. Arnold and John Waite Bowers. Boston: Allyn and Bacon.

Sklair, Leslie. 1998. Social movements and global capitalism. In *The cultures of globalization*, ed. Fredric Jameson and Masao Miyoshi. Durham: Duke University Press.

Slaughter, Anne-Marie. 1997. The real new world order. *Foreign Affairs* 76 (5): 183–97.

Smith, Dorothy E. 1984. Textually mediated social organization. *International Social Science Journal* 36:59–75.

Smith, Dorothy E. 1990. *Texts, facts, and femininity*. London: Routledge.

Spiro, Peter J. 1994. New global communities: Nongovernmental organizations in international decision-making institutions. *Washington Quarterly* 18:45–56.

Star, Susan Leigh. 1991. Power, technologies, and the phenomenology of conventions: On being allergic to onions. In *A sociology of monsters*, ed. John Law. London: Routledge.

Steiner, Henry J. 1991. *Diverse partners: Non-governmental organizations in the human rights movement*. Cambridge: Harvard Law School Human Rights Program.

Stienstra, Deborah. 1994. *Women's movements and international organizations*. New York: St. Martin's Press.

Stoler, Ann. 1995. "Mixed-bloods" and the cultural politics of European identity in colonial Southeast Asia. In *The decolonization of imagination: Culture, knowledge, and power*, ed. Jan Nederveen Pieterse and Bhikhu Parekh. London: Zed.

Strathern, Marilyn. 1988. *The gender of the gift: Problems with women and problems with society in Melanesia*. Berkeley: University of California Press.

Strathern, Marilyn. 1990. Artefacts of history: Events and the interpretation of images. In *Culture and history in the Pacific*, ed. Jukka Siikala. Helsinki: Finnish Anthropological Society.

Strathern, Marilyn. 1991. *Partial connections*. ASAO Special Publications, no. 3. Savage, Md.: Rowman and Littlefield.

Strathern, Marilyn. 1992a. *After nature: English kinship in the late twentieth century*. Cambridge: Cambridge University Press.

Strathern, Marilyn. 1992b. Parts and wholes: Refiguring relationships. In *Reproducing the future: Anthropology, kinship, and the new reproductive technologies*. New York: Routledge.

Strathern, Marilyn. 1996. Cutting the network. *Journal of the Royal Anthropological Institute* (n.s.) 2:517–35.

Subramani. 1998. The end of free states: On transnationalization of culture. In *The cultures of globalization,* ed. Fredric Jameson and Masao Miyoshi. Durham: Duke University Press.

Suva Y votes in new board and officials. 1976. *Fiji Times,* 7 December.

Szasz, Paul C. 1997. General law-making processes. In *The United Nations and international law.* Cambridge: Cambridge University Press.

Tabory, Mala. 1980. *Multilingualism in international law and institutions.* Alphen aan den Rijn, The Netherlands: Sijthoff and Noordhoff.

Tarrow, Sidney. 1998. *Power in movement: Social movements and contentious politics.* Cambridge: Cambridge University Press.

Taylor, Paul. 1993. *International organization in the modern world, the regional and the global process.* London and New York: Pinter.

Tennant, Chris. 1994. Indigenous peoples, international institutions, and the international legal literature from 1945–1993. *Human Rights Quarterly* 16:1–57.

Teubner, Gunther. 1993. The many-headed hydra: Networks as higher-order collective actors. In *Corporate control and accountability,* ed. Joseph McCahery, Sol Picciotto, and Colin Scott. Oxford: Clarendon.

Thomas, Nicholas. 1991. *Entangled objects: Exchange, material culture, and colonialism in the Pacific.* Cambridge: Harvard University Press.

Toren, Christina. 1990. *Making sense of hierarchy: Cognition as social process in Fiji.* London: Athlone.

Tsing, Anna. 1998. The global situation. Anthropology Board of Studies, University of California Santa Cruz. Manuscript.

Two more Y staff expelled. 1976. *Fiji Times,* 6 December.

Wagner, Roy. 1975. *The invention of culture.* Englewood Cliffs, N.J.: Prentice-Hall.

Wagner, Roy. 1981. *The invention of culture.* Rev. and expanded ed. Chicago: University of Chicago Press.

Wagner, Roy. 1986. *Symbols that stand for themselves.* Chicago: University of Chicago Press.

Wagner, Roy. 1991. The fractal person. In *Big men and great men,* ed. Marilyn Strathern and Maurice Godelier. Cambridge: Cambridge University Press.

Wagner, Roy. 1995. If you have the advertisement, you don't need the product. In *Rhetorics of self-making,* ed. D. Battaglia. Berkeley: University of California Press.

Walker, G. 1986. The standpoint of women and the dilemma of professionalism in action. *Resources for Feminist Research* 15:18–20.

Wapner, Paul. 1995. Politics beyond the state: Environmental activism and world civic politics. *World Politics* 47:311–40.

Warren, Kay B. 1998. *Indigenous movements and their critics: Pan-Maya activism in Guatemala.* Princeton: Princeton University Press.

Weiner, Annette. 1985. Inalienable wealth. *American Ethnologist* 12:210–27.

Weiner, James. 1995. Technology and techne in Trobriand and Yolngu art. *Social Analysis* 38:32–46.

Weisgrau, Maxine K. 1997. *Interpreting development: Local histories, local strategies.* Lanham: University of America Press.
Wheaton, Henry. 1866. *Elements of international law.* 8th ed. Boston: Little, Brown.
Wheeldon, P. D. 1969. The operation of voluntary associations and personal networks in the political processes of an inter-ethnic community. In *Social networks in urban situations,* ed. J. Clyde Mitchell. Manchester: Manchester University Press.
Whippy, William P. 1977. Land use on Naivevu copra estate, Macuata, Vanua Levu. Manuscript on file at the University of the South Pacific Library.
Willetts, Peter, ed. 1996. *The conscience of the world: The influence of non-governmental organisations in the UN system.* Washington, D.C.: Brookings Institution for the David Davies Memorial Institute of International Studies, London.
Winslow, Anne. 1995. *Women, politics, and the United Nations.* Westport, Conn.: Greenwood.
X looks back on ten years of help for girls. 1973. *Fiji Times,* 6 September.
Young, John. 1984. *Adventurous spirits: Australian migrant society in pre-cession Fiji.* St. Lucia: University of Queensland Press.
Zabusky, Stacy. 1995. *Launching Europe: An ethnography of European cooperation in space science.* Princeton: Princeton University Press.

Index

Academic analysis, contrast to institutional analysis, 81, 200nn. 9, 10
Acronyms, aesthetics of, 123
Action: as antithesis of analysis, 143–45, 169; in design pattern 134, 137, 155–70, 211n. 18; as Matrix inside out, 159–66. *See also* Network
Activism, 148–51; and donor institutions, 152–53; international, 2–4, 131
Actor-Network Theory, 26, 63–66, 126–27, 198n. 45, 208n. 20
Aesthetics: of analysis, 61–65; and brackets, 82–83, 85; of bureaucratic practices, 129–30; of collection, 124, 139, 207n. 12; definition of, 185–86n. 4; and epistemology, 139–39; and Fascism, 181, 214n. 11; of information, 16, 136–42, 185nn. 2, 4, 190n. 26; and modernist activism, 131–33; and politics, 182, 214n. 11; practice in conferences, 79–81, 114–16; of system, 120–24, 166, 173–74; technical, 87, 129; transnational character, 131–36
Agreements, international: displacement by informational practices, 178–81; negotiation of, 73–74, 78–89
Analysis: and action, 143–45, 169; point of ethnographic access, xiii–xiv, 1. *See also* Aacademic analysis, contrast to institutional analysis; Anthropological tools
Analytical forms, 21–22
Analytical tools, failure of. *See* Failure, as aesthetic device
Anonymous communication: simulation of, 52; suspicion of, 52
Anthropological tools: Network's appropriation of, 9–10, 65–69, 186n. 7; and representation, xiv
Artifacts: definition of, 186n. 5; and ethnographic practice, 186n. 5
Asia Foundation, 132, 151, 154–56, 173
Asia-Pacific Women in Politics (APWIP), 48, 172–73
Association for Progressive Communications (APC), 127–28, 195n. 26
AusAID, 33, 47, 53, 56, 152–54, 158–59

Barnes, J. A., 56 fig.7, 61–62, 65–66, 197n. 37
Bateson, Gregory, 62, 136, 185–86n. 4, 206n. 6
Baudrillard, Jean, 198n. 40
Beijing Conference. *See* United Nations Fourth World Conference on Women
Beijing Declaration, drafting of, 34 table 3, 147
Beneath Paradise, 131, 133–34
Benjamin, Walter, 181–82
Borrowing, and collection, 12, 17, 124–25, 207n. 10
Boundaries of land and truth, 106–8
Boutros-Ghali, Boutros, 9–10
Brackets: infinity within, 85–86; in negotiation of UN documents, 82–86; quantifying of, 88; removal of, 84–85; as visual phenomena, 85. *See also* Levels; Quotation
Bureaucratic practices, 194nn. 20, 21, 195n. 22, 200n. 13; aesthetics of, 129–30; documents as artifacts of, 17, 51. *See also* Institutions, knowledge in

235

Cairo Conference. *See* United Nations Conference on Population and Development
Capital: as analytical category, 93, 113; displacement by information, 92–94, 108–13, 201n. 2
Castells, Manuel, 92, 201n. 1
Change: perception of, among Part-Europeans, 95–96, 107–12; within networks, 213n. 7
Classification, 212n. 21
Clinton, Bill, 171
Colonial administration of Fiji and women's groups, 27–29
Commission on the Status of Women (CSW), 13 fig. 4, 190n. 21
Commitment, 161; and design, 180–81
Communication: skills, 23–25, 176, 192n. 5; as technical information processing, 125–29, 198n. 50
Comparison: and matrix form, 155; and negotiation, 155
Completion of matrix, 158–61
Complexity, 2–3, 62
Concreteness: and abstraction, 76, 127–29; of number, 99–109; of pattern, 161, 162–63 fig. 23, 164, 183
Conferences: academic critique of, 183; and documents, 77, 79–89; impact of, 10; language of, 86–89; as a network, 10; participants, 188n. 16. *See also* United Nations, global conferences
Consensus and form, 181–82
Context: as analytical form, 94, 200n. 12; failure of, 26–27
Convention on the Elimination of All Forms of Discrimination Against Women (CEDAW), 166
Counting and pattern, 76–77, 80, 87
Coups and nationalism in Fiji, 192n. 8
Critical areas of concern. *See* Global Platform for Action, critical areas of concern
Critique, displacement of, 3, 113, 182
Cultural relativism, 131–33, 181; and modernism, 3

Culture: absence of, 68, 141–42; as condition of activism, 133; as network, 194n. 21, 196n. 32
Customary international law, 76
Cybernetics, 63–64, 207n. 12

Data. *See* Information
Decolonization in the Pacific and women's activism, 175–78
Democracy and Network form, 2, 172–73
Department of Women and Culture, Fiji (DWC), 33, 48, 51, 67, 161–64, 198n. 47
Design: and activism, 130–36; and agency, 211n. 18; and cultural difference, 124–25, 133, 181; definition of, 20, 191n. 30; as distinct from art, 207n. 8; effectuation of global reality, 182–83; generation of political commitment, 131–33; and information, 114–16; as technical, 122–23, 125–30
Desire and technicality, 52, 143–51
Development Alternatives for Women in a New Era (DAWN), 48, 56
Development work: as a career, 32, 36–47; expatriates in, 28–30, 33, 152
Diagrams: as abstraction, 127–29; and meaning, 131, 134–36; and reality, 124, 142
Digital, definition of, 200
Dimensionality, 90–91, 136–37
Division: contrasted with collection, 110–13; and kinship, 93, 99–103, 203n. 16, 204n. 17; as legal exercise, 101–5; as markers of generations, 101–4; and number, 105; pattern of, 99–103
Documents: and action, 147–48; aesthetic of, 82, 89–91; as artifacts of bureaucratic practice, 17, 51; collating, 17; collecting, 95; drafting of, 78–89; formality of, 152–54; language of, 80–81, 86–89; as object, 90; and networks, 173; as pattern, 83–84, 90. *See also* United Nations

Donor-donee relationships, 152–55, 158–59, 199n. 3

Earth Summit. *See* United Nations Conference on Environment and Development
ECOSOC. *See* United Nations Economic and Social Council
ECOWOMAN, 32, 123, 188n. 16
Electronic mail, 195n. 26; establishment of network, 195n. 25
English language, 126, and diagrams, 207n. 7
Epistemology: and aesthetics, 138–39; modernist, 2–3
Essentialism, 187n. 10
Ethnography of already familiar phenomenon, 4–6, 12, 16–20, 73, 185n. 3, 186n. 5, 187n. 11, 190n. 24, 191nn. 28–29

Fact: and action, 156–57, 164, 169–70; competitive possibilities of, 178–80, 213n. 8; opacity of, 139–42, 208nn. 19, 21
Fact-finding procedures, United Nations, 171, 178–81
Failure as aesthetic device, 6, 19–20, 76–77, 89–90, 183–84, 212n. 23
Family trees, 111–12
Feminism: and funding, 149, 153, 209n. 6; as transnational issue, 17
Figure seen twice, 26–27, 68–69, 89–91, 183–84. *See also* Inside out
Fiji Land Claims Commission, 201–2n. 4
Fiji National Council of Women (FNCW), 117–18, 121, 192n. 12
Fiji Women in Politics, 59, 121–22, 153, 166–87
Fiji Women's Crisis Centre (FWCC), 47, 153
Fiji Women's Rights Movement (FWRM), 47, 153
Focal points: definition of, 130; designation of, in the Pacific, 23, 48; and information, 52, 134; linkages among, 49 fig. 6, 207n. 11; and scale, 49 fig. 6, 52–54; subjectivity of, 52–54, 195n. 24
Ford Foundation, 34 table 3, 172
Formality, and communication, 25, 64, 67–68, 116, 198n. 50; of system, 62–65
Formand action, 156–57, 169–70, 211n. 17; agency of, 69; appeal of, 64–66; and consensus, 181–82; incompleteness of, 158–59, 168–70, 183; internal spaces of, 151, 155–69; and politics, 181–82. *See also* Aesthetics; Formality; Network
Form-filling, 159–61
Frege, Gottlob, 108–9
Friendship, 60
Funding: and anonymity, 47; evaluation of, 153–55; form of, 153–55; practices, 153–55, 158–59; proposals, 153–55, 158–59

Gender, meaning of, in UN documents, 145–46, 196n. 29
Genealogical research among Part-Europeans, 110–13
Ginsburg, Faye, 129–30
Global conferences. *See* Conferences; United Nations, global conferences
Globalization: aesthetics of, 90–91; anthropology of, xiv, 4–6, 172, 186nn. 6, 7, 189n. 11; and complexity, 3–4; experience of, 184; in international institutions, 90–91, 201n. 15
Global Platform for Action, 13, 156–57; and action, 156–66; critical areas of concern, 13, 189n. 19; drafting of, 78–89; form of, 117; and implementation, 153–66; Mission Statement, 16, fig. 3; reception in Fiji, 118–19; strategic objectives, 13; and translation into vernacular, 148
Gore, Al, 201n. 2
Graphics. *See* Design
Grassroots, concept of, 164–65

Greenpeace, 33, 35 table 3
Grassroots Organizations Operating Together in Sisterhood (GROOTS), 55, 164–65

Haas, Peter, and Emanuel Adler, 212n. 1
Hannerz, Ulf, 62, 197–98n. 39
Haraway, Donna, 17, 63, 198n. 41
Heterogeneity of information and form, 117–20
Hierarchy, Fijian, 31, 198n. 47
Human rights, language of, 81, 201n. 15
Hybridic versus systemic conceptual devices, 62–63

Incommensurability, 204n. 23
Infinity: apprehension of, 95, 111–13; and globalization, 95
Information: academic treatment of, 62–63, 92, 93, 112–13; aesthetic agency of, 208n. 17; aesthetics of, 16, 136–42, 185nn. 2, 4, 190n. 26, 208n. 17; appeal of, 54–55, 63–64, 92, 114–16; blocking, 51–52, 195n. 22; collection of, 53, 89, 110–13, 171; comparison to capital, 92–94, 108–13, 201n. 2; and design, 114–16; digital quality of, 136, 200n. 7; in documents, 171, 199n. 6; dissemination of, 53–55, 171; as finite, 93, 94, 97–109; flow, 92, 113, 201n. 1; form of, 179–84; and gaps, 19–20; and networks, 4, 50–58, 92; and power, 175–78; and Rule of Law, 179–80; scale of, 18, 190nn. 26, 27; sharing, 25; technical processing of, 125–29; as universal, 180
Innovation in scholarship, 5–6
Inside out, 68–69, 190n. 25; and design, 126; matrices, 159–70; as a methodology 18–19; networks, 68–69, 115, 136–38. *See also* Dimensionality
Institutions: ethnography of, 16–18, 190n. 24, 191n. 28; knowledge in, 3, 194nn. 20, 21, 195n. 22, 200n. 13, 208nn. 17, 20. *See also* Bureaucratic practices; United Nations

Intergovernmental negotiations, 208n. 21
International institutions and networks, 172
International Labour Organization (ILO), 51, 155
International law: and fact, 179–80; and form, 181–83; and global conferences, 7–10; and information, 179–83
International legal document. *See* Documents
International Monetary Fund, 179
International Organization for Standardization, 179
International organizations. *See* International institutions and networks
International relations and networks, 172–73, 212n. 1
International Women's Development Agency (IWDA), 61, 131
International Women's Tribune Centre (IWTC): designs, 124–25, 135; role in Fiji, 127–29, 132–33
Issues: and networks, 67, 156–58; and matrix, 159, 169–70

Jay, Martin, 182, 214n. 11

Keck, Margaret, and Kathryn Sikkink, 173, 186n. 8, 212n. 2, 212–13n. 3
King, Lili, 117–19, 132
Kinship: failure of, as an analytical device, 196n. 31; Part-European, 95, 96, 99–104
Knowledge: anthropological, 81, 200nn. 9, 10; anthropology of, 18–19; as cumulative, 111; and gaps, 19–20; institutional and social organization, 92, 94, 106–7. *See also* Analysis; Globalization; Infinity; Information; Institutions, knowledge in

Land claims in Fiji, 201n. 4
Language: as abstract, 88; as concrete, 87–89; of documents, 199n. 5; and levels, 73, 86; in negotiation, 86–89;

as opaque, 86–88; and transparency, 200n. 13
Latour, Bruno, 63–64
Law, John, 65, 198n. 45
Levels, 73, 86; and brackets, 82–83; and globalization, 73, 82–83, 85, 90–91
Liberal rationalism, aesthetics of, 182
Linguistic anthropology, form and formality in, 191n. 1
Linkages. *See* Network, linkages in
Lists, 210n. 12
Literalization, 92, 112, 134–36
Lobbying practices, 87
Local and global. *See* Globalization

Manchester School anthropologists. *See* Social network analysis
Marcus, George, 2, 3, 186n. 4
Marriage and division of land among Part-Europeans, 99–101
Martin, Emily, 17, 201n. 1
Mathematics and formalism, 105, 108–9
Matrix, 159–66; and accountability, 212n. 21; and action, 156–66, 170; as activist tool, 156–61, 210n. 13; appeal of, 158–61; and commitment, 161; completion of, 158–61; and context, 156; and design, 159, 161–64; and fact, 164; and issues, 159, 169–70; and network, 166–70; systemic structure of, 156–58
Mats: collection of, 74; and counting, 76, 78; and documents, 70–75; and exchange, 75–78; layering of, 76–77; and pattern, 75; plaiting of, 75; as repetition, 75
Meaning, foreclosure of, in documents, 80–82, 200nn. 11, 13–14, 149
Methodist Church in Fiji, 192n. 9
Middle class in Fiji, 58, 195n. 27
Models: and anthropology, 112–13; and social relations, 211n. 17
Modernism, 23, 26–27, 131–33, 180
Modernity, theory of, 2–4
Mol, Anne-Marie, 65

Munn, Nancy, 1
Myers, Fred, 59, 186n. 4, 196nn. 30, 33

Nader, Laura, 213n. 4
National Council of Women, Fiji, 32, 60
Network analysis. *See* Actor-Network Theory; Social Network Analysis
Network diagrams, 24 fig. 5, 49 fig. 6, 56 fig. 7, 57 fig. 8, 121–23
Network: and academic knowledge, 113; and action, 166–70; activities, 47–58; as analysis, 66, 198nn. 42, 45; appeal of, 21–23; of conferences, 10; and cross-cultural communication, 131–36; definition of, 3, 172; and design, 191n. 30; as effect of design, 136–37; exclusion from, 55–56, 174–78; extension of, 110, 173–74, 212n. 22; formality in, 25, 64, 66–68, 116, 198n. 48; and friendship, 59–60, 62; and graphics, 117–28; and hierarchy, 51; and informational flows, 50–52, 92–93, 194n. 19, 195n. 25; inside out (*see* Sociality as Network Inside Out); of institutions, 172; in international relations theory, 2, 172–73, 212n. 1; linkages in, 197n. 38; and newsletters, 52; and NGO Forum, 48; as organizational form, 179–80, 192–93n. 11; self-descriptions, 172; skills, 25, 51, 54–55; and society, 59, 76; sociological appeal of, 2–3, 61–64, 92, 172–74, 201n. 1, 212n. 1; sociology of, 66–67, 172, 212n. 2; of terrorists, 171–72, 182; and transnationalism, 2–3, 186–7n. 8; visual appeal of, 114–36, 205n. 1; of women's organizations, 23–26. *See also* Focal points; Personal relationships; Recursivity
Newsletter: content of, 52; design of, 117–21; place of in networks, 122–23
New Zealand Overseas Development Agency (NZODA), 193n. 16
NGO Forum, 6; and heterogeneity, 189n. 18

240   Index

Nongovernmental Organization (NGO): accreditation of, at UN conferences, 188n. 16; aesthetic choices, 114–15; as career, 47; consultative status with UN, 188n. 17, 190n. 23; contribution to conferences, 10–12; and expertise, 214n. 10; networks, 23–26 table 3, 34–35, 36 table 4, 37–40, 47, 124–25
Norms and global conferences, 182
Nouméa conference. *See* Pacific Ministerial Conference on Women and Sustainable Development
Number: and equivalence, 105–6; as object, 108; as relational correspondence of, 94, 106–9; as representation, 109. *See also* Counting and pattern; Mathematics and formalism

Omomo Melen Pacific, 48, 56, 152, 175–78
Organizations. *See* Institutions
Ounei, Susanna, 175–78

Pacific Concerns Resource Centre, 175, 213n. 5
Pacific Ministerial Conference on Women and Sustainable Development, 199nn. 1, 2. *See also* Pacific Platform for Action
Pacific NGO Coordinating Group (PNGOCG), 32, 60, 156–57, 169–70, 193n. 17
Pacific Platform for Action: aesthetic quality of, 82; compilation of, 140–41, 189n. 21; design of, 70–72; negotiation of, 79
Pacific Population Information Network (POPIN), 53–54, 129
Pacific Sustainable Development Network Programme, 50, 54
Pacific Women's Association, 28
Pacific Women's Information/Communication Network (PAWORNET), 23–26, 36, 47, 50, 54, 69, 123, 142, 191n. 1, 198–99n. 50
Pacific Women's Resource Bureau (PWRB), 32, 36, 48, 50, 52, 192n. 10, 193n. 17
Pacific Women's Resource Centre (PWRC), 30, 32
Panel discussions, 51–52
Pan-Pacific and Southeast Asian Women's Association (PPSEAWA), 27–28, 192n. 3
Part-Europeans: clan membership, 202n. 6; demographics of, 201n. 3; kinship, 203nn. 11–14; status of in Fiji, 96; in urban areas, 202n. 5. *See also* Whippy clan; Division
Pattern: apprehension of, 76–78, 136; of communication, 123; and the concrete, 78, 83–84; digital and iconic, 78–79; in documents, 78–81, 123–25; extension of, 118–19; of language, 78–82, 86–89
PEACESAT satellite conferences, 36, 193n. 17
Personal relationships: anthropological study of, 61–62, 64; and the network, 59–61, 66–69, 196nn. 35, 36, 198n. 47
Perspective and information, 111
Phenomenon and analysis, 113
Platform for Action. *See* Global Platform for Action
Politics: and form, 181–82; neoliberal vision of, 2–3
Preparatory meetings. *See* United Nations Fourth World Conference on Women, preparation for
PrepCom, 12, 60, 79–87, 114–15, 190n. 21
Professionals. *See* Middle class in Fiji
Projects: academic critique of, 209n. 7; as units of development, 153, 209n. 7
Proposals. *See* Donor-donee relationships; Funding proposals
Public information symbols, 131

Quotation: aesthetic of, 88; and brackets, 86–89; as bridging device, 87, 89. *See also* Brackets; Language

Race among NGO participants in Fiji, 59
Real: absence of, 138, 143–45; and action, 145; and anthropological analysis, 143; as correspondence, 107; and design, 138, 142; desire for, 145–52; as effect of network, 172; as outside, 137
Recursivity, 3, 65–66, 172, 197–98nn. 39, 46
Regionalism, representation of, 33, 48–50, 198n. 42
Repetition of language, 80–81, 88
Replication of graphic designs, 99, 125, 187n. 11
Rio Conference. *See* United Nations Conference on Environment and Development

Scale: of analysis, 182–84; and globalization, 3–4, 182–84; in networks, 136–37
Scarry, Elaine, 91
Schematic diagrams. *See* Diagrams
Seen twice. *See* Figure seen twice
Sikkink, Kathryn. *See* Keck, Margaret, and Kathryn Sikkink
Simpson, William, 99–101
Simultaneous translation. *See* Translation
Smith, Dorothy, 139
Sociality as Network Inside Out, 59–61, 68–69, 115
Social Network Analysis, 61–62, 65–66, 115, 196n. 35, 197nn. 37–39, 198n. 44
Social scientific models: globalizing effect of, 4, 9, 174. *See also* Actor-Network Analysis; Anthropological tools; Social Network Analysis
Soft law, recognition of, 6, 7–8, 188n. 15
Soqosoqo Vakamarama, 27, 35 table 3
South Pacific Commission (SPC), 32–33, 49, 72–74, 190n. 23, 192n. 10, 193n. 13, 196n. 34
South Pacific Forum (SPF), 33, 190n. 22, 193n. 14
Spoken and written words in UN negotiation, 83
Statistics, 171; collection of, 140–41; and meaning, 141
Stereotypes, cultural, and design, 69, 124–25, 135 fig. 20
Strategic objectives. *See* Platform for Action
Strathern, Marilyn, 18–19, 94, 185n. 4, 186n. 5, 190nn. 26, 27, 212n. 23
Subregional caucuses. *See* United Nations Fourth World Conference on Women, preparation for
Surveys, 140–41
Sustainable Development, 199n. 2
Symbols and pattern, 127–29
System, 16–17, 201n. 1; aesthetic of, 121–25, 173

Tables. *See* Matrix
Technical skill and commitment, 125
Technology: attraction of, 187n. 11; and human labor, 125–29
Telephone conversations, 67–68
Teubner, Günther, 173
Text: and analogical reasoning, 199n. 6; dismantling of, 89; electronic hypertext, 199n. 6; and outline form, 129–30; translation of, 145–48. *See also* Language
Traditionalism in anthropology of globalization, 5
Training, 33, 36
Translation, 145–48
Transnationalism. *See* Globalization
Typeface in documents, 119

Uniformity in design practices in documents, 199n. 5
United Nations: aesthetic of, 184; Fiji's involvement in, 12, 14–15 table 2;

242   Index

United Nations (*continued*)
  global conferences, 6–12, 171; impact of, 9 fig. 2; and international law, 188n. 15; legitimacy of, 7–10; postwar history of, 66; procedures at conferences, 188n. 17; purpose of, 171. *See also* Fact-finding procedures, United Nations
United Nations Children's Fund (UNICEF), 32
United Nations Commission on the Status of Women, 190n. 21
United Nations Conference on Environment and Development, 8 table 1, 12, 188nn. 16, 17
United Nations Conference on Population and Development, 8 table 1, 214n. 10
United Nations Development Programme (UNDP), 32, 50, 205n. 1; Human Development Report, 178, 213n. 8
United Nations documents: analytical framework, 78–79; comparison of, 155; drafting of, 78–89; style of (*see* Brackets; Language; Quotation)
United Nations Economic and Social Council (ECOSOC), 190n. 21
United Nations Economic and Social Council for Asia and the Pacific (ESCAP), 192n. 12
United Nations Fourth World Conference on Women, 6–13; academic participation in, 81; and action, 147, 156–61, 165–66; and agreement, 174; computer facilities at, 195n. 26; impact of, 213–14n. 9; inclusiveness of, 184; and the media, 178; participants in, 175–78; preparation for, 12 fig. 4, 13, 189n. 20; and statistics, 171
United Nations Fund for Women (UNIFEM), 32, 49, 60, 67
United Nations Office for Research and the Collection of Information, 179
United Nations Population Fund (UNFPA), 32

United Nations women's conferences, history of, 7 fig.1, 8 table 1, 14 table 2, 30
University of the South Pacific (USP), 58
Urban society, anthropology of, 58

Visual language, as universal, 131–36
Vivivi, definition of, 75–76. *See also* Mats

Waghi battleshield designs, 181
Walbiri iconography, 1, 16
Whippy clan: ancestral stories, 202nn. 9, 10; family tree, 111–12; history of, 96–97; leadership among, 105–6, 204nn. 20, 21; and legal documents, 101–5; relations among urban and rural kin, 96, 97; reunion, 110–11. *See also* Change; Part-Europeans
Woman: 126–27, 137–38, 182; as analytical category, 17, 23, 196n. 29; as a word in documents, 80
Women and Fisheries Network (FISHNET), 48, 50
Women in Development, 32, 36, 47, 193n. 16; and academic critique, 209n. 7; and funding policy, 153, 209n. 6; and Gender in Development, 153
Women's Action for Change, 47
Women's Environment and Development Organization (WEDO), 156–57, 161
Women's Information Network, 117–19
Women's movement, history of in Fiji, 27–32
Women's Natural Medicinal Therapy Association (WAINIMATE), 123
Women Weaving the World Together, 72
World Conference on Human Rights (UN), 8 table 1
World Council of Churches (WCC), 33
World Summit for Social Development (UN), 8 table 1

YWCA in Fiji, 28–31, 59–60, 192nn. 5–7; Pacific Regional, 23, 25, 60